Against the
TIDE

Against the
TIDE

How to Raise Sexually Pure Kids in an "Anything-Goes" World

TIM AND BEVERLY
LAHAYE

Published in association with
the literary agency of
Alive Communications,
P.O. Box 49068,
Colorado Springs, CO 80949

AGAINST THE TIDE:
How to Raise Sexually Pure Kids in an Anything-Goes World

published by Multnomah Books
a part of the Questar publishing family

For information:
Questar Publishers, Inc.
Post Office Box 1720
Sisters, Oregon 97759

93 94 95 96 97 98 99 00 01 02 — 10 9 8 7 6 5 4 3 2

To our three married children, whose virtue
before marriage enabled us to write this book,
and to all those parents who wish the same
for their children.

Contents

INTRODUCTION

A s Bev and I drove our youngest daughter to the church on her wedding day we received the greatest compliment of our lives. Lori was sitting in the back amidst her wedding gear, her beautiful, long white dress filling the entire trunk. Leaning forward she surprised us with the words, "Mom and Dad, you can be proud of yourselves. You raised two daughters in Southern California and both of us were virgins on our wedding day!"

Tears of joy ran down both our faces as we realized that this dedicated Christian young woman of twenty-four had set the goal many years before to be a virgin bride, and she had achieved it. We did not realize that she got the idea from her sister, ten years older, who also had set and achieved that goal. We can't take credit for it. They, like Daniel of old, "resolved not to defile" themselves with the sexually permissive ways of our day. Today those girls, their husbands, and the seven children they have brought into this world have no regrets.

We are convinced that all parents want the same thing for their children. That is why we have written this book, to help you help them save themselves sexually for marriage. As the apostle John said, "I have no greater joy than to hear that my children are walking in the truth" (3 John 4). You can raise virtuous children in this permissive society, but you will have to work harder at it than any generation before you.

Our culture is one of the most sex-crazed this world has ever known. It is impossible to shield your child from it, for it is everywhere, from TV programming and commercials to school curricula to unbelievably early childhood conversation. Because of society's over-emphasis on sex, your children will probably show curiosity about it much earlier than you want them to.

Your child is going to be inundated with sex information, and much of it will be wrong, harmful, or inflammatory. If not from sex-obsessed friends or morally perverted TV or movie producers, such information may come from humanistic sex education teachers who insist it be taught in detail in mixed classes without the benefit of moral values.

That is why *you* should teach your children about sex. You should be well informed far in advance of their questions so that when they arise, you can use those opportunities to inform them correctly according to their age level. There are ways of answering and instructing them that will prepare them for marriage and the lifetime of enjoyment God intended for this important area of life.

Unfortunately, sex is a difficult subject for most people to discuss, particularly with their children. Many would prefer that the issue not come up. But ignoring this important subject could ruin a child's life. It is better that you, who gave them life, and people at your church, who share your moral values, be the only people who teach them about sex.

This book will help you be the best sex educator your child can have. The more you know about sex from a medical, moral, and scientific perspective, the better equipped you will be to teach it well and the easier it will be for you to discuss. We have tried to include almost everything you need to know to teach your children properly—from answering their curiosity in early childhood to explaining why and how they should save this exciting experience for the one person they will someday share their life with. On the other hand, this book will not teach you how to tell your teen to use a condom or where to get one before marriage. Nor will we advise them on how to terminate an unplanned pregnancy.

Like you, we think sex is for married partners. Everything in this book will be presented from that perspective. But we will equip you with valuable information on how you can prepare them to handle their turbulent hormones and to understand that single people can become sexually aroused (and what to do about it). Such training, while difficult, can save your child's life, or at least save him or her from the unnecessary tragedies caused by early sexual activity. It will also arm you with ways you can help your young child avoid the sex pervert who preys on innocent children before they are old enough to protect themselves. And you will be able to help them refrain from getting emotionally involved with someone who does not share their commitment to morality or decency.

Many people think Christians are not interested in sex. That is one of the big lies this world likes to convey about us. Another is that we are against sex. We think it is beautiful and a special gift of God to married partners only. But we know Christians are interested in it. Of the thirty-seven books we have written individually or together, *The Act of Marriage*, with almost two million copies in print, is our best seller and the third best seller in the history of Zondervan Publishing House. More evangelical pastors give or recommend that book to young people just before marriage than any other book of its kind. Now many of the readers who benefited from that book have children they want to inform properly about the gift of sex. We pray *Against the Tide* will be used as a tool of God in the hands of parents to raise up a generation of virtuous children even in this permissive society.

Part One

A CALL TO VIRTUE

VIRTUE: EVERY PARENT'S DREAM

Young people today are more permissive than at any time in American history. A case could be made that our society permits its young to begin sexual activity sooner than any society before it. A recent poll indicated that over 50 percent of the sexually active boys had their first sexual encounter between the ages of eleven and thirteen, two years earlier than in the 1950s.

One hundred years ago it was not so. The rate of teenage unwed pregnancy then was nothing in comparison to what it is today, meaning the promiscuity level was nothing like current sexual activity among young people.

A hundred years ago, the church was the conscience of the nation. At one time, the church, as a powerful, morally savoring influence on the nation, spoke out loud and effectively against any attempt to lower public moral standards. Today, Hollywood and Broadway have more influence on the morals of society than the church.

WHERE DID PERMISSIVENESS COME FROM?

The Multibillion Dollar Entertainment Industry

For about the last ninety years there has been a cultural war going on in this country between the entertainment industry and the church. Sexual permissiveness has been at the core of that cultural war. "Sex sells" is more than a cliché, it is a fact of life. Since its inception there have been those in the entertainment industry who have constantly tested the sexual mores of the nation. Today every moral standard is aggressively challenged by programmers. Christians are made to look ignorant, and sexual permissiveness is the "in" philosophy.

Not only are the morally depraved of the Hollywood cult (which have never represented the values of the average American family) held up to cult hero status, but the people they portray in their movies or programs arc Teflon characters who never pay for the sins of their permissive lifestyle. It is estimated that "on television every year, there are over 20,000 acts of implied intercourse. This season, every middle adolescent (character) in television lost their virginity."[1] None of them got pregnant. None of them got AIDS or a sexually transmitted disease. Such unrealistic results of promiscuity are not an accurate portrayal of life in the real world. It sends a false message to our children that they can play sexually permissive games and never get caught.

The Power of Television. Ted Turner is right. There has never been a vehicle to the mind as powerful as movies, TV, videos, or MTV, and it is almost completely controlled by the sexually permissive, at best, and anti-moralists or even anti-Christians at worst.

It is no secret why so many of this nation's youth are devoid of moral values. The messages many of them receive are just the opposite of what they should be hearing and what is good for them. Unless they are blessed with parents who take them to church, live a strong, morally committed life before them, and aggressively teach them how to remain virtuous, they will become as sexually permissive as the rest of society. The odds are that most young people will enter marriage sexually experienced beyond their age level. The entertainment industry is no friend of the family.

Explicit Sex Education

Sexual permissiveness and experimentation have gone up in direct proportion to the amount of time students spend in sex education classes. Children are curious, they want to experiment with what they learn. Without the benefit of strict adherence to abstinence, it should not be surprising that sexual permissiveness has reached all time high proportions for a civilized society.

Had it not been for courageous parents who fought a relentless battle in their public schools against compulsory explicit intercourse indoctrination programs, conditions would be far worse than they are. And the big lie in it all is that this radical brand of sex education, and the condoms given out to minors in school (often without parental consent), do not cut down on either unwed pregnancy or venereal disease. How could it? It promotes promiscuity.

The Sex Information Education Council of the United States (SIECUS) is the country's premier source for explicit amoral sex ed material. They believe in telling children "all" as explicitly and as early as possible under the pretext that it will slow unwed pregnancy and sexually transmitted diseases (STDs), although statistics prove quite the contrary. It is, however, an enormously profitable industry. Public schools have spent billions of tax dollars on sex education materials and training programs since SIECUS was founded. All we have to show for the time, effort, and money is a graphic increase in sexual promiscuity, unwed teen pregnancy, and venereal diseases. It is wise parents who fight vigorously to keep their children out of such classes and teach them what they need to know at home. (See Appendix A for more information about the dangers of sex education in our public schools.)

In some communities there are still some sane and responsible sex ed teachers who are trying to teach moral values and the benefits of virtue and abstinence. But they are few and far between. The explicit advocates out there are so numerous every parent should investigate thoroughly what his or her children are taught in those euphemistically titled "family ed" courses. It may be the worst thing your children can learn.

The Pornography Industry

The early 1970s saw an almost unknown pornography industry burst onto the social scene in this country promoting an "anything goes" mentality. In 1972, the U.S. Supreme Court legalized pornographic literature for the first time. Within ten years we became the "porn capital of the world."

The results of easily accessible porn are obvious to all but liberals and those within the industry itself who refuse to acknowledge it as the primary cause of rape, incest, and sexual permissiveness. Most police officers acknowledge that whenever they arrest rapists and bizarre sex criminals, they invariably find ample evidence the offenders are heavily into pornography.

There is little doubt that pornography, which can be obtained by almost any teen who is willing to pollute his mind, is having a sexually permissive impact on society. Only those who are committed to keeping their minds pure can resist the temptation to indulge in porn.

A *Child Sex Offender.* A "nice boy" in our Sunday school, fifteen years old, was taken to juvenile hall for sexually molesting a ten-year-old girl in his neighborhood. I could not believe it! I knew the boy and his parents and could not believe he was capable of such actions. But I was wrong.

In searching for why he would commit such a sin, I asked his parents if he read pornographic literature. They treated me as if I had insulted them. So I asked to see his room. Sure enough, in his drawers and under his mattress were stacks of porn. He had evidently found them in the alley and hid them. His emotional radiator overheated, and he lost control. When the lonely neighborhood girl (a latchkey child) came into his garage to while away the time, she got more than she bargained for—and he became a criminal.

Could that happen to a Christian? You bet, if he indulges in pornography. Actually, pornography may be even worse for teens than it is for adults. Because of their new raging hormones, teens' emotions can erupt at any time. This may occur when they are still so immature they do not have self-discipline. Pornography is to the mind what drugs and alcohol are to the body. It causes a person to be out of control emotionally. In that condition, all decisions are bad, and some young people can be marred for life.

The Increase in Divorce

Today's divorce rate of 51 percent has contributed greatly to teenage sexual promiscuity. Many of these couples have children who are adversely affected by the destruction of their home. Even the most friendly separation causes pain to children, and many go into rage, self-rejection, and depression. Most blame themselves for their parent's decision. Some hold it against the parent they live with and feel rejected by the parent who leaves. They experience a serious love deficiency that many think they can resolve through early sexual activity. Instead, they wake up to find themselves pregnant or infected with a sexually transmitted disease. Both of these results will adversely affect their entire lives.

Latchkey Children

Roughly 20 percent of today's children are raised at some period of their lives as "latchkey children." That is, over four million young children go home after school to an empty house. Many become bored, curious, or defiant and spend time with neighbors or friends their parents would never approve. Such children are vulnerable to sexual curiosity or experimentation and many are victims of child molesters or perverts.

The picture of our cultural future is not too promising; particularly for those who are serious about raising virtuous children. Unless God intervenes, our culture will become even more sexually permissive than it is today, with sexual perversion and child molestation becoming the next taboos to fall to modern degeneracy. With the decline in moral standards, serious parents are going to have to become more involved in the sexual education of their children.

THE DANGERS OF PREMARITAL SEX

Because children are our most prized possessions, it is devastating to us as parents when their lives are shattered by premarital sex. Except for drug addiction, nothing can ruin a teenager's life faster or more completely than premarital sexual activity (the two often go together). Since the sex drive is so powerful in all of us, particularly between the ages of fourteen and twenty-four, it is often a parent's greatest worry. Several times after performing weddings, I have heard the mothers of the brides say, "Thank God they are married; now I can relax!" It is obvious what they were afraid of—that their daughters might succumb to sexual temptation and either ruin their lives or start their marriage off with much harmful and unneeded baggage.

There are many reasons that justify this nearly universal concern parents have for their children's well being. Contrary to what our culture tells us, premarital sex is dangerous.

Premarital Sex Destroys Our Children's Spiritual Life

We have worked with enough young people of all ages to know that it is impossible for them to maintain a close relationship with God and be sexually active at the same time. In spite of what they may say when caught, everyone knows that premarital sex is wrong, particularly young people in the church. It creates a guilt complex that keeps them from reading their Bible devotionally and praying, and it usually estranges them from their other friends. Sex is so intimate that most sexually active teens pair off and spend their time almost exclusively together rather than with their other Christian friends. In doing so, they cut themselves off from the very people who could help them back into fellowship with God. It is all but impossible to imagine two high school teens having sex during a date on Saturday night and then willingly going to a prayer meeting or a Bible study on Sunday where they might be called on to give a testimony. That is hypocrisy most teens cannot handle.

The Most Important Time in Life. Somewhere between the ages of seventeen and twenty-five most people make their most important decisions, such as where they will go for additional training after high school, what will be their life's vocation, and who they will marry.

These are not all the decisions they will ever make, but you can easily see that your child's future will largely be determined by how they make them. If ever they need a vital relationship with God, it is when they are making these decisions. At this crucial time in life, the last thing they need is to be sexually involved.

Young people need to realize that premarital sex is not some harmless activity like baseball or tennis. The Bible calls it "fornication." It is impossible to be a fornicator and spiritual! God instructed us through the writer of Proverbs:

But a man who commits adultery lacks judgment;
whoever does so destroys himself (Prov. 6:32).

No parent wants that for his children.

Premarital Sex Has an Adverse Effect on Our Children's Education

It is crucial for young people to have a good education to prepare for their future. While it is possible to stumble through high school and still succeed in life, it is less common than a generation ago and always comes at great personal sacrifice. Colleges and universities and even Christian colleges are becoming more selective about those students they admit. If a young person does not do well in high school, it will be very difficult for them to get into the college of their choice. Sexually active students rarely do well in school—or at least as well as they could have done had they been able to concentrate on their education instead of on sex. Besides, "80 percent of the girls who get pregnant drop out of high school." [2]

The child who spends his teenage years cultivating the spiritual, academic, and sporting areas of life will be much further advanced when he or she graduates from high school than if he or she has developed a preoccupation with sex. Sexual activity has a way of possessing their brain at the exclusion of all other subjects. Those same young people, if they wait until marriage to become sexually active, can quickly learn all they need to know to experience a meaningful love life with that one person they will spend the rest of their life with. I have never met a person who refused to be sexually active before marriage who lived to regret it. Unfortunately, there are many who regret not waiting.

Premarital Sex Can Destroy Our Children Physically

We all want our children to enjoy good health. It is the first thing we look for at birth and protect all through life. Yet promiscuity makes our children incredibly vulnerable to STDs, including AIDS. (See the glossary for an overview of the most common STDs.) Sexual immorality has always exacted a price from one's physical health. It is as if the Creator established sexual commitment to one person for our physical survival as well as our spiritual and emotional well being.

Yet as one writer said, "Every day over 30,000 Americans become infected with a sexually transmitted disease. One problem with STDs is that people can have them and not know it. Often it is the person we least expect."[3] Some of these diseases, such as AIDS and gonorrhea, cannot be cured. No parent wants this for his child.

Premarital Sex Destroys Our Children's Reputation

The Bible says, "a good name [reputation] is more desirable than great riches" (Prov. 22:1). Nothing destroys a person's reputation faster than accusations of sexual promiscuity. Young people talk about each other. Boys are particularly braggadocios, and many a girl has lived to realize that when she surrendered her virtue to a boy she thought she loved, it cost her reputation. From then on she is often avoided by the good boys who are trying to live morally straight. Instead, she receives attention from the boys who want her body.

Premarital Sex Weakens Our Children's Character

More important than how well educated our children are is what they are. For what they are—their character—will determine what they do in life with what they know or have learned. In a vital sense, character development is the principal preparation in life, for character determines what we do under the pressures of life. Children and teens do not always react properly under pressure. They quit or explode or collapse emotionally and follow the path of least resistance. That is because they are children. Growing up is the process of learning to discipline ourselves as we grow into maturity.

Saying yes to premarital sex does nothing for one's character. It weakens one's resolve, unleashes adult passions in a child's body, and destroys self-esteem through guilt. Young people who say no to premarital sex tend to feel good about themselves and are prone to become winners in life.

One of the reasons God gave children parents is to protect them physically, mentally, and emotionally. He expects us to protect them from adult sexual temptations while they are young and immature and are developing character. All good parents protect their children from the fiery darts that would harm them—including sexual temptation. One way to do that is to teach them about their sexuality and how to maintain their virtue.

Premarital Sex Circumvents God's Perfect Will

You no doubt share the overriding desire we have for our four children. We do not care if they ever become rich or famous, we just want them to do in life whatever God has for them. We have found a lifetime of serving Christ to be an exciting and fulfilling experience, not because we are "full-time Christian workers" but because we were individually surrendered to Christ, to do His will, before we ever met. Next to accepting Christ, marrying each other was the best decision we ever made. Naturally we want the same for our children, and so do you.

Your Child's Body: A Temple. We do not hear much today about the important biblical principle that a Christian's body is the temple of God that must be kept holy. Scripture clearly emphasizes this principle in the following verses:

> Do you not know that your body is a temple of the Holy Spirit, who is in you, whom you have received from God? You are not your own; you were bought at a price. Therefore honor God with your body (1 Cor. 6:19-20).

If your child has received Jesus as his Lord and Savior, he is more than just a living human creature; he is the "temple of God." Therefore, he is commanded to honor and glorify God with his body. God has a wonderful plan for your child's life. You do not want him to miss that plan for that is his road to true happiness, one of the primary desires you have for your child. God's will cannot be found without sexual purity or virtue:

> The body is not meant for sexual immorality, but for the Lord....
> Do you not know that your bodies are members of Christ him-
> self? Shall I then take the members of Christ and unite them with
> a prostitute [immoral person]? Never! Do you not know that he
> who unites himself with a prostitute is one with her in body? For it
> is said, "The two will become one flesh." But he who unites him-
> self with the Lord is one with him in spirit (1 Cor. 6:13b,15-17).

Nothing circumvents the "perfect will of God" for a person's life like the sexual sins of fornication and adultery. Both have serious conse-quences that often adversely affect the rest of a person's life. It is inter-esting that one of our most powerful human drives is at its peak during our most vulnerable stage in life (ages fourteen through twenty-four). Perhaps that is why God gave young people parents, to help them save themselves for "the act of marriage" when they can enjoy that experience in the perfect will of God.

VIRTUE IS ITS OWN REWARD

Nothing worthwhile in life ever comes without sacrifice. Virtue is no exception. At some time in almost every child's growing up years, they will be faced with the tremendous temptation to engage in premarital sex. The path of least resistance always seems appealing at such a time. For many young people, only their strong moral and religious values, their commitment to maintaining virtue until their wedding night, or the fear of pregnancy or disease provides them the courage to say no when their glands are screaming yes.

At just such a time, young people need to know there are many advantages to living a virtuous life. Otherwise they may ask "why wait?"

Virtue Is the Will of God

First and foremost for Christians, virtue is the will of God for their lives regardless of the circumstances. Anything less will be a hindrance to their spiritual lives at a time when they need to hear the leading of the Holy Spirit clearly.

Once engaged in, sexual activity is almost impossible to halt without destroying the relationship, and it always has a detrimental effect on those involved. They withdraw from the group to spend more time together, they are filled with guilt, their prayer and devotional lives suffer, and they lose the keen edge of their spiritual dedication and participation with the youth group at the very time they need that strong spiritual influence.

Unless sexually active young people repent and resist, they will continue to deteriorate spiritually. If they do repent they usually break up with their girlfriend or boyfriend and then feel "used" or "defiled." Admittedly, God can and does completely forgive their sin of fornication, but it is impossible to return their virtue. When it's gone, it's gone. (Later in this book we shall describe the process of becoming "virtuous again." By God's grace, a new beginning is possible.)

Virtue Provides an AIDS-free and STD-free Body to Take into Marriage

When two Christians marry, they owe it to each other to bring into the marriage a healthy body that is free of sexually transmitted diseases, particularly AIDS. The only way to be certain of that is to be virgins when they marry.

Virtue Makes the Wedding Dress a Badge of Honor, Not a Hollow Mockery

White is the universally accepted color of the wedding dress and both biblically and traditionally indicates the bride is a virgin.

As early as five years of age, girls are incurable romantics. They often visualize themselves dressed in white, walking down the aisle of their church into the arms of a handsome Prince Charming. The vision usually lasts all through school, unless it is dashed to pieces by the guilt of premarital sex. Then the wedding dress becomes a cruel mockery the bride wears only to "save face" in front of her friends. What should be the happiest day of her life produces feelings of guilt that tarnish that wonderful occasion, and may get the couple off to a rocky start. Some brides cannot handle that hypocrisy emotionally.

The wife of a handsome lieutenant came to see me for counseling. Their eighteen-month long marriage was in serious trouble because, as she said, "I have become frigid." She and her husband-to-be had been having sex for several months before their wedding. She indicated she had been a virgin prior to meeting him, but after they became engaged she "gave in to his desire to go all the way." Admitting she enjoyed it before marriage, she could not understand why it was no longer pleasurable. It did not take long for her resentment to surface that the most difficult experience of her life "was to walk down the aisle of her home church in a white dress that was supposed to mean purity and virtue, but didn't!"

She felt like a hypocrite as she walked down the aisle with her father. She had a growing resentment toward her husband, thinking, *If he had just waited I could have been a virgin on my wedding day.* She would never have had to face the problem if she had said, "If you really love me, you will wait until we are married." Suppose he had received orders to be shipped overseas and was killed? Virtue before marriage is always the best policy.

The First Night Confrontation about Purity. Two very dear friends we will call Tom and Sue shared this intimate story. On their wedding night, Sue went into the bathroom to put on the lovely lace nightgown she had bought just for the occasion. When she stepped into the bedroom, Tom had never seen her more beautiful! Then she surprised him by saying, "Tom, I have saved myself for you until our wedding night. Are you a virgin, too?" Fortunately, he too had set his goal to save himself sexually for marriage and was honestly able to answer yes.

Suppose he could not have said yes to her question. Two options would have been open to him. One would be to lie, which would produce unnecessary guilt in him; the other would be to say, "No, honey, I'm sorry to say I'm not." That would have started their marriage off on a very unhappy note. It is comforting to know you brought a healthy and virtuous body into your marriage—and so did your partner.

Virgins Are Less Likely to Divorce

Those who were virgins at marriage are less likely to seek a divorce. According to an article in the November 1991 *Journal of Marriage and Family,* which examined the 1988 national Survey of Family Growth, "women who were sexually active prior to marriage faced a considerably higher risk of marital disruption than women who were virgin brides." These researchers discovered that "Catholics and Fundamentalist Protestants" were less likely to divorce and more likely to approach marriage as virgins. Perhaps the same principles of resolve that made a young person remain virtuous during their single years also help them through the difficult times of marriage. Virtue is maintained by self-control as a result of character strengths and moral commitment. These same character traits will help a couple maintain moral purity and fidelity to each other after marriage, regardless the amount of sexual temptation produced in today's permissive society.

Virgins Make Good Role Models for Their Children

Children are much more open with their parents today; in some cases they can be brutally frank. Many parents have acknowledged the icy chill that runs down their spine when their teenagers look them in the eye and ask, "Mom, were you and Dad virgins when you got married?" Again they are faced with one of life's moments of truth, even if their sin has been confessed and forgiven. For they either have to lie to their teen or stonewall them with "That is none of your business." Either response lowers the respect children have for their parents. However, if the parents played the game of life according to the rules of God, they can look their children in the eye and acknowledge their virtue. That is good role modeling.

Virtue Helps Produce Healthy, Normal Children

When I was a teen I had a friend (I'll call him Phil) whose father, like mine, was dead. Unlike my father, who died suddenly of a heart attack when I was nine, his father committed suicide when Phil was four. He could barely remember him. Phil had a scar on the side of his face that he eventually explained was the result of several operations to repair a hole in his cheek. Doctors said it was a birth defect caused by his father's syphilis contracted before he married. In his youth Phil's dad "sowed his wild oats" and incurred a sexually transmitted disease that disfigured his son for life. The father's guilt became so intense he hung himself—a high price to pay for a few minutes of illicit pleasure.

This list of virtue's rewards is not complete, but it does show the truth of the biblical aphorism, "The way of the transgressor is hard." From the beginning of time, immoral mankind has violated God's virtuous standard of behavior, but not without harmful side effects—mentally, emotionally, physically, and most of all spiritually. But all of the harmful results described here are avoided when a person saves sex for marriage. Virtue is its own reward.

VIRTUE: EVERY PARENT'S CONCERN, EVERY PARENT'S DREAM

Every good parent wants their children to be virgins when they marry. But it is not just the fear of pregnancy or STDs that makes virtue the universal dream of every parent. The ready availability of abortion, often without parental consent, poses yet another danger.

A *Fourteen-year-old with Adult Problems.* Beverly conducts a daily open-mike radio talk show from the nation's capital that is carried live on stations all over the country. One of her guests was the mother of a fourteen-year-old girl (we shall call Debbie) who is reasonably active in their church. Her mother had become concerned about Debbie, noting that she was not her usual bubbly self, "even refusing to go to the mall on Friday nights with her friends." One day her mother went in to tidy up Debbie's room and to her horror discovered under her pillow "a post abortion survey." When Debbie came home from school, she was running such a high fever, they decided she should see a doctor. At her mother's suggestion, Debbie took a bath first. While she was in the bathtub, she suddenly began screaming—human body parts were coming out of her, indicating a botched abortion. She was rushed to the hospital where she was put in the intensive care ward with a life-threatening infection. Finally, it became necessary to perform a hysterectomy to save her life, cheating her out of ever having the joy of being a biological mother. All this before her fifteenth birthday!

We heard about Debbie's case because she and her mother came to Washington, D.C., to appear before a Congressional committee to demand parental notification for children before they could legally get an abortion. As her mother explained to the Congressional panel, "The school advised our daughter to get an abortion without our consent but they were nowhere to be found when it came time to mortgage our home so we could pay the $28,000 medical bills to save Debbie's life."

You may think that this is an isolated case that could never happen to your fourteen-year-old child, but so did Debbie's parents. So did the California parents who contacted Concerned Women for America's Legal Defense Foundation for help with their eighteen-year-old daughter. She was paralyzed by an infection from a botched abortion, which was also recommended without parental consent.

No parents in their right minds want such heartache or suffering for their children, yet many are falling victim to such tragedies and at even earlier ages. You want to do everything you can to prevent heartache from striking your family, which is probably why you are reading this book. Thank God there are many things you can do to save your child from such suffering.

Christian Young People Speak Out on Sex

In preparation for writing this book, we held discussions with groups of high school students in California, Maryland, Virginia, and Oregon. All of the teens surveyed were active in their local churches. The most telling comment we heard from several was, "I wish my parents would talk to me more about sex." Many teens said, "My parents never talk to me about sex." That is tragic, and we are sure you agree.

Today, more than ever before, children need their parent to accept their role of family sex education instructors. This book will equip you for that role. The best way to insure that your children share your moral values is to teach those values to them. Then they can be fortified by your church and other Christian influences. But good sex education should always begin at home.

Some one is going to teach your children about sex. This book is designed to equip you, the most important person in your child's life, to be that teacher.

---

[1] Paul Hess, "They Call This Abstinence?" *Citizen Magazine*, 18 May 1992, 3.

[2] George B. Eager, *Love, Dating, and Sex: What Teens Want to Know* (Valdosta, Ga.: Mailbox Club Books, 1989), 73.

[3] Ibid., 72.

Chapter Two

HOW TO RAISE VIRTUOUS CHILDREN

Next to leading your children to Christ for salvation and teaching them to "walk in the Spirit" so they will live in the will of God, the best thing you can do for them is to raise them to be chaste. We have already seen that sexual purity saves them from a lot of heartache, guilt, and even physically destructive diseases.

But admittedly, that is easier said than done, for you cannot make life's decisions for them. You can do everything right in preparing them to make the right choices, but in the final analysis they will make their own decisions. That is what "free will" is all about. At best you can only help them prepare for the inevitable moments of temptation. When the lights are low, the music sweet, and their feelings hot, the final decision rests with them. They will have to live by the decisions they make. In many cases, so will you!

PREPARING YOUR CHILDREN FOR A LIFE OF VIRTUE

The following suggestions are some of the most important things you can do to prepare your children for those adult temptations that threaten to destroy them. Study them carefully.

Love Them

The best preparation you can give your children for life in an adult world is the assurance of your love. Everyone can afford that! As children grow up it is not uncommon for them to have strong feelings of inadequacy. That is why public educators talk so much about their need for self-acceptance. What they fail to understand is that such feelings are almost universal among children. They are little people in a big world where to them it seems everyone else can do things, but they are inept.

The best antidote for a child's inept feelings is genuine love from his mother and father. When children grow up with the consciousness they are important, because the two people most important in their world take time to love them, it gives them the realization of self-worth. We have found that children (particularly girls) who come from homes where they are loved usually make easy adjustments to marriage. Girls who were exposed to normal father-daughter love and were able to climb up on their father's lap anytime they chose and find his heart's door open, seldom have sexual hang-ups in marriage. Girls who were rejected by their fathers in childhood often show signs of frigidity within six to eighteen months of marriage or after the birth of their first child.

Family counselor Gary Smalley says that a woman needs "at least twelve touches a day" from her husband. Not only do we agree, but we also think children need twice that many touches. No matter how unaffectionate you are by temperament or background, with God's help you can give love to your children because they need it. The child that is given plenty of love at home is less likely to be sexually precocious because they are not love-starved. Many teens are so love-starved at home they trade their virtue for the hopes of finding love. Girls, particularly, seek love through sex, only to realize they had sex without love. Young people who are loved by Mom and Dad are less likely than the love-starved child to seek sex in all the wrong places, at the wrong times, and with the wrong people.

Our dear friend, Sarah Trollinger, runs the House of Hope in Orlando, Florida. She has taken in hundreds of teenage girls whose parents could no longer control them. Some have been sent to her by the courts as a last resort. Most of these girls testify that before receiving Christ they were "wild, rebellious, sexually active, and strung out on drugs." They used sexual activity to support their drug habits. One judge called them "throw-away girls." Fortunately, Sarah, in the name of Jesus, was there to catch them. It is incredible what God has done in these girls' lives after they accepted Christ, were discipled in the Word, and experienced the new life in Christ. Recently Sarah gave a survey to twenty-five of these girls and asked them what four things they wanted most from their parents. All twenty-five put "unconditional love" as number one. (Number two was total forgiveness).

A child does not have to be a runaway to want love from her parents. It is a universal desire. Take time to express love to your children every day. It helps to prepare them for life.

Provide Them Two Loving Role Models

The first two people of the opposite sex that children observe showing love to each other are their mother and father. They do not have to know the details about what their parents do in the sanctity of their love; in fact, it is better if they do not know. But they do need to pick up the signals from their parents that they genuinely love each other.

A case could be made for that kind of love-model being the best sex education there is. Millions of couples have gotten married without any knowledge of the opposite sex and went on to learn to experience a great love life. The key was their mental attitude toward the experience, and usually that was learned by watching the way their parents treated each other.

We also believe, based on our experience in counseling many married couples, that one of the reasons God gave human beings their powerful attraction toward the opposite sex is not only to propagate the race but to help smooth off their otherwise irritating personal differences. When properly consummated in marriage, sexual expression is so exciting, fulfilling, and enriching that it draws the two lovers ever closer together despite those differences that would otherwise drive them apart. Children can feel that love, and it makes them look forward to marriage with positive anticipation. It also stands in sharp contrast to the cheap and tawdry view of sex that is exhibited by Broadway and Hollywood.

Parents need to cultivate their love not just for themselves, but also for their children. For years we have encouraged couples to take mini-honeymoons as often as possible (preferably every three months). This is a time for them to get away from the children for a night or two and just enjoy each other emotionally, socially, and physically. When children see their parents going away just to be together, it reassures them that their parents still love each other and keeps the marriage mystique alive.

The Power of a Moral Example. The best insurance against immorality in a marriage is a warm love relationship between partners and the serious commitment to sexual exclusivity they made to each other and God on their wedding day. It is devastating to the moral practices of Christian youth when their parents are immoral. Many a girl has traded her virtue more out of revenge for her father's unfaithfulness to her mother than as an act of passion.

Two teens I know went down the moral sewer, ruined their lives, and married unbelievers after the news came out that their mother had an affair with her boss; both were professing Christians. Today the man and the woman have repented and broken off their relationship. The woman reconciled with her husband and changed jobs, but the affair cost her her two children. The boss divorced his wife, and although he too has repented and is walking with the Lord today after marrying again, he lost his five children; no small price to pay for sin. The children's morals went downhill immediately after the sin was revealed. The Bible challenges us to 'be examples to believers.' Nowhere is that more important than in the moral training of our own children.

Start Early Teaching Your Children about Sex

Sex is both the most exciting experience in the world and the most difficult to talk about. One reason it is the source of crude jokes with some people is because it is difficult for them to discuss on a serious level—so difficult that some couples rarely discuss it between themselves. We have found that usually couples who do not enjoy good sexual relationships are the ones who find it difficult to discuss. As a general rule, the better love life a couple has the easier it is to discuss it privately. Our mail indicates that one of the reasons God has so blessed our book, *The Act of Marriage*, is because for many couples, both newlyweds and those married as long as fifty years, it opens the conversational door on sex. One lady wrote, "Until we read your book we had not discussed our sex life for twenty-five years." Many times a free and honest discussion is the first step to resolving difficulties.

The reason sex is difficult to talk about even between loving partners is that it is intrinsically private. God intended it so! The normal instinct for modesty was given to us by God to protect our sexual body parts and activities. Sex was meant to be private.

It should not surprise us then that sex is difficult to talk about with our children. They instinctively want to keep it private and so do we. In this day and age, it is extremely important to talk to our children about sex. If we do not, someone, who probably does not share our values will.

Be Gently Aggressive. Take the initiative to talk to your children. Never show disapproval that they brought up something, even if they use some vulgar words to describe it. Usually, children do not realize those words are swear words. They simply overhear them and pick them up to add to their ever-growing vocabulary. They need to be taught in a loving atmosphere by their parents what is acceptable and what is not.

When children are little their curiosity about their own bodies and things they see in nature or on television make them ask questions. Use such occasions to convey the idea that they can talk to you about sexual matters just like they do about anything else. The natural tendency of parents is to "freeze" when they hear adult words about sex coming out of little mouths. That is why you should study the nuts and bolts information in the following chapters targeted to the age of your child. When those golden opportunities come along and your child throws open the conversational door, you are ready to walk right in.

Do not be like many parents who wait until they think their kids are old enough for "the big sex talk" and then dump the whole load on them in one session. More of this later. Just remember to be gently aggressive and occasional.

One of the best talks I had with our oldest daughter, who is today married to a minister and the mother of three children, was one night when she woke up in the car as we were traveling across the country. The rest of the family were asleep, and she crawled up in the front seat and began talking with me. Spontaneously, she brought up something that troubled her, and we discussed it openly in a relaxed atmosphere. Although I do not remember what it was we discussed, we opened a conversational door between us that has remained open ever since. You can be sure that when she became a teenager and boys began showing an interest in her, I was mighty glad that door was open. Somehow that door was open with all our kids. Maybe that is why having four teens at the same time was not traumatic but instead made it a fun time in life for us.

A Christian father heard me say we were writing this book and said, "Be sure and tell parents to start early!" Then he went on to tell how one Saturday morning their eleven-year-old daughter crawled into bed between him and his wife and said, "Dad, there is something I'd like to ask you about God. Why is it that He only wants us to have sex with one other person in life?" Stifling his temptation to panic, he used that open door to talk to her about things she was beginning to need to know. One subject lead to another, his wife added her thoughts as well, and the daughter got more than she asked for in a natural setting. Today at eighteen, she is a beautiful and well-balanced young lady who learned her values from the people in her life who love her the most: her parents. While this was their first in-depth sex talk, it was not the first time they had talked about it. They had discussed this subject for years whenever it came up.

Always Be Honest. It is incredible that so many parents do not tell the truth when their children bring up the subject of sex. Instead, they become flustered and either lie or teach the child by their nervousness that sexual topics are a "no-no" subject. This is flawed policy.

For example, note the difference in the following answers to the childish question: "Where did I come from?" The old answer was, "The stork brought you." A better answer is, "God gave you to us...and we are very glad He did!" Avoid teaching too much in response to these innocent questions. Make your answers matter of fact when your children are small, and use the proper words. Do not overload them when they are in lower elementary school. One mother became so flustered when her son asked, "Where did I come from?" that she told him the whole story. After she finished, he looked at her a bit bewildered and said, "I mean like Johnnie—his parents said he came from Texas."

Honesty is the best policy. Keep it simple. Answer their questions the best you can, and try to treat it like any other subject. The next several chapters should help you.

Keep Them Out of Public School Sex Education Classes

As we mentioned briefly in the previous chapter, sex education in public schools has gone from being a helpful hygiene course that included morality and abstinence to explicit "anything goes" classes that are at best amoral and at worst hostile to virtue. Formerly, the instuctors of these classes respected traditional Judeo-Christian moral values and were supportive of what parents were trying to teach their children at home. Today, these classes often shock the moral sensibilities of the students with explicit material that enrages parents throughout the country. They ridicule the old curriculum as "outdated biological plumbing courses," and have replaced it with what could honestly be called "intercourse education."

Educators present this new, radically explicit material under the pretext of reducing teenage pregnancy, but in actuality, teenage pregnancies have increased three-fold. They also insist on teaching the material in mixed classes, which destroys the moral mystique that naturally exists between the sexes. And as Appendix A makes clear, their latest plan for the future will only make it worse and morally unacceptable for Christians and other parents who share our moral values. If this wave-of-the-future material is not taught in your public school system yet, it soon will be. This shows how perverted some sex educators' morals can be.

When I first began opposing the radically explicit sex education changes in the California curriculum for elementary and high school children, I warned that the teaching of this curriculum would increase sexual promiscuity, teen pregnancy, and STDs. All three predictions have come true with a vengeance. Today, instead of 300,000 unwed teens each year, we have 1,100,000, and instead of STDs that were treatable by penicillin, we have incurable sexually transmitted diseases, including AIDS. Who needs this kind of sex education? Certainly not Christian young people.

In many public schools today, administrators and teachers require all students to take sex education. That is against the law! They cannot force children to take the course, but many administrators or teachers try to intimidate parents into forcing their children to do so. While there are still many dedicated teachers in the public school system, there are also many who do not respect your rights as a parent to be the primary teacher of this subject to your children. These self-appointed "sex experts" are literally evangelists of promiscuity. Most are convinced that everyone is doing it, which is quite untrue. This fallacy is an encouragement to some insecure young people to become involved in premarital sexual activity. Some sex education teachers or their recommended reading materials even endorse or speak favorably of homosexuality as "an optional sexual lifestyle."

Why Do They Do It? Why would intelligent people spend their lives in a branch of education that has proven to be so destructive to millions of children? Their explicit anything-goes teachings have produced an obsession with sex that has resulted in millions of unwed pregnancies and the subsequent heartaches, abortions, depression, suicides, and infection. Why do they do it? It is a matter of money, greed, and humanistic hatred for

Christianity and moral values.

Dr. James Dobson, a child psychologist, together with Gary Bauer, a Washington, D.C.-based lawyer, said in their book, *Children at Risk*:

> Let's deal with the obvious question head on: Why do bureaucrats and researchers and Planned Parenthood types fight so hard to preserve adolescent promiscuity? Why do they balk at the thought of intercourse occurring only in the context of marriage? Why have they completely removed the door marked 'Premarital Sex' for a generation of vulnerable teenagers?
>
> Their motivation is not difficult to understand. Multiplied millions of dollars are generated each year in direct response to teenage sexual irresponsibility. Kids jumping into bed with each other is supporting entire industries of grateful adults. The abortion business alone brings in an estimated $600 million annually. Do you really believe the physicians, nurses, medical suppliers and bureaucrats who owe their livelihood to the killing of unborn babies would prefer that adolescents abstain until marriage?...
>
> Imagine how many jobs would be lost if kids quit playing musical beds with one another! This is why professionals who advise young people about sex are so emotional about the word *abstinence*. If that idea ever caught on, who would need the services of Planned Parenthood and their ilk? It's a matter of self-preservation.[1]

For these and other reasons we recommend that parents be aggressive about keeping their children out of public school sex education classes. Instead, teach your children at home what you want them to know. Include not only the biological facts of life, but also moral values and reasons for abstinence and techniques on how to save themselves for marriage.

Teach Them Who They Are

We hear a lot from public educators today about self-image or self-acceptance. It is a problem for children because public educators reject or omit all references to God and teach children they are biological accidents—the result of "random chance as products of evolution." We know better. Our children are creatures of God! They need to know that. Talk about improving their self-image! Children who know they are creatures of God have much less trouble understanding "Who am I?" or "Where did I come from?" than those children who mistakenly think they evolved.

You should assure them of the following:

1. *They are children of God and coheirs with Jesus Christ* (John 1:12; Rom. 8:17). If they have received Christ personally, they have been born again into the family of God. Somewhere between six and twelve years old, you should make sure your child has received Christ personally. Then make sure they understand that "God loves them and has a wonderful plan for their life." Teach them that their body is not their own but is "the temple of God" and should be kept holy.

2. *They are your children.* It is reassuring to children to know they were wanted by their parents and are loved by them. Let them know that although you may not approve of everything they do, you do approve of them and love them. They are important to you and should know it. What they do in life is important to you, and their decisions will affect not only them but the whole family.

Their stand for virtue and integrity is a testimony for them, for their Lord, and for their family. Similarly, if they squander their integrity and lose their reputation by sexual promiscuity, it is a reproach to the whole family.

A sixteen-year-old tenth grader who attended one of our teen discussion groups had not opened his mouth until we brought up the following subject: "Do today's teens really understand the high cost of promiscuity?" He said, "I can tell you about that! My two older sisters got pregnant, one in college, the other in high school, and it changed our lives forever." He then related how it plunged both of them into an early adulthood and destroyed their vocational goals and dreams. While we don't want to give the impression that we want our children to remain virgins simply for the family's sake, we do want them to know that their moral conduct is important to God and to the entire family.

Teach Them Moral Values

If your children are going to learn Christian moral values, you and your church will have to teach them. The public school will not do it. In some cases, the public school does not teach moral values because they reject them. In other cases, since morals are based on the Bible, the schools have been intimidated by the threat of a lawsuit for "teaching religion." A federal judge in Louisiana recently decreed that teaching abstinence is unconstitutional because it is based on morals derived from religion. Consequently, he ruled that teaching abstinence in the public schools violates the First Amendment. For that reason, you must be the teacher of morals to your children, so that as they move into puberty, they are confronted with what the Bible teaches on the subject. They need to know that all sex outside marriage is condemned in the Bible. Lest they receive a wrong message, they should also be told that all references in the scriptures to sex in marriage are approved by God. You may wish to examine the Scripture references to Christian moral values found in Appendix B.

Keep Them Active in a Bible-teaching Church

The best friend your family has is your local church. That is the one place where the principles parents try to inculcate into the lives of their children are supported by everyone they meet. The teachers, pastors, and youth workers all teach from the same manual—the Bible. In the church we are on the same page as a family.

Dr. Jacqueline Kasun observed that regular church attendance is the strongest positive influence on the sexual behavior of girls over the age of seventeen. Her conclusions are confirmed by the 1986 Lou Harris poll for Planned Parenthood.

The Lutheran Brotherhood's "Respect Teen Program" had The Search Institute study forty-seven thousand sixth- through twelfth-grade students attending public schools. The study found that of those students who regularly attended church, 22 percent were sexually active, compared to 42 percent of those who occasionally attended church. Regular church attendance decreased the percentage of sexual activity by 20 percent. Evidently, the popularly quoted statistic that "51 percent of girls and 63 percent of boys" are sexually active in their teens is so high because many of these teens do not attend church.

Never Criticize Your Church within the Hearing of Your Children. Parents should never criticize their pastor, their church, or any of its leaders within the hearing of their children. The last thing you want when you take your teenager to church on Sunday is for them to filter everything your pastor teaches through the sound of last week's criticism of him at home. Parents who live on a diet of roast preacher for Sunday dinner usually raise children who are lost to the world before they get married.

Since your church is the best friend your family has, then use it to help you raise your children to love and serve God by attending regularly. Many of those parents who lamented they "lost their teens to the world," admitted they became careless about church attendance and involvement. Careless church attendance can be fatal to your children's lives. We taught our children that "unless you have a communicable disease that will endanger someone's health, we go as a family to church."

If your church is not a Bible-believing and teaching church, begin looking for one that is! Ages fourteen through twenty-four are the most important years in the spiritual training of your children. Provide them the best church experience your community offers.

Keep Them Active in Your Church Youth Group

Most teenagers are social creatures who crave the company of their peers. They will find such a group somewhere—their neighborhood, their school, or their church. We have found the church to be the best place for them to make friends who will have a positive influence on them.

The young people they will meet there will not be perfect. Some will be rebels who attend against their will, and rebels seem to attract each other. But generally, your teen will find moral and spiritual help in your church youth group.

One thing is certain—in that group they will associate with young people who are far less sexually active than other young people in almost any other environment. It is not too difficult to figure out which environment is best for your teens.

Send Them to Summer Youth Camp. One of the most effective programs youth and church groups provide young people is summer camping and weekend retreats. We realize these activities can be expensive, but they are among the most helpful programs you can provide for your children. Not only does camp allow them to get away to concentrate on spiritual matters, but at this crucial time in life they need to see themselves as part of a large body of Christian youth. In addition, the speakers at such events are usually among the most gifted leaders for reaching kids. Your children need such opportunities.

Many young people discover God's plan for their lives at camp. Some of the most important spiritual decisions young people make today are at summer youth camp.

Help Your Children Select Their Friends

Peer pressure today is strong, and it has the most influence on our young between the ages of fourteen and twenty-four. If there is ever a time your children need positive Christian friends, it is during those formative years.

Note these words of scripture: "Bad company corrupts good character" (1 Cor. 15:33). That verse is probably the main reason I am in the ministry today. When I was seventeen, my godly mother forced me to break off my close friendship with four boys I had played sports with, ran around with, and double-dated with for five years. However, she had noticed changes coming over me she did not like. Then God brought that verse to her attention one morning during her devotions and she saw it "as a message from God." I did not welcome that announcement and at first balked. But in her lovingly stern way, she said with tears in her eyes, "Young man, as long as you park your feet under my table, you will abide by my rules!" Naturally, I thought she was intolerant, mean-spirited, and unloving, but today I rise up to call her blessed! One of those friends has spent sixteen years in a federal penitentiary, and two have been divorced three times. I am still in love with my first and only wife and have what to me is the most fulfilling of all vocations. My mother and that verse saved my life. Your children, at the most important time in their lives (and probably when they least want it) will need your help in screening their friends. Don't fail them!

If Possible, Send Them to a Christian School or Teach Them at Home

For one hundred and fifty years the public school was as American as "motherhood and apple pie." Only a few ardently religious groups (Reformed churches, Catholics, Mennonites, and others) provided parochial school education. One generation ago Bible reading, prayer, Christian moral principles, and even creationism were common place in our schools. All this was changed with the advent of secular humanism in the curriculum. Now the practices and teachings of most public schools are not only void of anything Christian or religious but they are actually hostile to it.

The apostle Paul said, "See to it that no one takes you [or your children] captive through hollow and deceptive philosophy, which depends on human tradition and the basic principles of this world rather than on Christ" (Col. 2:8). That is exactly what is going on in the majority of our nation's schools today. Our children are being deceived by secular humanist philosophy and amoral traditions instead of being fortified with Christian principles and moral traditions.

It is time for Christians and churches to wake up and realize that in most instances the public school is an unfit place for our children to get their education. We should raise our young people according to our beliefs and principles, not theirs.

Home Schoolers. Currently there are 1.8 million parents who home school their children. Many do not have access to a local Christian school or cannot afford the cost. While some educators ridicule such parental attempts to protect the minds of their children, most parents of home-schoolers would be glad to compare their children's reading, writing, and math abilities to the average public school student. Home school can't be too bad an educational experience—twenty-nine of the fifty-five men who wrote our nation's constitution were home schooled. And today we have excellent materials available to help even inexperienced parents do an excellent job. (See *The Big Book of Home Learning*, vols. 1-4, by Mary Pride for the latest home education information.)

Churches to Start Christian Schools. My dream for the next decade is to see thousands of churches in both large and small communities work together to provide a Christian school for the children and youth who desperately need an alternative. In the first place, we have the biblical mandate to raise our children in the nurture of the Lord. Second, we have the buildings to accommodate such classrooms and some even have gymnasiums and playgrounds. Third, we have dedicated teachers and educators within our membership who would joyfully serve our Lord by teaching His children in church schools.

Although it cannot be said that young people who attend Christian schools never become sexually active, the percentage of those who do is much lower. The largest Christian school association in the country, representing over sixty-five hundred schools, took a national survey of high school students that included their response to sexual activity. Only 14 percent registered one or more sexual experiences.

Unquestionably Christian schools graduate more virgins than do public schools. That is reason enough for many parents to consider Christian school or home schooling worth the cost. They have no more precious possession than their children.

Warn Your Children about the Joys and Dangers of Sexual Attraction

When one of my daughters was in the seventh grade and not yet interested in boys, she was standing at my study window looking down on a group of ninth-grade young people gathered at the entrance of our church. Suddenly, she turned around and said, disgustedly, of one of the girls she deeply admired, "Diane just batted her eyes at those boys!" Two years later I stood at that window and saw my daughter batting her eyes at the boys. What made the difference? Hormone development.

It is not uncommon for boys and girls to dislike each other. But somewhere between the seventh and ninth grades, that repulsion becomes an attraction that often makes sex urges the most exciting feelings they have. The boy who "doesn't like girls because you can't wrestle or play football with them" suddenly cannot wait to get his arms around them and kiss them. He is not perverted; he is just being normal.

Without that urge for the opposite sex, the race would become extinct. During adolescence, your young person needs to be prepared to cope with these urges, feelings, and tendencies to sexual fantasies. He or she needs to know they are controllable, that they can produce great pleasure and bonding, but that they are also very dangerous.

Young people need to be taught that we human beings have many drives or urges that must be controlled in life, such as hunger, anger, and jealousy. The Ten Commandments are predominantly prohibitions against letting those urges control us. This is a good place to show them that one aspect of maturity is learning to control our urges. They have their proper place in our lives, but we should control them instead of letting them control us. Our appetite for food is a good example. We need food, and eating has a proper place in our lives, but we cannot eat anything and everything we want or we will destroy our health and appearance.

Young people must understand that God's will for all human beings is that they save the fulfillment of their sexual urges until marriage, after they each find the person God wants them to spend the rest of their life with. In the meantime, they should be taught that social contacts with the opposite sex are healthy and can produce much pleasure and fellowship so long as they are not intimate. Intimate sexual activity should always be taught as an expression of love that is reserved for marriage.

Premature sexual expression is the supreme example of sacrificing on the altar of the immediate that which is permanent. It may produce incomparable excitement and thrill for the moment, but in the long run it produces heartache, grief, and sometimes physical pain. It is not worth the risk, and young people need to know that.

Warn Them of the Law of Emotional Progression

Most young people who become sexually active never intended to "go all the way." Through their tears I have heard several say, "I don't know what happened to me, we just got carried away." They did not know or did not account for the progressive nature of sex. One writer who has addressed many youth groups on this subject calls it the Law of Progression:

> What is the Law of Progression as it relates to sexuality? It is this: When a guy and a girl spend time alone together, the relationship tends to move steadily toward greater physical intimacy.

> To begin with, just being together with the person you love is a happy and satisfying experience. But along with this is the desire for physical contact.

> The first physical contact in a guy-girl relationship is usually holding hands. This is exciting because it is physical contact and it feels great.

> In time, however, there will be a desire for greater intimacy. The guy may put his arm around the girl. Then comes the first kiss. It may be a simple goodnight kiss, but that can send a guy into orbit. That's wonderful, but the Law of Progression is working and what satisfies you now will not satisfy you later on.

> Each time you are alone, you start where you left off last time. The couple begins experimenting with "super kissing"—prolonged kissing. Then comes "French kissing"—kissing with your mouth open. You are now entering a phase where sexual desires are being aroused.

> Then comes prolonged sessions of hugging and kissing. The more time you spend together, the more intimate you become.

> Then comes "petting." This is where the hands get into the act. Petting is handling each other's body—parts normally covered by clothing. It does not include sexual intercourse. It has been defined as "everything but."

Petting is pleasurable to both the guy and the girl, but it's dangerous because it arouses strong genital feelings. In marriage this is the foreplay that prepares the couple for sex. But your body doesn't know that you are not married. The signal to your body is: Get ready for sexual intercourse.

Many a guy and a girl get involved in petting and see nothing wrong in it because they have no intention of going all the way. But invariably they end up doing what they never intended to do because they didn't understand the progressive nature of sex.

Petting is followed by "heavy petting." Then comes mutual sex play in which the guy and the girl are touching and handling each other's intimate parts. Sexual passions are further aroused and the couple proceeds to sexual intercourse—something that should be reserved for marriage[2]

Many Christians and other morally minded young people who "get carried away" erroneously justify having sex by thinking, "We're going to get married anyway," or "We love each other so its okay." But as Eager further points out, "[Premarital sex] marks the end of the relationship as it once was. The physical side of the relationship is now overpowering. After this, every time the couple gets alone, the tendency will be to go all the way—regardless of the dangers and problems."[3]

Once sexual intercourse has been experienced by unmarried couples, even if they were both virgins, it usually results in a desire for more intimacy or a breakup of their relationship. It is all but impossible for a couple that has "gone all the way" to back up in their relationship and stop having sex. Often it breaks down all their restraint and creates an emotional feeding frenzy that craves more and more sexual activity. Most newlyweds experience this intense sexual attraction which is right and good for them. However, single couples have the increased appetite without the opportunity or legitimacy.

It is not uncommon for couples engaging in premarital sex to become obsessed with sex, which comes at the expense of every other area of their life, including spiritual, educational, and family relationships. Most of their thoughts and activities now become sexually focused. This often creates conflict with their parents who become alarmed and suspicious. The parents may try to clamp down, and the young people rebel in

The Law of Progression

Start of Relationship

Being together & Holding Hands

Simple Good Night Kiss

Prolonged Kissing

Necking

Petting

Heavy Petting

Mutual Sex Play

Sexual Intercourse

Sexual Arousal

End of Relationship in Present Form

The progression of sexual feeling with increased physical intimacy an attempt to be together. This puts an ugly strain on family relationships that makes life miserable for all involved.

Many young people who lose their virginity experience strong guilt feelings that destroy their relationship and cause them to break up—not the strengthening of the love bond between them as they thought. Once they break up, it is almost impossible for one or both of them to remain active in the same church youth group. Every time they see each other they are reminded of their sexual intimacy. It is not that way with those who engage in light kissing or moderate hugging. They can break up and still face each other.

Sex is so intimate. Both nature and God teach us that sex before marriage is wrong and produces guilt. Sex was meant by God only for marriage.

That is why couples who engage in premarital sex pay such severe consequences, for this violates God's law which clearly says, "flee sexual immorality." Young people need to realize early on that all premarital sex is immoral. The Bible calls it "fornication," a very ugly name for a very harmful act.

The Death of Innocence. Once virtue is lost it can never be fully regained. Consequently, it makes it easier for those who have had premarital sex to "go all the way" with other dates. Soon a dangerous pattern of sexual promiscuity has begun. Unless the guilt they experience is followed by Christian counseling and the seeking of God's forgiveness for this sin—which, praise God, is always available for the repentant sinner (see 1 John 1:7-9)—the guilt will lead to either rebellion and flagrant promiscuity or a serious loss of self-worth, which is often followed by additional sexual escapades.

One beautiful girl, who was raised in a fine Christian home and professes to be a Christian, was expelled from her Christian high school for seducing three boys, who also were expelled. Upon counseling her, I discovered it all started with a boy she loved months before. They got "carried away" and she lost all respect for herself. She soon learned that her craving for approval could be satisfied temporarily by bringing others down to her level. Through the years I have watched that tragic soul go through three marriages. All ended because of her infidelity, a high price to pay for "getting carried away."

Your teens need to know that premarital intimacy is dangerous for many reasons, not the least of which is the Law of Progression. As

George Eager summarizes, "There is a progressive nature in sex. You tend to move steadily toward more and more physical intimacy unless you take definite steps to prevent this."[4]

Warn Them of the Dangers of Sexually Transmitted Diseases

In this promiscuous society of ours, where fornication is called "casual sex" or "sexual activity" (equating it almost to the level of sporting events), three million people contract sexually transmitted diseases each year. According to the Centers for Disease Control's latest report, "86% of all STDs occur among persons aged 15-29 years." Obviously, our youth need to know about their vulnerability to these diseases. It is one more reason you have to encourage them to remain virtuous until marriage.

We recommend a private, formal talk with your children at home to discuss these problems. Fifteen or sixteen is not too young, and if you suspect any sexual activity, twelve or thirteen is not too early. Please study the section on STDs in the Glossary and teach it to your children.

Provide Them with Clear Guidelines for Dating

It was surprising to us to find that many of the Christian young people who attended our discussion groups had no clearly defined rules for dating. Interestingly enough, the importance of such rules were not lost on the teens themselves for many of them responded to the question, "What suggestions would you like to see offered to parents?" by saying, "Give kids strict rules for dating." Many of these young people felt parents were too lax. One sixteen-year-old commented, "My parents are so naive," yet both her parents were dedicated Christians and leaders in the church. Because of the importance of this subject, we have dedicated an entire chapter (chapter 9) to it. Please read it carefully, develop your own dating rules, share them with your child, and lovingly enforce them. If you do not, someday you may wish you had.

Teach Them to Be the Moral Cop

Our macho society has bred the false notion that on a date a boy can go as far as a girl will let him. That, together with the usual male aggression complex and their growing sex drive, often makes girls a target of sexual conquest. That is, of course, morally wrong and should have no place in a Christian teen's attitude. After all, we individually are accountable to God for our behavior. Both the boy and the girl should be taught to be the moral police officer (the person who decides what is right or wrong) while on a date. This protects them both, and helps them to maintain their virtue regardless of sexual temptation.

Parents of boys ought to realize that just because a sweet looking young girl goes to church, that does not mean that under the right provocation she might not try to seduce him. She may have some psychological or emotional need you know nothing about. She may even have been sexually active before she met your son. If he does not have firmly established commitments to morality, he could be very vulnerable. Dr. Henrietta Mears, one of the greatest youth workers of her generation (when the level of sexual temptation was much less than it is today), said of the collegians with whom she worked, "I would never trust the best man we have with the wrong woman!" I agree. Unless they are deeply committed to morality for the Lord's sake, most men are vulnerable. Obviously, commitment to morality is necessary for our daughters also.

Two moral cops on a date can have lots of fun—they can even date seriously for awhile. But if their relationship breaks up, they can walk away from each other and still be friends, and they can look at themselves in the mirror each morning without guilt. Two moral cops on a date have the freedom to relax and enjoy life and each other in a wholesome manner, without worry. They have a clearly defined line for their conduct they will not violate. Believe it or not, that makes dating *more* enjoyable, not less.

Help Them Make a Formal Commitment to Virtue

During the last few years, popular child psychologist Dr. James Dobson and others have developed the idea of a formal commitment to virtue before marriage which we heartily recommend. It is an expansion of the idea my friend and youth evangelist Ken Poure popularized many years ago. After taking his sixteen-year-old daughter out for a formal dinner in a fancy restaurant, he had an intimate "father-daughter" talk and formally introduced her to the wonderful world of dating. That night she made a commitment to God and her dad to be a virgin on her wedding day.

One writer added the idea of presenting the teen with a ring or key, which symbolized their virtue. The young person (either a boy or girl) made a formal commitment to remain virtuous until marriage, and then both parent and child prayed and made that commitment to God. Then the child was given the ring or key to present to their marriage partner on their wedding night.

We believe this step in keeping them chaste for marriage is so important we have reserved an entire chapter for it. Please read chapter 8 carefully.

Teach Them to Purify Their Minds

All sin begins in the mind. If a person never sins in his mind, he will never sin with his body. That may be one of the reasons our Lord raised the moral level of adultery from the physical act of sex to the mental act of lust: "But I tell you that anyone who looks at a woman lustfully has already committed adultery with her in his heart" (Matt. 5:28). Note how different that is from the humanistic psychology which dominates our society and encourages fantasies even for school-age children.

Today, parents who would protect their children adequately must teach them how to and how not to use their minds. From the onset of puberty and the new exciting hormonal changes in their body, young people begin to have sexual thoughts that need to be resisted not culti- vated. The last thing they need is to cultivate these thoughts through fantasy trips. They need to bring every thought into captivity to Christ, as the scriptures teach. Particularly is that true of boys because of their intense sex drive. Their thoughts early on can become explicitly sexual.

All boys between thirteen and sixteen should have a parent talk about their thought life. We recommend that parents even ask them pri- vately if they ever think about sexual activity with other boys. While most boys are enamored with girls at the onset of their sex drive, some fanta- size male-male relationships. This must stop because it can lead to excluding male-female thoughts and fixate on male-male thoughts. Such a boy is easy prey for some homosexual "chicken hawk" who seeks young victims to lure into his perverted and very harmful lifestyle. As our society becomes more accepting of homosexuality for both men and women, parents must protect their children from it at all costs. It will destroy their relationship with God, their relationships with normal people, their own personal happiness, and usually their body through AIDS, hepatitis B, or other awful diseases. (See chapter 6 for a more thor- ough discussion of the problem of homosexuality.)

Girls' thoughts at first are more of romance and emotional and phys- ical surrender without the sexual details. But if cultivated, they too can learn the art of explicit sex fantasies. If indulged long enough this will lead to an increasing desire to find self-fulfillment in sexual activity.

Parents need to deal tenderly with these teens explaining that such thought temptations are natural. Everyone has them, but for Christians, who would be virtuous and pleasing to the Lord, they should be repented of and confessed. The human mind cannot entertain a vacuum; it must be active. Therefore, their thoughts should be directed to wholesome activities and eventually the goal of having a lifetime mate and a home of their own. The ideal would be for them to memorize scripture so they can review their verses as they drift off to sleep rather than entertain sexually provocative fantasies. My grandmother's classic statement is still true today: "An idle mind is the devil's workshop!"

Teach Them How to Say No!

It is not enough just to tell young people to say no to premarital sex; we must show them how. And we must show them while they are still young.

You should not make them wait until they get into a difficult situation to figure out what to do, but help them anticipate how to avoid such situations, which means they must follow the rules you lay down. That greatly reduces the number of sexually tempting situations they will face. Then urge them to say no emphatically. That means they say no with their mouth and body at the same time. The girl who says no but remains in a close embrace is sending the signal that she really does not mean it.

Some boys are demanding sexually. We hope your son has not bought into the idea that "all kids do it" and that the cost of a date entitles him to have sex. All kids are not doing it, and because of the AIDS and STD scare, the number who are doing it is decreasing and will probably continue to decrease as deaths and other traumas continue. We hope your daughter will not date boys who are sexually active or entertain the false notion that dating is for sex. She does not need that kind of pressure.

Young people need to think of dating as a time for fun, not just with one person but several. They should not be allowed to date without specific plans on where they are going and what they are going to do. Even couples who think they are in love do not have to be alone to have fun on a date. Sure intimacy is exciting, but it leads to the desire for more intimacy. "Research has shown that even with couples who do not intend to go all the way, they will be sexually involved after spending 300 hours alone with each other" [5]

Watch for Signs of Sexual Involvement

Most Christian parents naively think their children would never go all the way. Consequently, they often fail to see the signals their children send out when they start to get into trouble. Sometimes the signals are desperate calls for help. We believe all dating young people need to be watched carefully by the two people who love them most. When you see these signs, try to gently inject yourself into their life. If you are suspicious, find out where they went last night. If you are sure they are reaching the danger zone, come right out and ask them. The following are some of the signs to look for if your teen is dating the same person regularly:

1. *They become secretive about their relationship*. In the early stages of dating, your teen usually is so excited he or she likes to come home and tell you all about it—where they went, who they saw, and what they did. If later they begin to break any of your dating rules, their guilt makes them secretive and they begin to clam up. They may become sneaky, deceptive, and sometimes cunning in their efforts to get together with the person they are dating.

Of course, you have to ask yourself if in the past you showed interest in their excitement. If not, that could be why they no longer discuss it. Parents should be so grateful when their teens do talk to them freely that they drop whatever they're doing and join them in their world. However, when they shut you out, it is usually an indication there are things going on they don't want you to know.

2. *Watch for rebellion*. One of the easiest signs young people are doing what parents oppose is rebellion. This is caused by guilt, self-justification, the natural desire to be free, and the increasing appetite for sexual expression they may be cultivating.

We have the conviction that all teens go through a time of rebellion, often unrelated to dating. Our children's rebellion went from three weeks for one of the girls to two years for one of the boys. So be careful—what you detect may just be that natural rebellion Solomon had in mind when he said, "Folly is bound up in the heart of a child, but the rod of discipline will drive it far from him" (Prov. 22:15). The rebellion we mean here is children who have a free spirit generally but begin to become rebellious about their dating rules, sulk for long periods when opposed, and may become disrespectful.

There are only two commands for children in the Bible: "*Honor* and *obey* your parents in the Lord." We hope you have taught your children from early childhood to always respect you. Usually, this respect carries over into the teen years, though they frequently need to be reminded.

Likewise, the older they become, the more they need to see you show growing respect for them, not only as a person but as an almost adult person. If you have the right relationship with them, rebellion generally will not be long lasting. Rebellion due to secret dating practices will then be easier to detect.

3. *They become exclusive and develop an obsession to be with that person only.* This is one of the things that tends to make them rebellious. Many a parent has gotten a call from a youth pastor or Sunday school teacher to see why their child has not been coming to meetings of the youth group, meetings the parents thought they were attending. That sends a very dangerous signal.

4. *They decline spiritually.* Premarital sex, or even improper fondling, leaves Christians feeling so guilty they cannot continue their devotions, which further deteriorates their spiritual life.

5. *They drop out of church or attend only because you insist on it.*

Parents neglect these signals to their peril. When you recognize them, it is time for a loving confrontation. Ask your child, "What's wrong? You haven't been yourself lately." If he averts his eyes and finds it difficult to talk about it, the parent of the same sex as the child should ask, "Are you and _____ doing anything you are ashamed of or anything that will cause you to break your virtue vow?"

What If They Are Sexually Active? If your worst fears are confirmed and they are having sex, they must be broken up immediately, at least for a time. Their relationship needs to be cooled. Usually it is not enough to crack down on one; it is best to schedule a meeting with their partner's parents and bring their activity into the open. It causes great pain for the moment, but it averts greater hurt later on. Your hope is that you will come away from such a meeting with another set of parents willing to work on the situation. If not, at least they know why you are breaking off the relationship for the time being.

It is usually not wise to forbid the young people to ever see each other again; that leaves them with no hope. Make the separation temporary and indefinite. Your young person needs to get back in right relationship with God, which requires repentance and cessation of their fornication. Usually, after they have separated for a time, their ardor cools; they may even lose interest in each other or become interested in someone else. Even though this causes pain, it is far less harmful than the possibility of public disclosure, pregnancy, or even disease.

After the breakup, we suggest they talk frankly to the pastor or youth pastor and be given a formal opportunity to get right with God.

Don't Make Them Delay Marriage Too Long

Age does not change God's standards of righteousness, but according to current statistics, our society's practices do. Surveys indicate that about 50 percent of the young have had sex in high school; that figure skyrockets to 70 percent or more for those in college. Most students and professors just assume other students are sexually active by the time they leave home for college (or become so after they get there). The coed dorms are not only a convenient place for such activity but are one evidence of the official attitude toward it. Rarely are college kids encouraged to be chaste or practice abstinence. Instead, they are urged to practice "safe sex," which is a euphemism since even condom manufacturers admit to as high as a 12 percent failure rate.

A pastor friend shared a shattering experience that illustrates how the attitude on college campuses is so destructive of moral commitment. The most beautiful girl in his church came in to see him, a girl he had dedicated to the Lord. Her parents were very active in the church. As he looked at her he thought, "She is about as pretty as a girl can get in twenty-one years." But she shattered such thoughts by saying, "Pastor, how can I get this boy I'm living with at college to marry me?" When he recovered he said, "You mean you're no longer a virgin?" To which she responded, "Being a virgin is no big deal anymore!" I'm confident it was a big deal to her parents—and even more so to God.

If, however, your son or daughter has practiced the lessons you taught early and remained a virgin in high school, it is possible for him or her to continue that lifestyle in college. This is another reason for the formal commitment to virtue before they even start dating. (Be sure to read chapter 8.) Many young people meet at college the person they will share their life with. As one virtuous high school graduate said as she left home for college, "I've waited this long, I'm going to wait until I meet Mr. Right, and we get married."

What about the Deeply Committed Early? We all would love to see our young people date several people throughout high school and college while persistently maintaining their virtue. Then, just before graduation, have them meet their lifetime love, get a job, pay back their student loans, and then marry. It doesn't always happen that way. As someone said, "Love waits for no man." Instead, they may meet Miss or Mr. Right in high school, go off to college together, and grow steadily closer. Both parents may have the feeling they are meant for each other, "but not now; you can't afford it." After all, they must get an education.

It is an understatement that college students cannot afford to get married. Consequently, as the sincere lovers get older they may succumb to sexual temptation because "we've been going together for three years and plan to get married anyway." This, for good young people, may be the greatest temptation, for true love does seek sexual expression—God designed us that way. The longer they go together and grow in love, the more difficult it is to wait.

Somehow we parents have developed the idea that we will help our kids go to college financially as long as they do well and remain single. But since marriage is a sign of adulthood, we think our help should cease when they are old enough to get married. Bev and I do not think this is always a wise policy; consequently, we offer the following suggestion.

If your young person finds a Christian partner and you have the peace of God in your heart about their marriage, we think your financial support should be offered during the duration of their education whether they marry or not. Your objective is to help them get the best training they can. Marriage should not change that. It might even improve it. Many a young couple, under the above conditions, would do better in college married and helped by both parents than remaining single and spending four or five years fighting their hormones, libido, and sexually charged culture. Such a policy is not right for every pair of lovers, but neither should it be ruled out as a possibility by those who can afford it.

Provide Good Reading Material that Supports Your Values

Supplement your teaching and that of your church with good reading material. Focus on the Family has youth magazines of good quality for both boys and girls, and *Campus Life* magazine is good for high schoolers. In addition there are some excellent books in your local Christian bookstore. One that is written directly to teens is *Love, Dating, and Sex*, by George Eager. This book contains Eager's practical talks to thousands of teens and is written on their level. In addition, Josh McDowell's *Why Wait?* should be in every teen's library. (For a resource catalogue of videos, cassettes, and books, write to Josh McDowell Ministries, Box 1000, Dallas, TX 75221.)

The world, the flesh, and the devil are out to destroy your young people. You, your church, and some other Christians are their only source of human help. We need to be aggressive about protecting the minds and bodies of our children by providing them with alternatives to the ways of the world.

Surround Them with Prayer

Most of us prayed that God would give us children in the first place. Then we dedicated them to Him soon after they were born, much as Hannah dedicated Samuel to God in the Old Testament. Now we need to surround them in prayer that God will give them wisdom to hear and heed our parental advice to keep themselves pure and unspotted from the world.

At twenty years of age, after two years in the Air Force, I was more rebellious toward God than at any other time in my life. My mother's prayers kept me from going to the wrong college and instead directed me to a Christian university where I met Miss Right for my life. Together we have shared almost a lifetime of love and companionship for which we are both eternally grateful. I know you want no less for your children. Remember the words of scripture: "The prayer of a righteous man [or woman] is powerful and effective" (James 5:16b). Somehow I think God pays special attention to the prayers of parents for their children.

Summary

Well, there you have them—several suggestions for helping your child protect his or her virtue. Though it isn't easy today, it is still possible. Many Christian parents are doing it. You will, however, have to work at it harder than your parents did or your children may succumb to a tragic activity that could mar their whole life.

Think of it as a dangerous epidemic you would do anything to protect them from. Premature sexual activity is an epidemic in our times, and your children need to be protected from it. The day will come when they will thank you.

---

[1] Gary Bauer and James Dobson, *Children at Risk* (Waco, Tex.: Word Books), 11-12.

[2] George B. Eager, *Love, Dating, and Sex: What Teens Want to Know* (Valdosta, Ga.: Mailbox Club Books, 1989), 64-67.

[3] Ibid., 66.

[4] Ibid.

[5] Ibid., 127.

Part Two

WHAT YOUNG CHILDREN NEED TO KNOW ABOUT SEX

So far, we have examined why parents want their children and youth to save their virtue for marriage. Only on limited points have we addressed how to accomplish that goal. In Parts 2 and 3, we will go back and fill in the blanks on how sex education from early childhood to early adulthood is done at home by the parents. As your children ask questions—and they will—you should provide them with information according to their age group. We have divided the material according to age groups so you can be prepared to teach accordingly.

If your children are between two and thirteen, you should carefully study chapters 3 through 6 before you teach them.

If your children are teens, you may wish to skip chapters 3 through 5, which cover information small children need to know. You should familiarize yourself with the material in chapter 6 regarding preadolescence. This chapter includes basic information all teens should know. Then you can build on that foundation by teaching your teens to be sexually pure (Part 3).

Chapter Three

EVEN TODDLERS ARE CURIOUS ABOUT SEX

T he best way to teach sexual information to your children is to start early (before someone else beats you to it). Little children are usually curious about their sexuality. As they begin asking questions, give them clear and appropriate answers. Be honest. Use the proper nomenclature when referring to body parts and try to be relaxed. The best approach is to start with their earliest questions or signs of curiosity and let them set the pace. Give them just the information they need at the time.

The home provides the ideal place for such teaching because you can fill in the blanks of their curious little minds as the occasions present themselves. Do not set them down and dump the whole load on them all at once. Keep in mind, the younger a child is the shorter their interest span. In very early childhood, the most important thing for them to know is not all the details about sex but that he or she can come to you for them.

Dr. James Dobson tells the cute story of the little boy who needed his mother's help filling out a survey for school. Looking up from the paper he asked, "Mom, what is sex?" His mother took a deep breath and launched into a lengthy explanation, most of which went over his head. When she finished, he said, "I don't think there's room enough in this little square for all that!" The mistake many parents make is giving their child too much information at one time. The ideal is to maintain an open, ongoing discussion whenever it occurs to them to bring the subject up.

Experts in child development tell us that the most important period of human development is infancy through age four. Scientists estimate that at least one-half of a child's intellectual capacity has been obtained by the fifth year, and 80 percent by the age of eight. This refers to the intelligence level, not to the amount of information the child's mind accumulates. It is during this period of their life that a child is introduced to his or her sexual parts, how they function, and what is right and wrong to do. In a vital sense, absolute morals need to be firmly established during the early childhood years (birth to age eight).

During a child's first three months of life, they must have seven basic needs supplied in abundance by a loving mother and father. They must be regularly fed, kept warm, afforded plenty of sleep, cuddled and stroked, given bodily exercise, changed regularly, and provided with sensory and intellectual stimulation.

At the moment we first hold a wrinkly new baby in our arms, we inaugurate a sex-education program. We are teaching the baby about love, warmth, and comfort—three essential elements in developing close relationships. Dr. George E. Gardner, a Boston child psychiatrist, has observed that relating to other humans is the most important aspect of a child's development during the early years:

> It is the beginning of all the experiences that depend upon a positive feeling of love, affection, and trust toward other human beings.... The many pleasurable experiences the infant has very early in life with his own mother, or the one person who is responsible for his care, generate these feelings of trust and security.... From his mother he learns to trust others.[1]

From birth through the third year, a child is usually dependent primarily on his mother for such qualities as praise and comfort as well as feeding and diaper changing. During this period a child may develop a fear of strangers and cling tenaciously to his mother.

God designed the mother's breast so that an infant must be held and caressed to be fed. Emotional security gained during feeding is as important to the infant as the nutrition from mother's milk. The mother communicates her love to her child every time she nurses him.

To the benefit of this generation, breast feeding has returned to popularity. At the time our children were born, it was thought old-fashioned to nurse. Manufactured formula was substituted for mother's milk, so babies were weaned as quickly as possible and put on the bottle. Bottles, nipples, and formula may have been good for the economy, but they did little for a baby's emotions. Far too often the busy mother found it convenient to prop up the baby with his bottle while she continued on with other projects.

Children who feel unloved will have a higher rate of depression and attempted suicide than children who in infancy enjoy the emotional security of being nestled next to their mother's body while they are fed. Not only does a baby benefit, but mothers testify that they too enjoy the feelings aroused by such a clinging and dependent little life.

Mother is the principal sex-education teacher during these first three years of life. But modern research suggests that a father has a much more significant influence on his child sexually than was believed earlier. It is often from the father that a child gains his or her sexual identity.

What Is Normal Sexual Identity?

Normal sexual identity is the identity God gave you at birth. That is determined by your sexual parts. The problem is, the brain is the most important sex organ in any human being and, much like a computer, the brain is influenced by the data put into it.

The media, liberal educators, and some equally liberal sociologists have intimidated our nation against openly and honestly facing the issue of normal and abnormal sexual behavior. The Christian community sees the issue in true perspective because the Bible is so clear on the subject. Heterosexuality is God's design; homosexuality an abomination or a perversion of that design.

This is why it is important that infant and early childhood training be provided by both father and mother whenever possible. When a father accepts and loves his son or daughter, including the child's sexual identity, it is much easier for the child at puberty to accept his natural sex direction. These impressions are made at an early age.

This does not mean that boys raised without a father will be insecure about their identity. I am not suggesting that at all. My own father died before my tenth birthday, and my brother was only seven weeks old. He never knew his father, yet he is definitely a heterosexual. I point this out to encourage single mothers who are trying to raise their sons to have normal sexual identities. The odds are that they will. It is comforting, and was especially comforting to my mother, that the Lord promises to be "a father to the fatherless." (Single parents, see chapter 16).

Pleasure and Pain

Early in life a child realizes that he will experience two kinds of feelings: pleasure and pain. Accordingly he will elect to try to do things that give him pleasure. After receiving several spankings, he determines that some actions result in pain. He is learning from his parents the difference between right and wrong behavior. At this stage of development, the child is incapable of sophisticated reasoning. He learns moral behavior by being rewarded for good actions (hugs, kisses, loving approval) and by gently receiving the "rod of correction" for his disobedience.

At the age of two or three, the child is a bundle of energy, ceaseless in his quest for new information. He is constantly moving and assimilating what he sees around him. But until the child has developed the ability to use language, it is impossible to teach him specific information about sex. However, a wise mother and father will begin immediately after birth to teach him about obedience.

Two key elements must be present in any training of children: love and discipline. A child must know his boundaries; he must understand that certain behavior is acceptable, other actions unacceptable. He must also be made to understand that he will be dealt with consistently, lovingly, and firmly when he crosses the boundaries set for him.

There are only two commands in the Bible to children: To honor and obey their parents in the Lord" (Eph. 6:1-3). Do not expect your children to automatically honor (or respect) and obey you. These principles must be taught in the context of love. The parents who fail to teach their small children to obey are usually the ones who have trouble with rebellious teenagers. As James Dobson says, "The proper time to begin disarming the teenage time-bomb is twelve years before it arrives."[2]

Long before a parent can teach a child about sex, he begins to develop a sense of morality. As the child learns to speak and respond to his parents' directions, Mom and Dad slowly but surely are developing what will become his conscience.

Acquiring Sexual Knowledge

A two- or three-year-old will eventually begin to wonder where he came from. If his mother is expecting another child, curiosity will lead him to ask the first of an endless series of questions about sexual matters. Remember that sex education is a long-term process. A toddler has a short attention span and forgets easily. Most of the time he will assimilate only part of what we say, but we are building his sexual knowledge block by block through the years.

One of the golden keys of learning is repetition, for by it information becomes ingrained in a young child's mind. It is a process that begins at birth and lasts until they leave home.

Sex education lessons for a toddler may last no longer than five minutes, but you will gradually build an understanding of sexual matters in your child. Month by month, as the child grows, you can impart more information and at the same time repeat what he previously learned.

What is important at this stage is to treat a child's questions about sex as casually as we do his questions on any other subject. If we become tense, if our hands become sweaty and our voice cracks, he will sense the tension and assume he has raised a "taboo" subject. If we treat it as any ordinary matter, so will he.

Toddlers are literalists; their minds have not developed to the point where they can understand symbolism or abstract concepts such as honor or purity. However, they possess the kind of trust and faith our Lord admired so much (Matt. 18:2-4; 19:14). Unable to reason, they take everything at face value. Usually they will believe anything they are told, so it is important to be accurate in offering sexual information.

If, for example, a parent says that God placed a seed inside Mommy's tummy, a child will accept that as fact. He will believe that babies grow inside the mother's stomach instead of in the womb. If you have likened the mother's egg to a plant seed, the child will probably visualize a plant growing inside her. Don't be surprised if at dinnertime he may think the baby inside your tummy is being smothered by milk, vegetables, and roast beef!

When talking with your children, you should not enter into a complicated explanation of the reproduction process or sexual intercourse. When he asks a question such as "Where did I come from?" you need not spend an hour explaining everything you know about fetal development. You can simply give him a clear, matter-of-fact answer. (We suggest some simple answers to typical questions a bit later in this chapter.)

You should also initiate a conversation if you sense that your child has additional questions about his origin. To explain sexual reproduction plainly, you can introduce your children to the world of plants, animals, and insects. If a dog or cat is pregnant, you will have an excellent opportunity to explain how God has created life. We once bought a dog and had her bred so we could teach our children about sex.

Our children did the same thing for their children. We will never forget the time our three-year-old grandson took us out to the rabbit hutch in the backyard to explain "why Sugar is so fat." He knew the whole story. He told me how the family took Sugar over to see Thumper. "He is a daddy rabbit. He got Sugar pregnant and now she's going to have some babies."

We were impressed by how casual yet intrigued our grandson was about the mystery of life. That's why it is important for us to explain to our children the story of Creation—how God created male and female, plants and animals and insects—and how everything He made was "good." God fashioned every living creature with seeds inside to reproduce itself. Apples from apple seeds, chickens from eggs, butterflies from eggs that first turn into caterpillars, kittens from within the mother cat, and babies from human seeds called sperm and ova.

Teaching a Toddler about Sex

It is wise, even with toddlers, to begin familiarizing them with words such as *penis, vagina, vulva, ova,* and *sperm.* If they know the correct terms, they will be less likely to think there is something mysterious about them which can unnecessarily increase their curiosity. As you teach yourself to refer to the sex organs as casually as you do other parts of the body, you soon feel comfortable in dealing with this subject. We use correct terms for all the other parts of the body, why should we not be as accurate in describing sexual parts? After all, when God made Adam and Eve, including their sexual organs, He said, "It is very good."

The important thing for our children's well-being is to be accurate, natural, and relaxed about it. We can distinguish between what we discuss privately and among family and what we discuss with others.

Suggested Answers to Questions Toddlers Ask

Toddlers will eventually want to know the names of their sex organs. When a boy asks about his genitals—"*What is this?*"—give a matter-of-fact answer: "It's your penis. God made all boys to have penises, which is a tube you use to go to the toilet." For a girl, answer, "That part of your body is called the labia. It is two flaps of skin that help to keep germs out of the part of your body where you go to the toilet."

At ages two and three, the typical youngster is looking for simple answers to questions. For instance, if he asks "*Where did I come from?*" we suggest this answer: "You grew within a small bag inside your mommy, just below her tummy. When you were big enough to be born, you came out through an opening between Mommy's legs called the vagina."

If he asks, "*How did I get inside your body?*" you can answer, "When God created mommies and daddies, he put tiny cells inside each of us. The daddy has what is called sperm inside of his body, and mommy has tiny eggs. When the sperm from the daddy meets with the egg inside the mommy, a little baby begins to grow in a bag just below Mommy's tummy called the womb."

What if a toddler asks, "*How does the sperm get inside the mommy?*" We do not think it is necessary to explain sexual intercourse to two-or-three-year-olds. It may not traumatize them, but it could lead to confusion and an unhealthy preoccupation with a mature matter. Simply tell them that it is a good question but it is rather complicated and hard to understand. When they are older you will explain it to them. That will normally satisfy their curiosity.

If a child wonders, "*Why does Mommy have to go to the hospital to have a baby?*" a suitable answer is, "She must go to the hospital so the doctors can help her give birth to the baby. The doctors will make sure Mommy is comfortable and that the baby is born healthy."

"*Why does Mommy have breasts?*" Answer: "All grown-up women have breasts. God made women this way because a mommy's breasts will fill up with milk when she has a baby. This milk is food for the baby until it is old enough to take milk from a bottle or eat regular food."

"*Can any man and woman have babies?*" Answer: "Yes, most can, but God wants only men and women who are married to have babies. He wants every baby to have a safe home, where it is loved and cared for by a mother and father."

By the age of three, toddlers should have a simplistic understanding of how babies are born. They should have a general idea of how babies are made, have positive feelings about their own sex, and have a warm, trusting relationship with both mother and father. When you create this kind of climate in their mind, they will go to you and not to the child next door when questions arise. As children grow older, they will probably ask the same questions all over again. Each time you can provide more detailed answers.

A Christian psychologist has noted, "Good sex education begins with your attitudes, depends on the accuracy of your information, and is learned only in an atmosphere of responsibility."[3] We would add love to that atmosphere and a healthy respect for our Creator's ingenious design of human sexuality.

---

[1] George E. Gardner, *The Emerging Personality: Infancy through Adolescence* (New York: Delacorte Press, 1970), 24.

[2] James C. Dobson *Dare to Discipline* (Wheaton, Ill: Tyndale House Publishers, 1970), 33.

[3] Grace H. Ketterman, *How to Teach Your Child About Sex* (Old Tappan, N.J.: Fleming H. Revell, 1981), 8.

Chapter Four

PRESCHOOL: AGES FOUR TO FIVE

A t ages four and five a normal child develops the ability to use reason in coping with his world. Instead of merely reacting to his environment as he did as a toddler, he begins to think about the world around him—and question everything. He will gradually identify a cause-and-effect relationship to his environment.

The preschooler's developing language abilities enable him to learn about the seemingly endless array of objects, places, and people in his new world. Being able now to put thoughts into words, he begins a life-long quest for knowledge and understanding. If he is a typical child, he will probably get on his parents' nerves with incessant questioning: Why does the sun shine? Why is the grass green? How do birds fly? As he matures, he will invariably ask where babies come from.

During these years a child is mastering language, elementary thinking processes, and a concept of selfhood. In addition, if he has been disciplined properly in love, he develops a conscience, a moral sense of right and wrong. Dr. Selma Frailberg, writing in *The Magic Years*, discusses the formation of the conscience:

> Such a conscience does not emerge in the child until the fifth or sixth year. It will not become a stable part of his personality until the ninth or tenth year. It will not become completely

independent of outside authority until the child becomes independent of his parents in the last phase of adolescence."[1]

As Christians, we believe all people are born with a conscience that either accuses or excuses. Teaching Christian values at an early age fortifies that conscience. Likewise, as we teach a child about sex, it is absolutely essential that we include sound biblical principles of morality. Explaining reproduction without including a moral foundation will prove to be disastrous.

The four- to six-year-old should be gaining a sense of self-discipline and self-control as his conscience develops. Gardner explains that the development of these positive attributes should follow this pattern: 1) The child learns to control his bodily functions; 2) he is able to govern his aggression against others; 3) he gains a sense of property (not everything belongs to him); 4) he learns to control pleasurable drives or fantasies; 5) he is able to check infantile sexual impulses.[2] Not all children experience early sexual impulses, and those who do are not perverted or oversexed. The wise parent will be watchful of his child without reacting as if sexual impulses pose a significant problem.

Learning about Babies

During these years, a child is intensely interested in gaining the approval of his parents. He looks to them as the final authority on every subject. This attitude of receptivity provides an ideal opportunity to begin a graduated program of sex education geared to the interest level of the child. Remember to deal with each child as an individual. Not all five-year-olds are ready to accept the same information. In fact, you may find a younger child more receptive to a discussion of sex than an older sibling. Girls typically mature faster than boys. A five-year-old girl is a year or more ahead of a five-year-old boy in emotional and physical development. This difference doesn't level out until the late teenage years.

How can we decide whether our children are willing to talk about sexual matters? One way is to openly suggest that the preschooler sit down and chat with us. Then allow their reaction to direct you. Be careful not to force unwanted information on them at this age. By being sensitive in your communication about sexuality, you will lift the "taboo" stigma sometimes attached to this subject and make it easier for your child to ask more crucial questions at the onset of puberty.

In the sex-saturated society we live in, it is virtually impossible to keep children isolated from pictures, magazines, movies, or television programs that display sex in explicit and often offensive ways. Cable television movie channels often show R-rated movies that contain explicit sex, profanity, and violence. We can only wonder how many children are regularly exposed to sex scenes that are far beyond their ability to comprehend and evaluate.

At school our youngsters may be exposed to children who have acquired inaccurate sexual information from objectionable television programming. Older children often show off their sexual knowledge by describing sexual activities to younger, less-informed children.

The point is that our children—especially those in public schools— are going to learn about sex. It is far better that we convey accurate information and correct attitudes under controlled conditions than allow the child to acquire distorted views from their friends. Sex education on the school playground usually consists of a lurid description of sexual intercourse that totally ignores the emotions and commitments connected with it and strips it of its beauty. Our children should never be led to believe that the act of marriage is simply a biological function; rather, it is God's way of joining a husband and wife together in sacred unity.

Your most important asset in teaching your children about sex, love, and marriage is having a healthy attitude about these subjects yourself. Your mannerisms, tone of voice, and gestures will all convey either positive or negative feelings to your children. If you still carry any guilt about sexual matters from childhood, you would be wise to get your own feelings and thoughts in order before beginning to convey sex information to your offspring. A careful reading of The Act of Marriage will help to provide a positive biblical attitude toward this beautiful subject.

A relaxed, casual approach to sex education will remove many of the bad feelings children might have developed from premature exposure to sexual matters at school. Be sure to let your children know up front that you are willing to discuss sexual matters. We do not have to reveal everything at once, and we can tell them so.

At this age, our children do not need to know every last detail of the act of marriage from foreplay to climax. We should reveal this information as they require it. A direct question does not necessitate a detailed answer. If possible, we should respond to explicit questions briefly and to the point without adding unnecessary details. Usually a straightforward answer will satisfy the questioner. If not, you can tell them that you will be glad to discuss it when they are a little older and that they are free to remind you then.

EXPLAINING FETAL DEVELOPMENT

Where do we begin an explanation about sexual reproduction to our preschool children? A child who wants to know how a baby develops inside the mother can benefit from a simple explanation. With this explanation you may wish to use the diagrams included in this chapter or draw your own pictures to give your child a visual image of this miraculous event.

You might begin with the account of Creation in the Book of Genesis. Recount the story of the Garden of Eden, showing your child that God made both the male and the female, blessed His creation, and told Adam and Eve to multiply and subdue the earth. This plants in your child's mind the following truths: 1) God is his Creator, 2) He made us sexual creatures, and 3) reproduction is good, when preceded by marriage, because God made it.

Where Babies Come From

Inside every woman are thousands of tiny eggs smaller than the period at the end of this sentence. When one of these eggs meets with a sperm from the woman's husband, a new baby is created.

Our bodies are made up of trillions of cells, but when a baby is first created, it is only one cell—so small that we can't see it without looking through a microscope. But this cell splits into two cells, then four, continuing to grow and grow. In its early stages, the developing baby is called an *embryo*. Later in the baby's growth it is called a *fetus*, a word that means "young one."

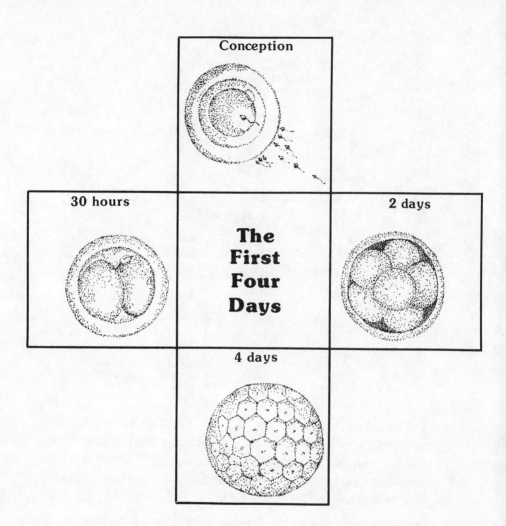

Conception

30 hours

The First Four Days

2 days

4 days

As the cells begin to multiply, this new baby finds a comfortable place in the soft lining of the uterus and begins to develop. Inside the mother's uterus (which is shaped like an upside-down pear), the baby grows until it is large enough to live outside the mother.

How does the baby eat? He is fed by his mother through a cord attached to his stomach. The other end of this umbilical cord is connected to the wall of the uterus. We can imagine what this is like by thinking of an astronaut walking out in space, attached to the spaceship by a cord. In space there is no air for the astronaut to breathe, so he gets his air through the cord attached to his suit. The baby gets his air and food through the umbilical cord.

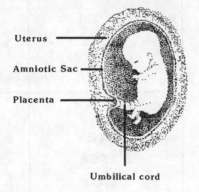

Baby is about this size at two months

Uterus

Amniotic Sac

Placenta

Umbilical cord

After about nine months, the baby is big enough to be born. The uterus begins to squeeze and squeeze (an action we call labor contractions). Slowly but surely the baby is squeezed out of the uterus and into the vagina and then out of the mother's body. A doctor, nurse, or midwife helps the mother to give birth to her baby.

As you explain these facts of reproduction to your children, stress the wonder of God's creation. It is important for them to understand that God made them and loves them very much. Most children are thrilled by this beautiful story and will ask you to tell it several times. Their questioning is an opportunity for you to see how they are progressing in their understanding.

NAMING THE BODY PARTS CORRECTLY

Some parents today fear the use of proper names for the sexual organs. If you do not use the technical names, your child may sense that sexual terms and bodily functions are "dirty" or "wrong." Each family has its own euphemisms for urination, defecation, penis, vagina, and so on. Unfortunately, this increases the difficulties of communicating healthful attitudes and avoiding negative impressions as parents teach their children about sexuality. By introducing them to the proper names, you can easily correct them when they use a dirty word they may have picked up from someone in the neighborhood.

Female Reproductive System

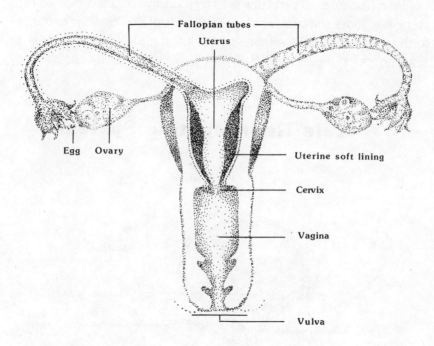

Ovaries. Two small containers in the mother's body that hold thousands of eggs. Each of these is called an ovary. When an egg leaves the ovary, it travels down a tube toward the uterus where it can meet the sperm.

Oviduct (Fallopian tubes). This is a tube through which an egg travels toward the uterus as it awaits fertilization.

Uterus. The uterus is like a little room where the baby grows inside the mother. This room, shaped like an upside-down pear, is like a balloon—that is, it gets bigger and bigger as the baby grows.

Cervix. This is a passageway between the uterus and the vagina. It is normally no wider than a pencil lead, but God has designed it to expand during childbirth.

Vagina. When the baby is large enough to be born and come out into the world, it descends from the uterus, enters a tube or tunnel called the vagina, and continues to the outside world. All girls have a vagina, uterus, and eggs. But God designed girls so they cannot have children until they are close to being teenagers.

Vulva. The external parts of a girl's reproductive organs are called the vulva. It includes the *labia*, which are two folds of skin over the entrance to the vagina to protect it from germs. Near the top of these folds is a sex organ called the *clitoris*.

Male Reproductive System

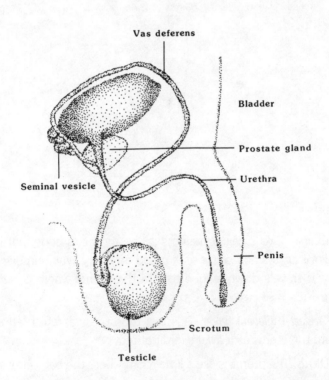

Testicles. These organs produce the sperm cells which, when joined to the mother's egg, form a new baby.

Scrotum. This is the bag of skin behind the penis which contains the testicles.

Spermatic duct (Vas deferens). This is a tube through which sperm pass from the testicles to and through the penis.

Penis. This is the male sex organ. Through this organ sperm cells and waste water, or urine, leave the body.

As the children grow older, they will need additional and more detailed information about reproduction. This is provided in later chapters.

PARENTAL CONCERNS

Masturbation

Masturbation sometimes becomes a primary concern of parents of four- to six-year-olds. According to Dr. Clyde Narramore, masturbation is practiced by some children between the ages of two to six and again between the ages of twelve and twenty. What should parents do if their children masturbate? Narramore advises,

> Infrequent acts of masturbation should be ignored. This is not easy to do when one has been taught that masturbation causes all sorts of dreadful things. But try your best to accept the fact that there is no physical basis for being afraid or worried. Your *attitude* will more than likely determine the end results.[3]

A child who masturbates is not demonstrating a depraved mind. He is just giving evidence that he has discovered a pleasurable aspect of his body. If he fondles himself in public, a parent should speak to him calmly in private about it, explaining that such behavior is not polite and should not be done in public. You should be diplomatic so that your response does not foster negative feelings about the sex organs. But neither should you let a child become an exhibitionist.

A compulsive or chronic practice of masturbation might indicate an emotional difficulty of some kind. You should consult a trusted physician if you feel your child is overly preoccupied with his genitals.

Sex Play

Sex play often alarms parents, but at ages four, five, or six it is quite common for children to satisfy their curiosity by exploring each other's bodies. Playing "doctor" or "nurse" is one of the ways children investigate the anatomy of the opposite sex.

This sex play should be firmly discouraged, but resist the temptation to get angry or indignant. By simply telling our children and those involved that this is inappropriate behavior, we should be able to eliminate casual or secretive sex play. We should let the child know that he should learn about male and female differences from us, not from personal investigation. We can help him to realize that our bodies are private and that therefore we are not to expose them to others or touch the private parts of another person.

Sex Roles

Sex roles are a greater concern than they once were. Feminists, humanists, and "sexologists" in our culture often advocate a unisex society where men and women will supposedly dress alike, think alike, and be able to choose sexual lifestyles freely. Our children are being bombarded with this propaganda through transvestite rock stars and Hollywood actors and actresses who do not share our moral values.

Little boys often dress in their mother's clothing, and girls sometimes don their father's outfits. Before our society was assaulted by sex revolutionaries, this would have been considered harmless play, for children love to put on costumes. Unfortunately, in our day harmless play could lead to sex-role confusion. Without making a big issue out of it, try to encourage your children to play make-believe in the clothes of their own gender.

In addition, both mothers and fathers should be reinforcing specific sex roles for their children. In his book *Sex Roles and the Christian Family*, W. Peter Blitchington writes:

> During the first five or six years of life, the young child's sexual identity will be formed. A boy needs contact with his father in order for his sexual identity to be developed properly. Boys whose fathers are absent, passive, or rejecting often find it harder to identify with the male role. Overly dominating mothers may also lead a young boy to identify too strongly with his mother and to reject masculinity.[4]

If you are a single mother or father of small children, don't worry if your children do not have a same-sex role model. Provide them with a loving, non-smothering relationship, and the Lord will make up the difference.

[1] Selma H. Frailberg, *The Magic Years: Understanding and Handling the Problems of Early Childhood* (New York: Scribners, 1984), 59.

[2] George E. Gardner, *The Emerging Personality: Infancy through Adolescence* (New York: Delacorte Press, 1970), 92.

[3] Clyde M. Narramore, *Understanding Your Children* (Grand Rapids: Zondervan Publishing House, 1978), 123.

[4] W. Peter Blitchington, *Sex Roles and the Christian Family* (Wheaton, Ill.: Tyndale House Publishers, 1984), 107.

Chapter Five

MIDDLE CHILDHOOD: AGES SIX TO TEN

From ages six to ten, a typical child is learning to reason, to think things through on his own, and to discern right from wrong behavior. If he has received sufficient discipline and love during early childhood, his conscience, or inner control mechanism, should become well developed. At this stage, children will begin to control their emotions, postpone gratification, and check outbursts of anger when they cannot get their way. The soundness of a child's values or morals will depend in large measure on our effectiveness as parents in conveying Christian truth. We cannot entrust the moral training of our children to the ungodly or others who do not share our moral values. It is our responsibility to "civilize" our children by teaching them to follow the Lord through our example and through the lessons we teach them from the Word of God.

During these years a child becomes a social individual, learning to cooperate and interrelate with others—at school, at church, or at play with neighbors. Children begin to realize that their actions have consequences. They discover that some behavior is unacceptable and will get them into serious trouble; other behavior is affirmed and will be rewarded. They look to adults for approval. By age seven, the child is becoming a well-adjusted member of society, wanting to interact with others. At eight and nine, children will join clubs and participate in group activities (usually with members of their own sex). By age ten, segregation between boys and girls is the norm. This is only temporary. Within a few years, the opposite sex will gradually become an obsession.

At age six, children normally display an awareness of and interest in the physical differences between boys and girls. As previously pointed out, they may sometimes play "doctor" or "nurse" in order to explore the bodies of the opposite sex. There may be episodes of sex play or instances in which boys and girls will agree to show each other their genitals to satisfy their curiosity. Naturally this kind of behavior should be discouraged. But we should beware of making a bigger issue out of it than necessary. We should make it clear to our children, without being severe, that only doctors or parents are allowed to see them in the nude. If necessary, we can satisfy our children's curiosity by showing them drawings of male and female organs, such as those included in this book.

Seven-year-olds show less interest in sex, but some exploration still takes place. From ages eight to ten, children normally look at sex and elimination as a source of crude jokes. At nine they will begin to talk about sex with their friends and use sexual terms in swearing or in creating poetry. They are fascinated to learn about their own sex organs.

By age ten most girls and some boys have learned from their friends about menstruation and sexual intercourse—if we haven't already informed them. Wise parents will share this information briefly, by the eighth or ninth year, to ensure that their child is accurately informed. It is far better that details of sexual reproduction come from parents than from bathroom walls or misinformed friends.

INFORMATION ON HOW LIFE BEGINS

What are children aged six to ten interested in knowing about sexual reproduction? They are normally curious about conception and the process by which a baby grows inside the mother's body. Many will also inquire about the role of the father in conceiving the child.

When God created this world, He fashioned all manner of life forms. He created bugs, fish, turtles, hamsters, elephants, birds, and thousands of other animals. He made all kinds of plants. His crowning creation was man and women. The book of Genesis tells us that God created every creature with the ability to reproduce itself, or create new life from within its own body. Within every plant are the seeds to create new plants. Within the bodies of animals and humans, God designed what we call a *reproductive system* so that each animal and human can create more life.

The sexes have different reproductive systems that complement each other for the propagation of new life. Two males cannot conceive babies, nor can two females. In mammals, life can be created only when the sperm from the male joins with the egg from the female. A male has millions of sperm cells; a female has thousands of eggs.

Inside the sperm cell and the egg are tiny objects called *chromosomes*. Under a powerful microscope these chromosomes look like little bits of string. On the chromosomes are *genes*, which determine what the child is going to look like: his hair color, eye color, intelligence, physical abilities, body build and height, temperament, and more—every physical and mental characteristic of the person.

Sperm cells and eggs contain twenty-three chromosomes apiece. When they join together in conception, therefore, there are forty-six. Within each set of chromosomes are fifteen thousand genes. Scientists who study how human life begins have discovered that at least eighteen million different combinations could be made in creating a baby. That is, every child that was ever born had the potential to be different in eighteen million different ways! With that many choices, it is easy to understand why no two human beings are exactly alike. Even identical twins are not identical! So every human—in fact, every creation of God—is unique.

In explaining chromosomes and genes to our children, we can compare genes to the instruction booklet we receive with a new bicycle. Upon opening the carton, we pull out all the different parts and then begin to read the instruction booklet to learn how to put the bicycle together. The instruction booklet provides a step-by-step plan for successfully assembling the machine. Without instructions we would have a difficult time making any sense of the various bicycle parts. The same holds true within a male's sperm cell and a female's egg. The genes act as little instruction booklets, forming a blueprint as to how a baby will look and how he will think, his creative tendencies, and his temperament, which has a profound effect on his personality and actions.

A Baby Begins to Grow

The following explanation of conception and development can either be read to your child or rephrased in your own words. The illustrations in this chapter will be helpful as well.

A mother's egg is usually fertilized by the sperm inside a tube in the mother's body known as the *Fallopian tube*. This is like a short, rubbery pipe that leads from the mother's ovaries, where the eggs are kept, down into the uterus, where the baby will grow. Every woman has approximately 400,000 eggs in her ovaries, but only three hundred to four hundred of them pass out of the ovaries and into the uterus during a woman's lifetime.

Conception

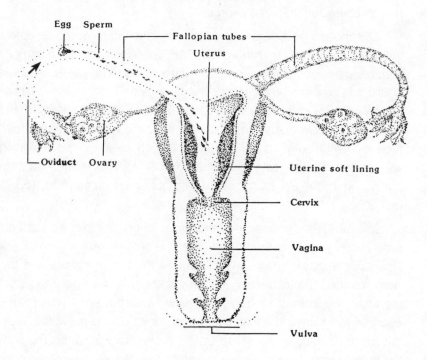

After growing for a few days, the fertilized egg attaches itself to the side of the uterus and begins to develop into a baby. To help the baby mature, a special organ called the *placenta* grows on the inner wall of the uterus. This is made up of many, many blood vessels that help to feed the baby. Connecting the placenta to the baby's stomach is a long tube called the *umbilical cord*. Through this cord the baby receives his food and oxygen from the mother's bloodstream. The baby's waste also passes through this cord into the mother's body; her liver and kidneys will dispose of these waste products. The placenta also acts as a barrier protecting the baby from many harmful substances that might travel in the mother's bloodstream.

During the second week, a special protective covering surrounds the baby as he grows in the uterus. Called the *amniotic sac*, this covering is filled with a watery substance called *amniotic fluid*. This fluid protects the baby from being injured in the uterus and also helps to keep him warm. In this dark, warm, protected nest the baby grows for nine months until he is ready to be born.

The Growth Stages of a Baby

At conception a new baby is smaller than the dot of an "i." Within six to twelve hours the fertilized egg divides into two cells which then continue to divide. Within two months, the baby has grown to 240 times its original size and a million times heavier than its original weight as one cell. A newborn baby has millions of cells; an adult has sixty trillion.

When the fetus is about five days old, the cluster of cells resembles a berry. This stage of development is called a *morula*, derived from the Latin word for mulberry. As the morula continues to grow, the cells begin to take on different jobs in forming the baby. Some cells become part of the brain; others become muscle tissue and nerve endings. Still other cells join together to form the eyeballs, ears, nose, mouth, hands, and sexual organs. Through a mysterious process called *differentiation*, which scientists still haven't figured out, each cell knows exactly where to go and what part of the body to become.

In the first month of life, the *embryo*, (a Greek word meaning "to swell") is about the size of an apple seed. The baby already has a heart, and the brain is beginning to form. The backbone, spinal column, and nervous system are also developing. New scientific research is demonstrating that even from this early stage of development, the embryo is a real, living person.

In the second month, the brain is formed. Ears, eyes, nose, lips, and tongue are taking shape. At this point the baby is called a *fetus*, a Latin term for "young one" or "offspring." By month's end, all the baby's features are in place. By the ninth week, the fetus has a reproductive system and can be identified as a girl or a boy.

The Developing Fetus

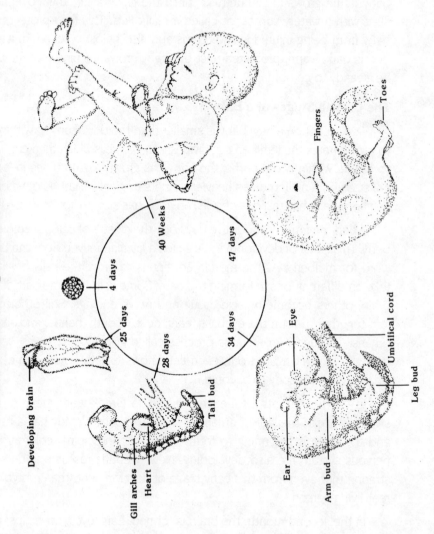

Fingers

Toes

40 Weeks

4 days

47 days

25 days

28 days

34 days

Developing brain

Tail bud

Gill arches

Heart

Eye

Umbilical cord

Leg bud

Ear

Arm bud

By the third month the baby, more than two inches in length, develops fingernails and toenails. During the fourth month, eyebrows and eyelashes form, and the baby will suck his thumb for the first time.

In the fifth and sixth months, the fetus develops nostrils, and the ears begin to function. The growing baby can hear his mother's voice and can even open his eyes and see. During the seventh through ninth months, the baby completes the final stages of development before birth. In his booklet, *When You Were Formed in Secret*, Gary Bergel describes these final months:

> The skin of the infant thickens and begins to look polished. A layer of fat is produced and stored beneath the skin, both for insulation and as a food supply. Antibodies that give immunity to diseases are built up. A gallon per day of amniotic fluid is absorbed by the baby and the fluid is totally replaced every three hours. The baby's heart now pumps three hundred gallons of blood per day and the placenta begins to age.

> Approximately one week before the two hundred and sixtieth day the infant stops growing and "drops," usually head downward, into the pelvic cavity. All preparations are finished and both the mother and child can but wait for the drama of birth.[1]

Baby in late stage of pregnancy

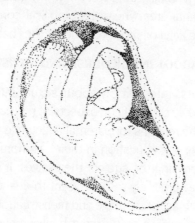

The Baby Is Born

No one is sure how the baby knows when it is time for his passage to the outside world, but the typical human baby is born nine months after conception. The uterus, which is the largest and most powerful muscle in the mother's body, begins to squeeze together to push the baby down through the bottom of the uterus, through an opening called the cervix, and into the birth canal (the vagina), and out into the world.

Usually before the baby is born, the mother knows it is time to go to the hospital because the amniotic sac breaks and the fluid flows out of her body. When the mother's *water breaks*, as it is called, it is important that she reach the hospital as rapidly as possible to protect the baby. The amniotic sac and fluid provide protection for the baby, but when the water is gone, the baby must be delivered quickly. Most doctors prefer that the mother reach the hospital before the sac is broken.

When the mother is taken into the operating room, the doctors and nurses help her deliver the baby. She usually has to push to get the baby to come out. A baby is usually born headfirst, and when he comes through the cervix, his head is squeezed. But God has created the baby's skull with a series of interlocking bones that can be pushed together. Several days after the baby is born, his head is back to normal shape, and the process does no harm to his brain.

At the moment of birth, when the baby is outside the mother's body, he is still attached to the placenta by the umbilical cord. The doctor cuts off the cord, leaving a small stub. After a few days this stub dries up and falls off. The abdominal area where the umbilical cord was attached to the baby is called the *navel* or, more commonly, the "belly button."

TEACHING ABOUT INTERCOURSE AND MENSTRUATION

For most parents, information about sexual intercourse and the menstrual cycle are the most difficult aspects of reproduction to communicate to children. The reasons for parental reluctance vary. Many parents never received proper sex education in their own homes and have never felt comfortable discussing the subject themselves. If it was taboo when they were young, they are likely to be reticent to deal with the subject as adults. In addition, the act of marriage and menstruation are very personal issues, seldom or never discussed except between spouses. A third reason may be that parents are worried about traumatizing their youngsters with images of "making love" or with fearful thoughts of "bleeding" when the menstrual cycle begins.

How should parents approach these issues? In discussing sexual intercourse, you can first describe sexual reproduction among animals, then lead into a discussion of how mothers and fathers create new life. The following explanation builds on the discussion of reproduction included in the previous chapter. Of course, you will be the judge of how much of this material you should use.

Sexual Intercourse

In warm-blooded animals such as elephants, horses, dogs, cats, and hamsters, God has equipped the male with a penis. During certain times of the year, male and female animals *mate* or have *sexual intercourse*. In the case of dogs and cats, for example, this is when they are "in heat." When a female dog is in heat, the male dog places his penis inside the female dog's vagina and they mate. The sperm from the dog enters the female's body and meets with the egg, creating a puppy. Usually a female dog has several puppies, which we call a litter, and it takes only a few months for these puppies to become fully developed in the mother's womb.

All animals mate by *instinct*; they do it without even thinking about it. No animals can think like a human being, but God has put instructions in their brains telling them when to mate, how to find food, how to protect themselves from enemies, how to build their homes—everything they need to live and survive.

Unlike animals, we humans use our brains to reason. Admittedly, we possess certain instincts for survival, including automatic reactions when we find ourselves in danger. But God has also given us a free will and the ability to reason. Free will means that we have the freedom and ability to choose how we are going to live. Having granted us the capacity to differentiate between good and evil, God prefers that we choose to obey Him.

An important part of God's plan for mankind is reproduction—bearing children to carry on the human race. He wants men and women to have children, but only if they are married and have committed themselves to raising their children within the family. God condemns sexual intercourse outside of marriage as a sin. Unfortunately, many people who do not know God choose to mate without being married.

When a husband and wife love each other very much and want to have a baby, they go to bed, hug each other closely, and kiss. During the time of hugging and kissing, the husband places his penis inside his wife's vagina. When sperm come out of the man's penis, they travel up into the Fallopian tubes. If one sperm cell meets an egg, conception occurs. This is how babies are made. Nine months after conception, a beautiful chubby baby is born—the result of a mom and dad's love for each other.

Menstruation

For an undetermined reason, girls in America are experiencing their first periods at an increasingly earlier age. Some girls as young as nine years old begin to menstruate. The following information is essential in preparing girls for this momentous event.

Deep inside a woman's body are two *ovaries* where the body stores eggs, or *ova*. Each month, when a girl or woman experiences her period, one egg is released from the ovary and travels down her Fallopian tube in preparation to meet a sperm cell. Likewise, every month the women's uterus gets prepared to hold a fertilized egg. During this time she is *fertile* and can become pregnant. But most of the time the egg is not fertilized by a sperm; it simply disintegrates or falls apart and leaves the woman's body through her vagina.

When the uterus prepares to receive the fertilized egg, its lining becomes thick with many blood veins. If a fertilized egg attaches itself to the side of the uterus, these veins are ready to begin providing food for the developing baby. But when no fertilized egg appears, this lining falls apart and is discarded out of the woman's body.

For several days during the month, this thick lining flows out of the woman's body. This is called a *menstrual flow* and happens to a woman whether she is married or not. The menstrual flow is commonly called a *period*, and it occurs as a monthly event until a woman reaches forty-five or fifty years of age. To catch this menstrual flow, women use sanitary pads or tampons.

Menstruation should be explained by a girl's mother at about her eighth birthday. It does an injustice to a girl not to convey these truths before she experiences her first period. She should be reassured that this is a perfectly natural occurrence, a sign that she is becoming mature enough to bear children. She should also understand that there is nothing unclean or filthy about her period.

Tell the Truth

If we deal with reproduction and menstruation with a relaxed attitude, our children will accept the information we give them without being upset or thinking sex is somehow a dirty secret. By emphasizing God's role in designing this creative process, we will show our children that sex is a wholesome and positive aspect of their lives. By talking to them freely, you build a special bond with your children that, as they mature and see or hear things that make them curious, will help them feel comfortable asking you questions. If you do not discuss sex or you make it some deep, unexplainable mystery, you will only increase your children's curiosity. Someone is going to tell them about this wonderful area of life, and who would be a better choice than you?

---

[1] Gary Bergel, *When You Were Formed in Secret* (Elyria, Ohio: Intercessors for Life, 1980), 1-13.

C h a p t e r   S i x

PREADOLESCENCE: AGES ELEVEN TO THIRTEEN

Adolescence is the most difficult period of youth. It hits at about twelve years old, seems to take forever to get through, but lasts for only two to three years. When twelve-year-old Chelsea Clinton moved to Washington, D.C., a *Washington Post* staff writer, Elizabeth Kastor, wrote a clever piece titled "The Eternity of Being Twelve." In the article, she described what it is like to "be a girl of 12 going on 13":

> The old childhood laws of friendship and loyalty tremble and crack. Parents become dictators with perverse ideas about wardrobe. The hair-sprayed sophistication of the black-draped melodrama of adolescence beckons. You are told to behave like an adult but are still relegated to the children's table at Thanksgiving. You are, in one girl's words, too young to drive but too old to be cute.[1]

She points out that at that stage in youth the only things that matter are friends and clothes—not nice fancy clothes but stylish ones. If the wild scuzzy look is in, that is what they want so they can look like everyone else.

As our children enter puberty and adolescence, we will face some new and unique challenges. The little one we once cradled in our arms is now blossoming into adolescence and will begin to show adultlike thinking on some occasions. But we will discover quickly that preadolescents vacillate between childlike thinking and adult reasoning. Conflicts are inevitable; we must be ready for them. This is a normal stage of life. Adolescence is also a time when our children begin to pull away from us to establish their own identity.

If the level of closeness between parents and children could be measured during this stage, it would not be unusual for it to drop from 100 percent to 50 percent, even in the best families. From the child's perspective, parent's opinions, intelligence, and customs fall into a deep dark hole and what matters most is what his or her friends think. Parents cannot believe their children would prize the opinions of a pimply faced friend who thinks his parents are "stupid" just because they do not want him to cut holes in his new jeans or put scuff marks on his new tennis shoes. They tend to want adult rights and liberties with childlike responsibilities.

One pretty fourteen-year-old (going on seventeen) who attended one of our discussion groups had already become attractive to older boys. She said, disgustedly, "My parents don't trust me to go on dates with some of the most popular guys in school!" I looked at her and thought, "Neither would any parent in their right mind." If it had not been for her loving parents, she could have easily been eaten alive on the altar of lust and cast off like a rag doll. Someday, she may thank them for their parental protection, but right now they are the object of her anger.

Adolescence is not a total loss; it only seems that way. Sometimes, teenagers can enjoy their families, but unless they are taught the facts of life thoroughly when they and their parents have a close loving relationship, this stage of growth may be the most trying time of your life. Often they want answers for everything: "Why can't I go to this movie? Everyone else is!" or "Why can't I buy that CD (or video)? All my friends have it!" Their questions may indicate they have the wrong type of friends. Most parents would be shocked if they knew what some of the lyrics or video messages are saying to their kids. At this stage in youth, many parents learn a new dimension to prayer!

Adolescence is that time in a person's life when he is changing from a child into an adult. It is a period that roughly parallels the teenage years, but sometimes begins as early as nine years old in girls. The beginning of adolescence is known as *puberty.* This stage of development is characterized by the maturing of the sexual organs in preparation for reproduction—menstruation in girls and the first presence of sperm in boys—as well as secondary sex characteristics such as pubic hair, underarm hair, enlarged breasts in girls, and deepened voices in boys.

THE TRAUMA OF PUBERTY

Puberty signifies a definite physical and emotional change in a person, moving him from childhood into adulthood. Puberty can be especially disturbing for boys and girls who have not been properly prepared for it by their parents. Just imagine how horrible it would be if your daughter were sitting in a classroom and she experienced *menarche*—the beginning of menstruation—but hadn't been prepared for it. How well would we cope with that situation if we thought we were bleeding to death in front of our friends? Or imagine the guilt and fear your son would experience after waking to find his sheets soiled with semen if he had not been told about "wet dreams."

We should not put off telling our children about sexual matters as they approach puberty. A little knowledge will go a long way in protecting them from unnecessary trauma. Going through puberty or preadolescence is difficult even when a person has been informed what to expect. In general we will have to tell girls the facts of life earlier than boys. Boys do not usually reach puberty until around age twelve, normally one to two years later than girls.

Puberty begins with significant hormonal changes that trigger physical changes in boys and girls. Every body has its own internal mechanism for determining when puberty starts, and this moment differs with each child. Puberty can start as early as age nine, as has been stated, but also as late as age sixteen. There is no right time chronologically for a child to enter puberty; it depends on the individual's makeup.

The onset of puberty is governed by the *endocrine system*, which consists of several glands, including the hypothalamus, the pituitary, the thyroid, the parathyroid, the adrenal glands, and the ovaries or testicles. All these work together to bring about physical and emotional changes.

In a boy the hypothalamus signals the pituitary gland, which in turn releases three key hormones, the *androgens.* These hormones give the boy his masculine qualities, both physical and emotional. The male hormones stimulate aggressiveness, ambition, and drive. The three hormones released by the pituitary stimulate the adrenal glands and cause a boy's testicles to begin producing the hormone *testosterone*, the most potent of the male hormones. Testosterone induces the production of sperm cells and the growth of body hair. In addition, the boy's voice box or larynx grows and his voice deepens. Boys may also experience a temporary enlargement of the breasts during puberty. This enlargement is called *gynecomastia* and can sometimes be painful, but is a normal occurrence and should not be cause for alarm.

In a girl the pituitary gland stimulates the production of two primary hormones, *estrogen* and *progesterone*, in the ovaries. Both hormones work to change a girl into a woman physically and emotionally. They stimulate what we consider naturally feminine qualities, such as gentleness and nurturance. Estrogen causes growth of the breasts, widening of the hips, and maturation of the genitals, including the clitoris and the labia (which will be discussed later). In addition, a special lining called the *endometrium* in the girl's uterus begins to form in preparation for child bearing. One of the primary signs of puberty in a girl, however, is the onset of menstruation, which we discussed in chapter 5.

Puberty brings sexual maturity to both boys and girls. It does not, however, bring emotional maturity. That is a lifelong process.

EMOTIONAL INSTABILITY

As our children begin to mature sexually and change physically, they also experience emotional traumas. In most children, passage into adolescence is characterized by tremendous highs and lows of emotion. They become acutely aware of pressure to conform to what is considered "in" among their classmates.

Teenagers gradually begin to think independently of their parents and choose to make up their own mind about the world, their values, and religious convictions. Fortunately, this can also be a time of great spiritual sensitivity when they are open to challenges from God about what to do with their lives. Many a missionary or minister heard the first call of God during or shortly after adolescence. It is essential that teenagers be active in a vital church youth group during this stage so that some of the strongest influences from outside do not conflict with the family's values. Those families who attend church regularly during this stage have less trouble keeping their children active in the church during high school.

An adolescent's mental processes fluctuate from childlike to adultlike. He often feels confused about himself, his goals, his reason for living, and his relationships. He fights to be treated as an adult, but there is still that part of him that needs the comfort and security he knew as a child. In many ways, he wants the benefits of adulthood but not its responsibilities.

As he changes physically, an adolescent typically becomes uncomfortable with his looks. With his hormones in a state of flux, he will begin to notice oily skin, blackheads, or acne. He may not like the shape of his nose. He may be embarrassed by his sudden growth spurt that sends him towering above everyone else in the classroom. Sudden growth often leaves an adolescent clumsy and uncoordinated for a time, which compounds his problems. Or he may feel like a dwarf because everyone else has grown three inches during the year and he is still four-eleven. What is worse, the girl he wanted to be friends with is suddenly six inches taller than he. So he worries about his attractiveness to girls.

It is doubtful that anything is more traumatic for a preadolescent boy or girl than the junior high school locker room. Early developers have the emotional edge over the late bloomers in the locker room, where everyone's physical attributes become painfully obvious. Those who have not yet entered puberty invariably compare their bodies with those who are physically more mature. The results can be disastrous. Depression and poor self-esteem are natural consequences when children unwisely compare their bodies with others in the locker room.

Children troubled by their lack of development should be reassured that their hormonal clocks are not broken—they are merely slower than others. Although a child who develops early has a slight advantage over a late bloomer, the former can also develop self-esteem problems if he grows too tall or too wide.

As parents we need to understand the confusion, peer pressure, hormonal imbalances, and self-esteem problems that face our preadolescent children. They need extra amounts of loving patience from us. All children need love, but our love is going to be severely tested during their adolescence. We should be prepared for this.

Communicating with our children in an open, responsive way is one of the keys to getting through this traumatic time. We have to let our preadolescents know that they can come to us at any time and discuss any subject on their minds. They need to know that we are going to love them, pray for them, and comfort them during their journey from childhood to adulthood. They also need to know that we are going to continue to set guidelines for their behavior. These guidelines include such concerns as what kinds of friends they have, how they entertain themselves, and what their spiritual obligations are. Your first big, pre-dating test will come when you are forced to demonstrate your love for them by saying "no" to something they want to do because it would be harmful.

SEXUAL MATURITY

Before your children enter adolescence, they should have a good understanding of their reproductive organs and how they are supposed to function. The following description builds on the information provided in previous chapters. The diagrams in chapter 4 will be helpful and should be used again when presenting this information to your son or daughter. Though boys usually feel more comfortable learning this information from their father and girls from their mother, it can be shared by either the mother or father.

The Male Reproductive System

The male reproductive system includes the penis, glans penis, scrotum, sperm, Cowper's gland, urethra, testicles, vas deferens, ampulla, seminal vesicles, epididymis, and the prostate gland.

The *penis* is, of course, a dual-purpose organ, used not only for sexual reproduction but also for eliminating waste liquids from the bladder. The tube inside the penis is call the *urethra*. The sperm cells pass through the penis into the woman's vagina during sexual intercourse. The inside of the penis is somewhat like a sponge, honeycombed with an intricate network of tiny blood vessels. When a man is sexually aroused, these vessels fill with blood and the penis enlarges and becomes stiff. Valves within the blood vessels close, preventing the blood from leaving. This enlarged, stiff state is called an *erection*. An erection can occur at almost any time once a boy has entered puberty. It can occur not only from sexual arousal but also from such things as wearing tight-fitting clothing.

The head of the penis, called the *glans penis*, is one of the most sensitive areas of the boy's body. This "erogenous zone" contains densely packed nerves and is the main source of physical pleasure for a man in sexual intercourse.

The *scrotum* is the bag of skin that contains the *testicles*. Also called *testes*, the testicles are oval glands about the size and shape of large nuts. Inside each testicle is a long tube about one-thousandth of an inch in diameter and about a thousand feet long. One testicle can produce as many as 500 million sperm cells each day. For sperm to be healthy, they must be manufactured in an environment about four degrees cooler than the normal human body temperature. That is why they hang outside the body. In cold weather, the muscles of the scrotum draw the testicles closer to the body to maintain the proper temperature. The scrotum itself has a unique design; the left part of the scrotum is slightly lower than the right one. This is to prevent the testicles from rubbing together when a man walks.

The testicles manufacture sperm cells every day. As they fill up, the sperm cells pass into a tube known as the *epididymis*, inside the scrotal sac, where they mature. This is like an incubator or storage area.

As more and more sperm are produced, the mature sperm cells are transferred from the epididymis into a tube called the *vas deferens*. (In Latin, vas means "vessel" and deferens means "carry."). From this tube they are deposited in another storage area called the *ampulla chamber*. The sperm eventually leave the ampulla chamber and enter the *seminal vesicles*, two organs that manufacture seminal fluid, or *semen*.

The male reproductive system includes two other important glands: the *prostate* and *Cowper's gland*. The prostate lies between the bladder and the base of the penis. It produces seminal fluid and contains nerves that control penile erections. It also contracts to help ejaculate sperm from the penis. Cowper's gland is the first gland to function when a man becomes sexually aroused. It sends a few drops of slippery fluid into the urethra, preparing it for the safe passage of sperm by neutralizing the acids of the urine that would otherwise kill the sperm. A valve at the top of the urethra opens to let urine out, but automatically shuts when sperm cells are on the way.

A *sperm* cell is an amazing creation. Under a microscope it looks like a tadpole with three parts. The head contains the chromosomes that will help determine the characteristics of the child should an egg be fertilized during intercourse. The neck contains the energy source to propel the sperm. The tail provides the sperm with the ability to travel through the vagina and into the Fallopian tube to meet the egg.

The egg is surrounded by several layers of protective material that the sperm must penetrate in order for conception to occur. The sperm has chemicals called enzymes that dissolve the layers around the egg and permit a sperm cell to burrow its way inside. The layers are so tough, it takes literally millions of these sperm to surround the egg and weaken the layers enough for one sperm to enter and fertilize the egg.

Intercourse does not always result in conception. When it does, there are normally only one sperm cell and one egg involved. In rare instances, however, the fertilized egg divides in such a way that two babies begin to grow; this is how identical twins form. These babies will look exactly alike because they have the same combination of genes. At other times, two eggs are fertilized by different sperm at the same time; this is how fraternal twins are conceived. Fraternal twins do not look exactly alike because they have a different combination of genes.

The Female Reproductive System

The female reproductive system is made up of the external genitalia and the internal reproductive organs. The *vulva,* the external sexual parts, consists of several organs. The two large, fleshy folds of skin are called the *labia majora.* (In Latin, labia means "lips" and majora means "large.") Located just inside the labia majora are two smaller folds of skin, the *labia minora.* Right at the top of the labia minora is a small organ called the *clitoris.* The clitoris is located just above the opening of the *urethra,* where waste liquid is eliminated.

The clitoris is equivalent to a man's penis except that it is much smaller. Like a penis, it has a *glans* at the top and a small shaft. As in a man, the glans is densely filled with nerve endings; this makes it a woman's most sensitive sexual organ. Unlike the penis, however, the clitoris has no opening at the end and plays no part in reproduction itself.

The *hymen,* deriving its name from the mythical Greek god of marriage, is a membrane which partially blocks the opening to the vagina of a virgin.

A women's internal sexual organs include the vagina, ovaries, Fallopian tubes, uterus, and cervix. The *vagina* is the receptor for the penis during intercourse and the birth canal through which the baby passes from the uterus to the outside of the mother's body. (Vagina is Latin for "sheath.") The vagina is from three to five inches long. Its walls contain many tiny glands that secrete a cleansing liquid to keep it free from germs.

The *uterus* (a Latin word meaning "womb" or "belly") is the size and shape of a pear, about four inches long. This is where the baby will grow for nine months until he is ready to be born. Two *Fallopian tubes* are attached to the top of the uterus. These tubes lead toward the *ovaries,* where unfertilized eggs are stored. Although it is not directly connected to the ovary, a Fallopian tube catches the egg when it is released from the ovary.

An egg is normally in the Fallopian tube when fertilization takes place. It then continues its journey into the uterus, propelled through the Fallopian tube by tiny hairs called *cilia*. If the egg is not fertilized, it dissolves and comes out of the women's body during the *menstrual period*. If the egg is fertilized, it will attach itself to the uterine wall in a few days for the gestation process.

At the lower end of the uterus is the *cervix*, which is Latin for "neck." This connects the uterus to the vagina. The opening of the cervix is usually only about the diameter of a pencil lead, but it expands greatly when the baby is ready to be born.

CONTROLLING THE SEX DRIVE

Adolescents' sex drives are strong. They are healthy drives as long as they are kept under control and channeled in the right direction. It is important your children understand that their sex drive, even when it seems very powerful, is normal and controllable. First Corinthians 10:13 informs us that we need not be overpowered sexually and violate the laws and principles of God. Moreover, medical experts tell us that no physical damage results when sexual tension is not released. We should communicate this to our preadolescents and inform them as well of the unique release mechanism for boys known as nocturnal emission.

Nocturnal Emissions

If a boy is not properly prepared for it, a *nocturnal emission*, or "wet dream," can be a disturbing experience. Awakening in the middle of the night to find his sheets wet from semen is unsettling and often produces feelings of guilt or shame. These feelings can be alleviated if a boy is given a simple explanation of what is happening. In the male reproductive system, God created a unique release mechanism for unused sperm cells, which are produced by the thousands every day.

Eventually there are so many sperm cells that the storage places (the epididymis, seminal vesicles, and prostate gland) are full. What happens then is a little like what happens when a pot boils over on the stove. When the male reproductive system is filled to overflowing, the penis becomes particularly sensitive to any external stimulation—even something as simple as rubbing against bedsheets at night. A little stimulation is enough to expel some of the sperm to relieve the pressure on the storage places. In many cases, a full bladder pressing against the seminal vesicles will result in ejaculation at night.

Often a nocturnal emission is accompanied by a sexually oriented dream. Ejaculation is a sexual experience, so it's not unusual that a sexually stimulating dream would accompany it. Dreams are subconscious, and a boy need not feel guilt or shame when this experience occurs, for God knows he has no control over his brain while sleeping. However, he should be aware that sexually stimulating pictures, movies, or stories can create dreams that bring on these experiences more frequently.

The "wet dream" is God's method of releasing the buildup of sperm cells and sexual energy in an adolescent boy or in a man. It is easier for a boy to learn about this from his father, but frequently a mother discovers the signs of a wet dream when changing her son's sheets. You should reassure your sons that this is very normal and they need not feel embarrassed.

By keeping a casual, matter-of-fact attitude we can convey positive feelings about wet dreams to our sons. They should come to see them as a gift from God for helping the body take care of itself.

Masturbation

Masturbation is a common practice among teens, particularly boys. Is it wrong for a Christian to masturbate? There is probably no more controversial question in the field of sex than this. A few years ago, every Christian would have given an unqualified yes, but that was before the sexual revolution and before doctors declared that the practice is not harmful to health. No longer can a father honestly warn his son that it will cause "brain damage, weakness, baldness, blindness, epilepsy, or insanity." Some still refer to it as "self-abuse" and "sinful behavior"; others advocate it as a necessary relief for the single man and a help for the married man whose wife is pregnant or whose business forces him to be away from home for long periods of time.

The Bible is silent on this subject; therefore it is dangerous to be dogmatic. Although we are sympathetic with those who would remove the time-honored taboos against the practice, we do not feel it is an acceptable practice for Christians for the following reasons:

1. Fantasizing and lustful thinking are usually involved in masturbation, and the Bible clearly condemns such thoughts (Matt. 5:28).

2. Sexual expression was designed by God to be performed jointly by two people of the opposite sex, resulting in a necessary

and healthy dependence on each other for the experience. Masturbation frustrates the designed dependence.

3. Guilt is a universal aftermath of masturbation unless one has been brainwashed by the humanistic philosophy that does not believe in a God-given conscience or in right and wrong. Such guilt interferes with spiritual growth and produces defeat in single young people particularly. To them it is usually a self-discipline hurdle they must scale in order to grow in Christ and walk in the Spirit.

4. It violates 1 Corinthians 7:9: "For it is better to marry than to burn with passion." If a young man practices masturbation, it tends to nullify a necessary and important motivation for marriage. There are already enough social, educational, and financial demotivators on young men now; they don't need this one.

5. It creates a habit before marriage that can easily be resorted to afterward as a cop-out when a husband and wife have sexual or other conflicts that make coitus difficult.

6. It defrauds a wife (1 Cor. 7:3-5). No married man should relieve his mounting, God-given desire for his wife except through coitus. She will feel unloved and insecure, and many little problems will unnecessarily be magnified by this artificial draining of his sex drive. This becomes increasingly true as a couple reaches middle age.[2]

Differing Opinions. There are many differences of opinion on this subject among Christian pastors, doctors, psychologists, and psychiatrists. In his book, *Sexual Understanding Before Marriage*, Herbert J. Miles, a sociologist and former pastor, states that a young man should depend on nocturnal emissions to release his pent-up sexual energy. He also believes, however, that a "limited and temporary" program of masturbation is appropriate for late adolescents. Miles believes that it is permissible as long as the masturbation is done for purposes of self-control and is not based on lustful thoughts. However, many counselors are not sure it is possible to masturbate with a pure mind.

Psychologist James Dobson writes in his book, *Preparing for Adolescence*:

It is my opinion that masturbation is not much of an issue with God. It's a normal part of adolescence which involves no one else. It does not cause disease, it does not produce babies, and Jesus did not mention it in the Bible. I'm not telling you to masturbate, and I hope you won't feel the need for it. But if you do, it is my opinion that you should not struggle with guilt over it.[3]

Several youth pastors were meeting to share methods of helping young people get into the Word on a regular basis. The subject of masturbation came up as a sure deterrent to a young man's spiritual life. The single men present all agree that masturbation was not wise because of the guilt it produced, but even they admitted using it to keep their natural sex drive under control. After much honest discussion, they agreed that the real problem was mental and not physical. They concluded that if an unmarried man could masturbate for physical release only and without entertaining lustful thoughts, it should not be prohibited or associated with guilt. Even then, it should not become an addictive habit.

WHAT PARENTS SHOULD KNOW ABOUT HOMOSEXUALITY

In recent years we have heard a great deal about homosexuals and their lifestyles. They are not a new phenomenon; they have been with us at least since the days of Lot (Genesis 19). However, in recent years they have "come out of their closets" and are demanding the right to be recognized as normal. Homosexual couples are demanding to be recognized as "families" with the right to marry and adopt children.

Although they would like us to believe they are "born homosexual," no undisputed scientific evidence has come to light to confirm that conclusion. As I noted in my book *What Everyone Should Know About Homosexuality*, there are several factors that may predispose a young man or woman to turn to homosexual behavior.

1. *Temperament.* I have found that most homosexual men reflect a high degree of melancholy temperament. They are usually sensitive, artistic, gifted, introverted perfectionists who were very impressionable in their youth. Most were rejected by one parent or sibling, and by the time they reached adulthood were extremely angry. Not all "melancholy" boys have homosexual tendencies, but perhaps 15 to 20 percent may. Many of these young men do not become homosexual, indulge in male-male sexual fantasies, or think of themselves as homosexuals because they believe it is wrong.

2. *Inadequate parental relationships.* One professor of psychiatry notes,

Current research indicates that the family most likely to produce a homosexual comprises a very intimate, possessive and dominating mother and a detached, hostile father. Many mothers of lesbians tend to be hostile and competitive with their daughters. The fathers of female homosexuals seldom appear to play a dominant role in the family and have considerable difficulty being openly affectionate with their daughters.[4]

Some fathers rejected their daughters, particularly for not being boys, which has caused some girls to view themselves as boys and thus to take on male characteristics. Proper parental love is one of the best preventatives of homosexuality.

3. *Insecurity about sexual identity.* Many parents have unknowingly damaged their children by refusing to accept them for who they are. Often when a father has a daughter but wanted a son, he will treat her like a boy. This kind of rejection from parents can make children reject their own sex and seek to imitate the opposite sex. "It is important for girls to accept their femininity and enjoy being women, while boys should be trained to esteem their manhood. Learning to love and accept yourself is fundamental to learning to love someone else."[5]

4. *Childhood sexual trauma.* Sexual exploitation or molestation damages children and may lead them into a homosexual or promiscuous lifestyle. Many boys are led into homosexuality by older boys or men who have befriended them for sexual reasons before puberty begins. Consequently they are guided in the wrong direction and develop the habit of homosexuality. In all likelihood, if they had been left alone, they would naturally have grown up heterosexual. Unfortunately, each experience fosters habits, guilt patterns, and thought processes that may lead to homosexual practices. The wooing of a young boy by a homosexual man is called "chicken hawking." Today, this activity is hardly mentioned by educators or the media though it is the most common way to produce a homosexual.

5. *Youth masturbation.* Most of the homosexuals I know indulged in masturbation early and frequently. This seems to be a crucial step in adopting a homosexual lifestyle. As frequent masturbators, they learn to associate their genitals with sexual pleasure. This association can overcome heterosexual leanings and destroy a natural attraction toward females. Masturbation can divert a child from normal sexual desires and serve as a catalyst that will provide him with a mental attitude favorable to homosexuality.

6. *Sexual fantasizing.* Almost all homosexuals indulge homosexual thoughts and fantasies, contrary to scripture. The more they do it the better they are at it; some even look at same-sex pornography. The more

a person fantasizes about members of his own sex, the easier it becomes to try to fulfill the fantasies. With repeated episodes of homosexual behavior, the boy's sexual orientation is gradually steered away from heterosexuality. If homosexual thought patterns become entrenched in a child's mind before he reaches puberty, his increased sex drive after puberty will intensify toward his own sex—not, as it should, toward the opposite sex. I have counseled many homosexuals, and all were same-sex fantasizers. Of the thirty homosexual men I have seen come to Christ and forsake that lifestyle, those who have had a temporary relapse admitted it started in their minds.

7. *Childhood associates and peer pressure*. Many young boys possessing feminine characteristics have been unmercifully teased as children. This teasing or rejection can result in self-hatred. If a boy has been rejected by his friends—or worse still, by his father—he may accentuate his feminine characteristics and drift toward homosexuality. Our children's friends may also be a bad influence on them by introducing them to sexual experimentation.

These are some of the factors that may lead children into a homosexual lifestyle. Homosexuality is not a biological reality; it is a learned behavior. It is the result of a process that begins with a combination of these factors, is reinforced by an initial homosexual experience, and becomes a habit because of increasingly pleasurable thoughts and feelings and experiences with members of the same sex. The more our children expose themselves to homosexual thoughts, the more likely they are to be drawn into that lifestyle. Once involved in homosexuality, a person finds the habit difficult to break.

How to Protect Your Child from Homosexuality

A child is best protected from homosexuality by being brought up in a Christian home where the father is the loving head of the home, where the mother is supportive of the father's role, and where both parents have warm and affectionate relationships with their sons and daughters.

In his excellent study of homosexuality, Growing Up Straight, George Rekers writes, "A secure and normal sexual identity in a child is best fostered by a stable home where both father and mother provide affection, attention, and security for their children."[6] If children are growing up in a home where there is a single parent of the opposite sex, every effort should be made to provide a same-sex role model for them. A boy could look to an uncle or grandfather as a role model. A girl could look to her grandmother, aunt, or another positive female as a model for her behavior.

The key to protecting our children from homosexuality is for us to study and obey the Scriptures and to live the Word of God in our own lives. By paying attention to our children, by loving them, communicating with them, and listening to them, we will most likely have success in raising sons and daughters who have no sex-role confusion or leanings toward homosexuality. I say "most likely," because no matter how good we are as parents, our children will eventually exercise their free wills and choose one lifestyle over another. If we are committed believers who have done everything in our power to bring up godly children and one goes astray, we should not take the blame on ourselves. God gave each of us a free will either to accept or to reject His salvation. That same free will allows our children to reject everything we have taught them, regardless of how hard we have tried to help them live according to God's Word.

If you have a child or teen who you believe is involved in homosexuality, do not ignore the problem. Find a biblical counselor who has experience in this field, and get him or her into counseling as soon as possible. There are many "exit" groups and other groups throughout the country that have good success in bringing homosexuals out of that lifestyle. These groups have one thing in common: they are all based upon a personal confrontation with Jesus the living Christ and the power He gives that enables a person to come out of a homosexual lifestyle (1 Cor. 1:18).

DOING OUR JOBS

Just teaching our children is not enough. We must protect them from the wrong influences at this tender age. It is a wise parent who knows where and with whom his eleven- to thirteen-year-old is at all times—and is "watchful," as the Scriptures teach.

As parents we have the responsibility to convey our moral values and these truths about sexual matters to our preadolescents to prepare them for adulthood. Waiting for them to bring up the subject may prove fruitless. We need to initiate the discussion. How to do this is considered in the next chapter.

---

[1] Elizabeth Kastor, "The Eternity of Being Twelve," *Washington Post*, 14 January 1993.

[2] Tim LaHaye and Beverly LaHaye, *The Act of Marriage* (Grand Rapids, Mich.: Zondervan Publishing House, 1976), 269-70.

[3] James C. Dobson, *Preparing for Adolescence* (Venture, Calif.: Vision House, 1978), 86-87.

[4] Tim LaHaye, *What Everyone Should Know about Homosexuality* (Wheaton, Ill.: Tyndale House Publishers, 1980).

[5] Ibid., 78.

[6] George Rekers, *Growing Up Straight*, 75.

Part Three

HOW TO TEACH YOUR TEENS TO BE SEXUALLY PURE

Chapter   Seven

TEACHING
YOUR TEENS
ABOUT SEX

Surveys indicate that four out of five teenagers rarely talk to their parents about sex. Yet most parents and teens indicate they would like to discuss the subject more freely. One of the survey questions we asked those who attended our discussion groups was, "Whom would you most like to talk to you about sex: teachers, counselors, ministers, friends, or parents?" The majority responded, "My parents."

As a child grows into his or her teen years, both his or her interest in the subject of sex and the need to know increase dramatically. Because of the changing forces going on inside them, they think more about sex than any other subject and talk about it with their friends, who are probably as uninformed as they are. Teenagers have adult physical capabilities but are still developing character traits and dealing with turbulent emotions. Because of the enormous sexual pressures placed on teenagers by our culture, it is imperative that parents begin talking to their children before their teenage years not only about sex, but also about morality and abstinence. Be sure to discuss it in a relaxed way so they will feel comfortable talking with you about sex as they grow older.

Nothing stifles communication between teens and parents like repeated adult criticism. Teens are fond of shocking their parents with off-the-wall ideas they have borrowed from their peers. If parents respond by condemnation or harsh criticism, future communication may be jeopardized. At times silence is the golden key to communication. By silence you are not giving assent to your children's latest "pipe dream," but you let the sound of their own voice filter down into their base of reasoning while in your presence. That might be the time to ask, "How do you feel about that?" or "What do you think about that?" These two questions are normally asked only by parents who communicate well with their teens. Parents should realize that these questions are excellent ways to help an emotionally bottled-up teen express herself. If you develop the habit of asking these two questions and listening without interruption, you will find the gates of communication opening wide and your children will display an openness and receptivity. Listening, not giving advice, is an essential ingredient in parent-child relationships.

One simple technique to help promote conversation is to repeat in your own words what your child has said to you. This lets him know that you really heard and care about his feelings and thoughts. It takes concentration, but it is well worth it.

Be sure to develop one other quality: be shockproof. Teens offer many pronouncements with a minimum of thought and express feelings that are temporary. Some simply love to shock their parents. Try responding, "Is that what you really think?" or "Do you agree?" If you become shockproof, few barriers will be raised between you and your child, and he will feel he can share anything with you—as long as he can trust you. Like any good counselor, you must grant your "client" the sacred counseling privilege: "never betray a confidence."

If after reading this book you realize you are already late, you should prayerfully select a time to have a long talk with your child. It may be difficult at first, but it gets easier as you both get over your embarrassment. They will find the details of their sexuality and that of the opposite sex very fascinating. No matter how difficult it is to initiate such a session, it is essential they get this information from you. If you present your talk carefully and discreetly, you will build a rapport with him or her that will help your teen face this turbulent time in life and allow either of you the opportunity to bring the subject up anytime new questions or challenges arise, particularly as they begin dating. Leave your son and daughter with the impression that "anytime you want to talk, I am ready to do so. No subject is too small or too personal for you to discuss with me."

Do not wait too long! An evangelist friend of ours said, "At thirteen, my dad nervously sat me down for the big 'S' talk. When it was almost over, I realized I knew more about the subject than he did, for he didn't tell me one thing I didn't already know." This will not happen if you study the subject carefully and then share the information with your child.

Whose job is it to begin the discussion of sex? Most parents have the mistaken idea that "if my son wants to talk to me about sex, he will ask." Actually, he will not unless you have had such talks during their growing up years. If a parent who is waiting for his teenager to bring up the subject really understood the conflict going on in his youngster, he would force himself to open the conversational door. After all, he has a vested interest in whether or not his teen is prepared for this major facet of life. Teenagers have developed feelings never experienced before and sometimes have to fight off impure thoughts not wrestled with earlier in life. As one young person admitted, "I'm afraid my parents will think I'm doing the things I ask them about."

We have discovered a great amount of hostility toward parents from teenagers who are in trouble over sex. While it is true that many get into trouble because they rebel against their parents, they may also feel resentful toward parents who never warned them how dangerous sex can be. One survey indicated that while most young people prefer to learn about sex from their parents, four out of five who were in trouble at the time did not want to talk to their parents about it. When a teen's world collapses around him, he wants to blame someone else for his problems, and usually his or her parents receive the blame.

Probably the best way to initiate a conversation is to ask your teen the questions that are most likely to be on his or her mind. This should be done by the parent of the same sex when possible. The following questions reflect the major concerns of most young people, depending on their ages.

FATHERS' QUESTIONS TO SONS

When introducing the subject of sex into a conversation with your son, try to be as casual as possible. Remember, you know in advance what you are going to talk about, but your son may be surprised. You should look him in the eye and say something like the following.

Question: *We haven't talked about sex for some time now. Would you mind if I asked you a question?* Usually the teen thinks, "Good grief, he's going to ask if I've had sex with a girl!" so he is relieved when we ask a much less threatening question. The day may come when you should ask that question, but it is hardly the one for opening the conversational door.

You may also begin, *I'd like to have a talk with you about sex, Jim. It may be uncomfortable for both of us at first, but it's so important that I think we should discuss it anyway. You are approaching manhood, and you will find that the sexual forces and changes going on inside you will have a powerful effect on your whole life.*

Question (early teens): *Have you started to feel your sex drive increase lately?* Let him respond. You might add, *Does it bother you?* Notice how unthreatening that question is. It assumes these are natural feelings and if he hasn't experienced them yet, he will. Never lecture or preach at him, but offer brief explanations of things you feel he is old enough to ask. At times you can identify with him by observing, *I remember when I was your age. I felt guilty when I had these feelings, and it wasn't until later that I found it was natural ——all the guys have them.*

Perhaps you can add, *When I was your age, my dad and I enjoyed some great talks about sex that really helped me prepare for manhood. I hope we can have talks like that too.* If you can't say that, you can at least set the stage so he can make that remark to his son some day.

Question: *Have your new sexual feelings made it difficult for you to concentrate on your studies, your spiritual life, or Bible reading?*

Question: *Do you think a lot about girls?* You may wish to add, *Do you know what Jesus meant when He talked about lust being as bad as adultery? What is the difference between lusting and looking?* With this you might wish to read Matthew 5:27-28.

Question: *Do you know what causes a man to have a sex drive?* If he does not understand, it will be helpful to review the material in preceding chapters. He needs to identify the sex drive as a gift of God, a natural drive that must be controlled.

Question: *Have you had any wet dreams yet?* Most boys awaken from a wet dream feeling guilty. They should understand that this is God's merciful gift of "overflow" when his body manufactures more sperm cells and semen than his system can handle. He should also be told that the dream does not cause the emission but it is caused by the sexual overflow. If his body had not manufactured so much sexual fluid, he would not have experienced the dream. However, he does need to be counseled to avoid pornography or sexually lurid TV programs and movies, for they can cause the dreams as well. (For additional information on this important subject, see the section on nocturnal emissions in chapter 6 and in the glossary.)

Question: *Have you masturbated yet?* This is probably one of the toughest questions for your son to answer. He needs your assurance that as a man you understand that almost all men have masturbated. According to an old saying, "99 percent of all men have masturbated at one time or another, and the other 1 percent are liars." I did meet one young man who claimed he had never done it, and because of the dedicated minister he is today, I believe him. But he is rare indeed. This too is a subject you should study in chapter 6 to be properly informed.

Question: *Do you fully understand how babies are conceived?* Be sure to listen intently to his description, letting him describe what he knows. If you have done your work well in the lower grades, you will not have to teach much here. It is important, however, that you are not critical of what he doesn't know. Tell him, *That's good, son. There are just a couple of things I'd like to add.* Then provide the necessary additions.

Question: *How old does a girl have to be before she can get pregnant?* You may be surprised by his answer. Explain that she becomes fertile after she has started to menstruate.

Question: *How many teens your age do you think are sexually active?* The statistics on this are alarming. Surveys are so diverse that they prove nothing except that young people are more active today than at any time in American history. Some estimates go as high as 63 percent for boys and 51 percent for girls before graduating from high school. These percentages were confirmed by the groups of young people we met with. It is assumed that 50 percent or more have had at least one sexual experience before high school graduation.

As we have already seen, even Christian young people are more active sexually than they used to be. Most parents, ministers, and Christian school officials would be amazed at the sexual activity of youth coming from Christian homes. Do not assume that your son "would not do it." It is important for both of you to start talking early so that he will know that some day you will look him in the eye and ask if he has ever had intercourse with a girl. That prospect alone might cool him down some night when his passions have all but run away with him.

Question: *Do you know any promiscuous girls?* You don't need any names. Indeed it is important to assure your son that you will keep his confidence. Don't even tell your wife what he shares privately unless you get his permission.

Question: *Would you date a promiscuous girl?*

Question: *Do you know any girls who have become pregnant in high school?*

Question: *What do you know about sexually transmitted diseases?* Your son should know something about AIDS, syphilis, gonorrhea, and herpes and should understand that both AIDS and herpes are extremely contagious and incurable. While most young people do not think their peers would ever have AIDS, it only takes one to have sex with a carrier to introduce it into his school. One West Texas high school senior class of only ninety-eight students had six students who tested positive for the AIDS virus. Yes, one person could start an epidemic. The glossary has more information on these diseases if you need it.

Question: *Do you have any homosexual friends?* or *Do you know any boys who are gay?* You do not want to implant hatred for homosexuals in the heart of your son, but you don't want him to make them his dearest friends either. Unless they are repentant homosexuals seeking God's grace and power to overcome their homosexuality, you should not permit your son to run around with them. Remember the apostle Paul's words, "Bad company corrupts good character."

Additional Questions You May Want to Ask Your Son

Question: *What do you think about oral sex?* This question should be asked of him at about age sixteen or seventeen if he is dating a girl regularly. It should not be asked by itself and should be introduced discretely. But you should inquire, because oral sex is probably the most common form of birth control used today by teens before marriage. It is also being introduced into some sex education courses as a form of abstinence (see Appendix A).

Did God give us sex only for making babies?

Do you know why girls menstruate?

Are you aware of the emotional pressure a girl feels just before and during her period?

How should a boy treat a girl if he knows she is having her period?

Does a young man need premarital sex experience in order to be a good love partner when he gets married?

What do you know about abortion? What is your honest feeling about abortion for an unwed teenage girl?

What do you think is the boy's responsibility if he has gotten a girl pregnant?

Do you know what the Bible teaches about premarital sex? What passages come to mind?

Is there a difference between adultery and fornication?

How far can an unwed couple go?

Reasons You Can Give Your Son for Waiting to Have Sex

In an age when teens are subjected to enormous pressures to experiment with sex and treat it casually, a boy needs some reasons why he should delay that activity until marriage. He may be in a school where sex educators openly teach or infer that teens "ought to practice their sexuality" or "have the right to control their own bodies" or "make their own choices." Then parents are left with the responsibility of helping their teens pick up the pieces of their shattered lives.

As already noted, a teenager can hardly watch television without viewing a passionate show of affection that includes or implies sexual relations. Whose moral values are under attack? Yours. And your son's. With this and the many other sexually stimulating pressures of our society, not the least of which may be the pretty girlfriend he dates, he needs your help. She may be as innocent as he, but to remain that way, they both need to be armed with logical reasons for not engaging in life's most exciting experience.

Many of their friends may already be promiscuous, and some may be pressuring them to conform to the new-age morality, which is really the old immorality. Your son needs to hear from you why he should not engage in premarital sex. You can give him the following reasons for not having sex. Some of these reasons are adapted from previous chapters.

1. *Your body belongs to God, not to you.* Every teenager needs to understand that intercourse other than between married partners is a sin against his body, which (if he is a Christian) is the temple of God. He defiles not only himself, but God's temple (1 Cor. 6:15-20). (See Appendix B for additional scriptures about sexual sins.)

2. *You are to be the spiritual leader in any close relationship you have.* It is impossible to lead a girl spiritually if you have illicit sex with her. You have a responsibility toward God, your parents, her parents, the girl herself, and even her future husband to help her spiritually while you are going together. Dating can be an exciting time even without sexual activity. It supplies a vital need in the maturing process of every young person. Don't waste those months or years in adult behavior. You will cheat not only the future, but also the present.

3. *Your spiritual life depends on holiness of thought and practice.* To become the spiritually mature man God wants you to be, you must give time to Bible study, witnessing, and prayer. The adolescent years form a special period of development mentally, vocationally, socially, and spiritually. If your social life involves premarital sex, you will not develop spiritually at this crucial period in your life.

4. *Premarital sex clouds your judgment at what could be the most important time of your life.* You are going to be making some life-long decisions in the next few years. Engaging in premarital sex keeps you from making these decisions with God's blessing. Your choices will likely chart the course of your life for the next fifty years. This is the time for clear-headed, Spirit-filled thinking. It is not the time to fall prey to an obsession with sex.

5. *Premarital sex could cause you to be faced with the responsibility of an illegitimate child.* God has given you the gift of procreating life. Do you want a child you have fathered raised by someone else? Or do you wish to marry a girl before you can adequately support her and your child? What future is there for an illegitimate child compared with the happy home you have been raised in?

6. *Do you want the responsibility for ruining a girl's life?* Nothing can damage a young woman's life like an unplanned, unwanted pregnancy. This is a heavy weight to carry on your conscience. No amount of immediate excitement and pleasure can compensate for years of grief that such an

act would cause so many people (the two of you, the child, and your parents).

7. *Do you want the responsibility of teaching a young girl to be promiscuous?* Premarital sex is usually initiated by two young people who love each other very much. They justify it by insisting that they would never give themselves to anyone else and that intimacy is permissible between two people in love. However, statistics indicate they will probably fall out of love and breakup. In the meantime, they have likely awakened an appetite for sex that will make it easier to be intimate with others.

Although it may seem unthinkable now, many prostitutes and promiscuous women gave their virtue to a man they loved during their teen years. You should never do on a date what you would not want another young man to do with your future wife.

8. *Treat every girl the way you wish other boys to treat your sister.* Dating is a sacred trust. You bear responsibility for another man's most treasured possession. Grant her the respect and decency that accompanies such trust.

9. *You must learn self-control and self-discipline.* Everyone knows that sex is exciting and pleasurable, but the foremost human trait every person needs to acquire is self-discipline. Denying yourself the opportunity of sex before marriage will never hurt you; it will build your character and teach you that passions and desires can be controlled. Self-discipline in this matter will enable you to gain it in other areas of life. It takes a better man to say no than to say yes.

10. *You need to save your sexual expression for your one true love.* If your future mate asks you, "Have you ever had sex with another woman?" will you be able to look her straight in the eye and say no with a clear conscience? If you can, her respect for you will soar, for she will realize that you are someone special. It is estimated that only 20 percent of the males in the United States enter marriage without sexual experience.

One advantage of your obvious self-control prior to marriage is that she can trust you more after marriage. If a man restrains himself from premarital sex, it is very likely he will resist the temptation to extramarital sex.

11. *You can give your bride your gift of virtue.* If you present your son with a special virtue ring as he enters his teens (see chapter 8), you can remind him that in addition to the wedding ring he will someday present

to his bride, he can give her the virtue ring as a tangible expression of his love. You hope his Christian bride can do the same. This little ceremony will bring joy to their hearts for years to come.

Note to Fathers

If fathers will study the above questions and reasons to wait, they will be armed to prepare their sons for the dating years. They do not have to be delivered all at once but can be spread over time. You will find that even though it is difficult to initiate this subject with your son, having such a talk with him will build a vital relationship between you that will last a lifetime. The older he gets the more he will treasure how well you prepared him for this exciting but precarious stage in life.

MOTHERS' QUESTIONS TO DAUGHTERS

Mothers and daughters often have an easier time than fathers and sons in communicating about sex. Unless their temperaments are seriously in conflict, a daughter often looks to her mother for advice if she feels that her parents enjoy a positive relationship and if mother is not too critical and judgmental.

Some of the questions that fathers ask their sons are appropriate for mothers to use with slight modifications. You may wish to make your own adaptations of these. Of course, the weight of the questions will depend on the age of your daughter. You will notice that some of the questions have been adapted, for your use, from previous chapters.

Questions about Menstruation

The onset of menstruation requires discussion and explanation. It is rare that a girl, no matter how close she is to her father, would go to him for counseling on this matter. The first painful cramps usually cause her to seek her mother's help. We assume that you as a mother have prepared your daughter for this event. If you have not, consider her first female cramps as a signal that you are behind and need to catch up. Apart from menstruation, a girl's development of breasts and pubic hair will necessitate frank mother-daughter talks around ages twelve to fourteen. Again, it is the mother's duty to open the conversational door, not the daughter's. By raising questions, you can attract her interest and make it easier for her to ask about things that are troubling her.

Question: *One of the subjects we should discuss is menstruation. Would you like to talk about it now?* This could be a tactful opening for a discussion with an eleven- to thirteen-year-old. You may want to refresh your knowledge on the subject by reading chapter 6 and then discuss with her the cause, process, and results. Be sure to include her emotional reactions—depression, irritability, tears. The better you prepare her, the less apt she is to suffer an embarrassing experience.

Question: *Are any of your girlfriends starting to get interested in boys?* Then you can ask, *Have you found yourself more interested in boys than you used to be?* This may initiate talk about girls "prettying up" or dressing to attract boys shortly after the beginning of menstruation. Concentration on school work becomes difficult, their grades may suffer, and they will probably be more self-conscious in school and more easily embarrassed around boys than previously. Explaining this probably will not change anything for your daughter, but it will explain to her the nature of the forces going on inside her, and it will let her know you understand. Be sure to clarify that menstruation is part of nature's process in preparing her for maturity.

Question: *Do you know what "turns boys on"?* Most innocent girls have no idea that tight-fitting sweaters over a shapely emerging bustline is a visual turn-on to boys, as are tight-fitting jeans, short skirts, sexually provocative movements, and skimpy swimsuits.

Some Christian women and their daughters are very naive about what boys find stimulating. Our Lord declared that if a man looks on a woman to lust after her, he is committing adultery in his mind (Matt. 5:28). Explain to your daughter that her body can be a symbol of femininity that ennobles men or a symbol of lust that inflames and causes them to stumble spiritually. She may object to the idea that she is "her brother's keeper," but even that becomes an opportunity for you to explain that godly women are modest women. Most innocent girls are confused about the thin line between modest femininity and flirtatious provocativeness. Be sure to discuss with her Paul's advice to all Christians: "Therefore, if what I eat causes my brother to fall into sin, I will never eat meat again, so that I will not cause him to fall" (1 Cor. 8:13).

Our daughter Linda has been a youth pastor's wife for twenty years. When we discussed with her some of the subjects we were going to include in this book, she spontaneously offered some advice for parents of teenage girls: "Tell them to stop being so naive. I can't believe how some parents, even fine Christian parents, let their girls dress. Sometimes they are so provocative they drive spiritual boys away and attract the wrong kind of guys. Some of them let their daughters come to youth meetings and even to church in outfits that shouldn't be seen outside the bedroom! And some of the swimsuits they buy them to wear to the beach are downright indecent! I don't know what they are thinking of."

In contrast, I think of the words of a deacon who arrived fifteen minutes late for a meeting before church service one Sunday morning. He apologized for being late and said, "We were all set to come to church early, and I took one look at my teenage daughter and told her to go back in the house and get dressed!" That dad and mother, for his wife supported his decision, had their priorities straight. Encourage your teens to wear proper attire. If they will not, then insist on it. Always remember you are the parent; they are the child. For some reason (maybe Adam and Eve's nature), they usually insist on testing your standards.

Question: *Are you aware of the sexual stimulus you give a boy when your body comes in contact with his?* Every girl should realize that boys develop a sensitivity to female touch. Explain to her that a mature woman's breasts are sensitive and are used in married lovemaking as a means of sexual arousal. But in some girls, that sensitivity does not begin as soon as the breasts develop. If a girl is not careful she can inadvertently arouse a boy simply by bumping or brushing against him.

Question: *Are you aware of how the sex drive in a boy takes place and what arouses it?* This may be the means of explaining to your daughter how males function so she can cooperate with nature and not let her body be a cause for sexual fantasy or lust. Go back to the chart in chapter 2 and go over the principle of the Law of Progression.

Question: *Do you talk about sex with boys?* There seems to be an increasing tendency for people of both sexes to talk openly about this very private subject. Such cross-sexual conversation is cultivated today under the guise of freedom of expression and openness. We believe this is harmful—not because sex is shameful, but because it is private and open discussion about it is stimulating to both sexes. Such conversation should be saved until marriage and limited to one's partner.

Question: *Have you ever had amorous feelings?* Introduce this question when you think your daughter has been inadvertently exposed to sexually suggestive material via TV, a book, or a movie. It is important that she analyze her feelings. This might be a good time to explain to her "the cycle of a woman" in relation to her monthly period. Many girls will find that they are generally more affectionate during certain times of the month. Your daughter needs to understand the nature of this feeling and its relation to her fertility cycle.

Question: *Are any of the girls your age sexually active?* This might be followed with, *Do your girlfriends talk much about sexual activity?* You need to be aware of your daughter's view of this issue, the status of her moral values, and the type of values held by her friends. She also needs to know your family rules on dating (see chapter 9) and that she will be held to them.

Question: *Do you know any girls who got pregnant before marriage?* Ask her how she thinks the girl felt and what she should do with the baby. You might also address the current fad of some girls getting pregnant deliberately. You might inquire whether she feels this is fair to the child. Let your daughter talk freely without your becoming judgmental. If you automatically declare "what's right," you are apt to shut the conversational door. Do not be upset if she ventures an off-the-wall answer to shock you. Try to respect her opinion, and keep asking questions: *Do you think...?* or *How do you feel about...?* Ask her what she thinks pregnancy costs an unmarried girl.

Question: *Have you or any of the girls you run around with heard the old fable that boys like to use after a girl arouses him—that if she doesn't have sex with him, he will be injured physically or psychologically?* Even though your daughter would be disobedient to your dating rules if she did get a boy that worked up, she should know that the "stone ache" a boy gets is a physical phenomenon that has no lasting effect. More than anything else, it should show her that she is playing with fire.

Explain that physical intimacy was intended by God to prepare married couples for intercourse, and point out that many "friendship rapes" are caused by boys who get overheated and use their superior force to overpower a girl. That she never intended to "go all the way" does not lessen the fact that she has lost her virtue, exposed herself to pregnancy, and is partially responsible for the unpleasant situation. Many an unhappy marriage has started this way, and numerous broken dreams were similarly ignited by heavy petting that was never intended to get out of control. Your daughter needs to know that the sex drive is nothing to play with. Like any power, it can get out of control.

Question: *Do you or girls your age think you must have sex with a boy to keep his interest?* Your daughter should know that such reasoning is false. If she must have sex with a boy to retain his interest, he is primarily interested in her body, and their attachment will be short-lived. Many women do not understand that the male who refuses to wait until marriage for sex is not worth having. One reason a young woman, who is eager to marry, has such a difficult time getting a boy to take her to the altar is that she unwisely submits to his sexual desires before marriage.

Question: *Can a girl remain a virgin and still be popular?* There is strong peer pressure today to engage in premarital sex. It takes strong commitment to moral and spiritual values and encouragement from their parents for girls to see that popularity is not nearly so important as integrity and character. At certain times in teenagers' lives, they might sacrifice almost anything to be popular. They need to realize that some things are more important than popularity, and giving in to teenage sex is not one of them. We hope that your daughter has been trained to demand character and quality in a young man and to recognize that giving in to him sexually may create in him a disgust with both her and himself. That will immediately kill her popularity in his eyes.

In addition, your daughter should be alerted to another teenage certainty: boys brag about their female exploits. They may promise to keep her confidence while they are going steady, but after they break up the entire school will know she is an easy mark. Promiscuous girls are popular only for sex, whereas virtuous girls are admired for themselves.

Additional Questions You May Want to Ask Your Daughter

By the time your daughter is seventeen, she may know far more than you realize, and her questions may be heavier than yours. A survey of high school girls revealed that the following questions were paramount in their minds:

How do you avoid sex and still keep a boyfriend?

If I turn a boy on, will it harm him physically?

How far can a girl go without getting into trouble?

How does intercourse feel?

How can I tell if I am ready for sex?

What is the best method of birth control?

Is it better to masturbate each other than have premarital sex?

Is it wrong to have oral sex?

Why should I remain a virgin?

Have you provided your high school daughter with the answers to these questions?

Reasons You Can Give Your Daughter for Waiting

Emotions often dominate the decision-making process between the ages of fifteen and nineteen, but you underestimate your children if you think that logic and reason do not enter into their decisions. Since they are bombarded emotionally on every side to have sex before marriage, only their parents, the church, and some responsible adult friends will provide adequate reasons why they should wait. The following list of reasons why teenage girls should wait is not exhaustive but should give you a good start.

1. *Your body is not your own, but God's.* Young people need to be told that they serve as the central prize in a war for control of their body. On one side God wants to keep it holy, which involves not having sex until marriage. He offers a reward in this life and the life to come for those who keep themselves pure. Those who do so have a better chance of love and happiness in marriage, a guarantee of freedom from STDs, and eternal reward. On the other hand, Satan wants to use their bodies for sexual violation of God's laws and to fan their emotions to yield to his will. But as our Lord warned, Satan is a liar. Instead of premarital sex being all pleasure as he promises, it becomes short-term ecstasy and long-term misery. It breeds guilt, fear, and shame and can lead to premarital pregnancy and incurable disease.

Actually, a Christian young woman has no option if she has committed her body to Jesus Christ. The Bible is very clear. If we obey Christ, we will keep our bodies pure; if we engage in premarital sex, we disobey and dishonor God (see Appendix B).

Your daughter needs to hear from you what she probably already knows—that God wants to keep her body pure for His service. If she has this principle impressed into her brain, it will help to strengthen her resolve when she is confronted by temptation.

2. *Virtue helps to maintain self-respect.* One of the greatest problems among modern teens is a lack of self-image. What we think about ourselves profoundly influences our view of God, man, the future, and everything else in our lives. Once a girl violates her virtue, she loses self-respect, making it difficult to come to grips with who she is and thus retarding self-acceptance.

3. *When it's gone, it's gone.* No girl ever became promiscuous until she lost her virtue. Once virginity is gone, however, a powerful spiritual and psychological reason for refusing to engage in premarital sex has also vanished. It is natural for a virgin to want to tell the man she marries that she has saved herself exclusively for him. But that is something only virgins can do. (See chapter 8 for a discussion of how a boy or girl can become virtuous again after losing his or her virginity.)

4. *Virginity helps you learn self-control.* The girl who does not gain sexual self-control will probably have a difficult time developing self-control in other areas of life, including food, finances, academics, and work. Sex is such a major concern of life that self-mastery is absolutely essential.

One Christian girl who really had her act together was continually pressured by her peers to break her virginity. Finally she said to her friends, "I can be like you any time I wish. You can never be like me." Not bad thinking for a seventeen-year-old!

5. *Promiscuity usually leads to unwed pregnancy.* Every mother of a teenage girl worries that her daughter could get pregnant prior to marriage. No single event can affect a teen's life and family more critically than this. All her dreams of a beautiful church wedding—usually the happiest day of a girl's life—vanish forever.

The most tragic impact is the damage inflicted on the girl. She is confined at a time in life when she craves activity. Adult responsibilities are thrust upon her prematurely. Education will become difficult at best, impossible at worst. She may miss "Mr. Right," and she may have sentenced herself to a lifetime of economic mediocrity because she had not adequately developed her skills. This is an exorbitant price to pay for a few rapturous moments.

6. *Your Christian testimony will be destroyed.* It is difficult for a girl to survive an unwed pregnancy without ruining her Christian witness. While it is admittedly unjust for boys not to share equally the full impact of a pregnancy, girls suffer more. This one act and its natural consequences can undo a lifetime of positive testimony.

7. *Disease is a risk.* Sexually transmitted diseases have always been with us, confirming that promiscuity is as old as mankind. The two major strains, syphilis and gonorrhea, have caused untold suffering—birth defects, brain damage, impotence, infertility, and other human miseries. But promiscuity has increased so much in recent years that two new strains, Herpes Simplex II and AIDS, have arrived on the scene as incurable maladies. Millions of people have forsaken promiscuity out of fear. This same fear ought to motivate young women to maintain virtue. Discuss with your daughter the sexually transmitted diseases dominant in our society, which we describe in the glossary under "Sexually Transmitted Diseases."

8. A *hasty marriage becomes likely.* A friend told me "There's a family in our church that I wish could have read this a year ago. Their fifteen-year-old daughter married the seventeen-year-old boy who impregnated her with twins. Now they live in her parents' home, and the boy won't work." Is that the lifestyle those parents had planned for their fifteen-year-old? You cannot keep your daughter from ruining her life through premarital sex, but you can try. An ounce of prevention (parental sex education) is always worth a pound of cure. Whether to marry the teenage father is a subject in itself, which we will consider in chapter 15. The odds are stacked against such a marriage working. God meant children to be a blessing. A hasty teenage marriage as a result of promiscuity is usually a hindrance instead, and the unhappiness young people create for themselves is incalculable.

9. *Once begun, teenage sex is difficult to stop.* Once teens begin to have sex, it is all but impossible for them to stop unless they break off their relationship. The ensuing obsession prevents a couple from getting to know each other on any other level, and unwed pregnancy is almost inevitable. If the truth were known, only a small percentage of couples who engage in teenage sex eventually marry each other.

10. *A teenage girl risks cancer of the cervix.* The very nature of a girl's body seems to indicate that God never intended for her to have sex at a young age. Dr. Rhoda Lorand, a New York psychiatrist, says that girls who engage in sex prior to the age of eighteen have an incidence of cancer of the cervix several times greater than those who do not. She concludes that nature built in a protective device for mature women to offset the introduction of the male organ that could bring foreign matter and germs into her vagina. Before the age of eighteen, a woman does not have that immunity. It is reasonable to conclude that God did not intend young girls to have sex at all.

11. *You can give your husband your virtue ring on your wedding day.* If you have given your daughter a virtue ring and led her to make a commitment to virtue (as described in chapter 12), this is a good time to remind her she will have such a gift to give to the man of her dreams on their wedding night. Not only will it be an emotionally fulfilling experience for them both, but it is tangible evidence that she is bringing an AIDS-free and a STD-free body into their marriage. Today that should be reason enough to remain virtuous prior to marriage.

These are some of the reasons you can share with your daughter to save her sexuality for marriage. Informed parents are the best sex educators in their children's lives. It is no longer optional; it is a matter of moral survival. We must arm our sons or daughters with all the information they need to make the important decisions in life. Next to the spiritual dimension, nothing affects them more than their sexuality.

Here's a rule of thumb for parentally guided sex education: Start early, be accurate, answer all questions honestly to the best of your ability, maintain an open relationship, and offer a good example of real love in your marriage.

Chapter Eight

HOW TO HELP YOUR TEEN MAKE A COMMITMENT TO

T wenty years ago, Dr. James Dobson wrote in his best-selling book, *Dare to Discipline*, that he and his wife took their daughter to a fancy restaurant and presented her with a challenge to maintain her virtue until marriage. Then they presented her with a gold key on a chain as a memento of the event. That idea has caught on, and others have added to the concept. Dr. Richard C. Durfield, another Christian psychologist, has popularized the idea in his book, *Raising Them Chaste*. Today thousands of Christian parents who want their children to enter marriage as virgins have adopted the idea.

A commitment to virtue is so important today because of the enormous pressures young people face. Many of these pressures are much stronger and different than the pressures we faced when we were their age. Today's kids are encouraged to throw away their virtue and express their sexuality. We believe that a formal commitment to virtue is both a needed and powerful tool that can help safeguard your teen from premarital sexual involvement. When emotions get out of control and threaten to overpower common sense, a strong resolve or commitment to virtue can prevent your teen (and your family) from experiencing enormous heartache.

A sexual misstep at this stage in your son's or daughter's life can be enormously expensive to him or her spiritually, emotionally, physically, and vocationally. They do not understand that now, even though they may think they do.

Your child may receive from his or her future mate a virtue token on their wedding day; you want to do all you can to make sure your son or daughter can reciprocate. The gift of a ring, locket, or key on a chain as a token of virtue is a beautiful way for your child to start off a marriage that you pray will last a lifetime.

WHAT IS A COMMITMENT TO VIRTUE?

Your children's commitment to virtue should be the biggest event in their life since their conversion to Christ. It should be well planned and carried out with dignity—a night they will always remember. It is the big night when Mom or Dad schedules a date with their teen of the same sex to present to him or her the capstone of his or her sex education. We recommend this event be planned for the early teen years, possibly as early as thirteen. We hope you have taught your children the material covered in Part 2 of this book as they proceed through childhood, so by this time they do not need a detailed explanation of the basics. They already know them.

This event will help them celebrate their emergence into the adult world of hormones, drives, and passions. By this time they are usually aware that they are increasingly interested in the opposite sex. Many of the girls will have experienced menstruation and the boys a wet dream. So a special night out, fathers with sons and mothers with daughters, to celebrate their emerging sexuality puts it on the table for free and open discussion. It is important for them to know that this is a time when they can bring up any question, make any statement, and tell how they really feel to someone who is interested and who knows and understands. As Durfield says, let them know that "no subject is off limits, no question is too dumb." This is the time for them to have their sex questions answered and for you to further open the conversational door.

Even more than that, it is the time for a dad to challenge his son and a mother to challenge her daughter to make a formal commitment to God, to them as parents, and to their future partner that they will be a virgin when they marry. Such a commitment may enable them, at some highly pressured moment, to keep themselves pure.

We suggest you schedule this night quite a ways in advance and build anticipation for it by referring to it as a special event you are looking forward to. Make advance reservations at a nice restaurant, perhaps one the child has never been to or one that is his favorite. This will help make the event stand out in his mind for the rest of his life.

Some very wonderful parents do not feel adequate to lead such an event by themselves. In that case both parents should take their teen on this special date. In families where only one parent is a Christian, it may be wise for the believing parent to take the son or daughter. In single-parent families, the parent the child is living with should take the child for the big date. I was raised in a single-parent family and would have welcomed such an event. Unfortunately in those days, parents rarely talked to their kids about sex. Today that omission can be fatal.

One thing this event is not. It is not a welcome into the world of dating. That too could be cause for a special night out when your child is fifteen or sixteen (whatever is your set time for dating). The only kind of dating they should be doing after the commitment to virtue is group dating such as church youth activities. Dating, like getting your driver's license, should be a set time, but it should not be confused with the commitment to virtue that should occur two or three years earlier. Your children need the time in between to realize the seriousness and importance of their commitment.

Planning the Event

I am a goal-oriented person. Unfortunately, I do not always plan very well. Bev is totally different. When she has a goal she plans it out very carefully and then works her plan. It usually takes her longer to get there, but I have learned that it is much easier and better if we plan our attack and then execute it. We have developed a slogan, "Anything that needs to be done can be done better if it is well planned and organized." That is especially true of the father-son or mother-daughter big night out. Plan it carefully; you will be much happier with the results. We suggest the following steps.

1. *Pray about it together.* You have no doubt learned never to do anything without asking God's blessing. He says in His Word, "in all your ways acknowledge *him* and *he* will make your paths straight" (Prov. 3:6). Since your children are really the Lord's children on loan to you, and since their virtue is so under attack today, you can be sure God is vitally interested in helping you make this a most significant event in your

children's lives. Ask Him for wisdom in the planning and a receptive spirit on the part of your teen.

2. *Schedule the event with great ceremony.* Since this is such an important event to you and your child, you should sit down with your teen, just as you would any adult you make appointments with, and write the event on your calendar. Tell him or her that you want to take them out that night for a very special dinner and talk. This is the time to ask them where their favorite restaurant is or where in the city they would rather go than any other (within the capability of your budget). Inform your teen that he or she can order whatever they want that night. It should be far enough in advance (three to four weeks) to build up anticipation. It does not hurt for them to overhear you tell someone that you cannot do something when they ask because you have a special date scheduled with your son or daughter. A few days before the event, call the restaurant and ask for a quiet booth or table where you can have privacy.

3. *Pick out a virtue ring.* You should purchase a good quality ring—as good as you can afford—so that it will be of unique significance to the teen. You may want one with your teen's initials on it, or a fish or a cross—whatever you think they will be most proud to wear, even when they are eighteen or older. Then have their initials and the date inscribed on the inside. You might also put an appropriate scripture reference on it.

When I went into the military, my mother gave me an identification bracelet with "1 Cor. 10:13" stamped on the underside. When I finished my flight training, I put my wings on the front side and wore it all through the Air Force and college. To me it was a badge of honor and a special gift from my mother.

It is surprising sometimes what our teens appreciate. When rings were not popular with teenagers, our son Larry was given his deceased grandfather's initialed ring by his grandmother because he shared the same first initial. When I saw her present it to him (he was seventeen at the time), I figured he would accept in politely and then never wear it. I was wrong! He was elated, gave his grandmother a big hug, then put the ring on his finger and wore it while he was in the military and at college. Do not underestimate your teens' potential to appreciate the significance of this special celebration of their emerging adulthood.

4. *Prepare yourself thoroughly.* Do not assume that because you know all about sex that you can wing it on this date. Study the material presented earlier in this book about your child's sexuality and that of the opposite

sex. Read about some of the sexually transmitted diseases discussed in the glossary. Write down some of the reasons your son or daughter should remain virtuous. Make some notes of what you want to present on a four-by-six card and refer to them during the discussion with your teen. You should prepare your talk every bit as much as any speech you will ever make. You may even want to practice it on your spouse.

5. *The big night!* The first part for this dress-up occasion should be to relax and enjoy the evening. Talk to your teen about things he or she is interested in and get the ordering out of the way. For the next hour you should have the most serious, profitable, and enjoyable time you have ever had with your teen. We assure you, they will not forget it

You can start by telling him how much you love him and are proud of him. Tell him that you thank God for sending him into your family. Then point out that you realize he has taken the first big step into adulthood and is developing and will develop adult feelings of sexuality. Then emphasize the importance of keeping his body holy and honoring God's standards of morality. Christians are not to live according to the standards of the world but are held by God to higher standards. You should also talk to him about why God wants him to keep himself sexually pure until marriage by elaborating on the spiritual, emotional, and physical benefits of not engaging in premarital sex.

Be sure to tell him that he will someday find a Christian woman with whom he believes God wants him to spend the rest of his life. He may have many girlfriends through school, but sex should be shared only with the person he marries. Particularly, bring in the problem of "making out" and how dangerous petting can be. This is a good place to show him the Law of Progression chart (see chapter 2) if he has not already seen it. If he has, refer to it.

At some point, ask if he has any questions about sex. Tell him that nothing is off limits and that, to the best of your ability, you will try to answer them. Leave the door open by saying "Well, if any question comes up, and it probably will, please feel free to talk to me about it." One boy who did not even like girls yet, amazed his father by asking, "When I date a girl, how far can I go?" This provided the dad a chance to warn his son that passionate kissing was dangerous and that light kissing was all he should ever plan to engage in until marriage. This is also a good time to challenge your son or daughter to always act as the moral cop (see chapters 10 and 11).

Then challenge your teen to purpose in his or her heart not to become sexually defiled, the same way Daniel "resolved not to defile himself with the royal food" (Dan. 1:8). Then teach him or her the importance of making a covenant or commitment to God and the importance of keeping those vows.

You can encourage him to make such a commitment in prayer. By this time, the meal is probably over, and you can pause to order dessert. While waiting, you can ask him to take your hand and pray out loud as he makes his commitment to virtue until marriage. When the teen has finished, you can pray in agreement and then pray pointedly about his future mate and how important it is for him to find that special person God has for him. Pray that your child will conduct his life in such a way that he can look his future partner in the eye without guilt. He needs to hear from the most important people in his life that abstinence is the best policy—even if it is not popular.

6. *Make the virtue ring presentation*. After your teen has formally committed himself or herself to God, you, as the parent, should formally present the virtue ring as a visible symbol of that commitment. Encourage him to wear it as a badge of honor and openly tell his friends what it is when they ask. Tell him to be proud of his virtue. If his sexually active friends make fun of him, encourage him to say, "I can become like you any time I want, but you can never become like me." He can also say that he is determined to be AIDS and STD-free when he marries.

Then encourage your teen to set as his goal to wear that ring until his wedding night, when he will give it to his new mate as a symbol that he has kept himself pure. You can assure him it will be a treasured keepsake for many years.

Ask one more time, "Do you have any more questions you want to ask?" Then assure him that you are praying for "the perfect will of God" for his life, both his future life's partner and his vocation.

You both will long treasure this night and its significance!

THE WAY ONE FATHER DID IT

Focus on the Family Magazine carried the charming account of Dr. Richard Durfield and how he had his big father-son night with his son, Jonathan. It was so well done we've chosen to reproduce it here, with permission. We pick up the story after they were seated, not in the secluded spot they asked for, but in a rather crowded restaurant where others were obviously watching:

> "Tonight is your night, Jonathan," I began. "This is a special time for you and Dad to talk about any sexual questions that might still be on your mind. Whatever might seem a little awkward at times, well, tonight is the right time to ask. Nothing is off limits tonight.

> "If something's been bothering you about marriage or adolescence or whatever, it's okay to talk about it. As we eat through the courses of the evening, I want you to just be thinking about any questions you might have."

Jonathan's all boy. He'd much rather ride his mountain bike in the hills than chase after girls. When we first sat down, he had seemed a little uncomfortable because I saw him looking around. But as we began talking, he relaxed a bit.

My son, who has never been on a date, wanted to know *for sure* what 'the line' was. How far was *too far*? He had a good idea, but he wanted to hear it from me.

"A light kiss is about as far as you can go," I replied. "Sexual emotions are very strong, and if you're not careful, you'll do things you don't want to do. So you need to avoid anything that leads you up to that."

For instance, I explained, certain types of kissing are going too far. Kissing a girl on the neck can lead to going much further.

The 'Key Talk' Beginnings

Jonathan has two older sisters and one brother: Kimberli, 23, Anna, 19, and Tim, 18. About 10 years ago, when Kimberli was entering adolescence, Renee' and I had an idea: have a private, personal and intimate time with the child to explain conception, the biblical view of marriage and the sacredness of sexual purity. A time when a mom and daughter or a dad and son can candidly discuss the questions, fears and anxieties of adolescence. I called it a 'key talk.'

We also had another idea. At the time of the key talk, the

parent presents a specially made 'key' ring to the son or daughter. The ring, which symbolizes a commitment with God, is worn by the adolescent during the difficult teen and young adult years.

What is a key ring? The purpose of a key is to unlock a door, and the ring symbolizes the key to one's heart and virginity. The ring is a powerful reminder of the value and beauty of virginity, of the importance of reserving sex for marriage.

The ring also represents a covenant between the child and God. A covenant not only obligates us to God, but it obligates God to us. As long as we honor a covenant, God will also honor it. Throughout history, God has blessed those who have remained faithful.

The son or daughter wears the key ring until he or she is married. Then the ring is taken off and presented to the new spouse on their wedding night—that sacred evening when a life of sexual experience begins.

Renee' had open and frank key talks with Kimberli and Anna. She described just about everything a child would want to know about sex. Because our daughters are attractive, intelligent and sought-after, they needed important reasons to remain virgins until their wedding nights.

The pressure of society and its "well, they're going to do it anyway" attitude pushes millions of teenagers into a world of promiscuity. Sadly, our daughters are members of a shrinking minority....

Jonathan's Ring

As the main dishes were taken away, I told Jonathan it was time to make a commitment before the Lord. Yes, we lacked privacy, but I felt it added to the significance of what he was about to do.

I wanted Jonathan to pray—right there at the table—but I had to set things up a little bit. "Now this covenant is going to be something between you and God until you are married," I said. "We're going to include whoever your wife will be in this prayer. We're going to ask God that wherever she is and whoever she is, that He'll be with her also. We'll ask Him to help her to be chaste until the time you're married. I want you to ask God for His grace to keep this covenant pure, because even though you may have right intentions, sometimes things go wrong. I want you to pray and then Dad will pray."

Jonathan turned to me and took my hands. It surprised me that he would be so bold in a public restaurant, but I realized that was exactly what he needed in order to stand alone.

Jonathan bowed his head and prayed fervently. Then it was my turn. Before I prayed, I said "Jonathan, I have something for you." I took a custom-made 14K gold ring and slipped it on his finger. Bowing our heads, I asked the Lord to honor the covenant Jonathan was making and help him resist temptation in the coming years....

A Parent's Influence

My key talk with Jonathan was one of the most memorable and moving experiences I've ever had. It seemed our hearts were bonded together.

Young people are romantics. They have a real need to identify their personal self-worth. Wholesome, biblical thoughts instilled during their tender years open an avenue for parents to discuss sex with their children. The importance a parent places on the key talk will greatly influence the child's sexual behavior prior to marriage.

Key talks should happen when the child becomes interested in the opposite sex. That can be as young as 10 or as old as 17.

Obviously, the key is a powerful day-in-and-day-out reminder for the child. The more the child values his or her virginity, the more the key ring becomes a precious symbol of the commitment to God and the future spouse.

As I've shared the key ring idea with many families, I've

learned that it is also a good idea for teens who have lost their virginity. Although they have jumped the gun, they can commit themselves to God to remain pure until their wedding day.

Teens who have fallen short can become virgins again in the sight of God. Once they're forgiven, it is as though they have never sinned. The Lord tells us in Isaiah 43:25 that "I, even I, am He who blots and cancels your transgressions, for My own sake, and I will not remember your sins."

As Jonathan and I left El Encanto's that night, a couple sitting at a nearby table stopped us. They couldn't help but notice something special had happened, they said.

Something special *had* happened, and it was between Jonathan, his wife-to-be and the Lord.[1]

REPENTANT TEENS NEED A CHALLENGE TO BE VIRTUOUS AGAIN

You may be too late for your teen. Like some of those who attended our discussion groups, your teen may have became sexually active frighteningly early. It is unbelievable how early young people are having sex today. Besides, your child may have been sexually active before becoming a Christian. Now that he or she is a Christian, your child needs to be challenged to a new life of virtue.

If this describes your situation, you should preface the presentation of the virtue ring with an acknowledgment that your child's virtue was lost before they accepted Christ or came back to walk with Him. Then read them several verses on forgiveness and what God does with our sin, such as 1 John 1:7-9. Because of the enormous sacrifice of Christ on Calvary, God has removed our sins from us "as far as the east is from the west" (Ps. 103:12), and He "remembers [our] sins no more" (Isa. 43:25). The Christian faith is strong on forgiveness; our Lord has commanded it so.

Recently a good friend who had fallen into sin, now forgiven by the grace and mercy of God, confessed, "It is easier for God to forgive me than it is for me to forgive myself." He is still struggling with guilt, but not because God has not forgiven him. Once we confess our sin, God "remembers it no more."

Do not be surprised if your once sexually active teen, who is now living an exemplary life, still struggles with guilt. Every time he goes to church or youth camp, he hears challenges to live a holy life and is reminded that he did not. Your teen needs your encouragement to accept God's forgiveness and your forgiveness and to go on to live a whole new life. It is important that once your teen has dealt with his or her sin, that you never bring it up to them again.

Our Lord did not hold it against the woman caught in the very act of adultery once she came to Him in repentance. He said, "Go now and leave your life of sin." Your young person is a new creature in Christ Jesus and should accept himself or herself as such. They also should be offered a virtue ring (or "virtuous again ring") to safeguard them from future indiscretions. The day will come when they can say, "I am not the same person I once was. Jesus Christ has made me a new creature."

GIVE THEM A SALVATION CHECK

This is an ideal time to make sure your son or daughter has had a personal "born-again" experience with Jesus Christ. The best way to find out is just to ask: "Tom, can you remember a time when you personally invited Jesus Christ into your life to become your Lord and Savior?" If the answer he or she gives is not too positive or reassuring to you, then follow it up with the classic question from Evangelism Explosion: "If you died right now and woke up at the gate of heaven, and the Lord Jesus asked you, 'Tom, can you give Me one good reason why I should let you into My heaven?' what would you say?" Then wait for his answer. If your teen knows the Bible, he or she may reply, "Lord, You promised that if I believed in my heart that You died for my sins and rose from the dead and invited You into my heart, You would come in and save me." There are many good answers from scripture that they can give, but they should have one.

If they have not been born again, you need to invite them to do so. If they cannot give a positive witness of their faith, their conversion is more important than giving them a virtue ring. I can't think of a greater joy than to lead your own child to Christ. Right there, where you are having this discussion, you could lead them to bow their head and invite the Savior in. Ask them, "Wouldn't you like to receive Christ and know that your sins are forgiven and that you are His child?" The Bible says, "Yet to all who received him, to those who believed in his name, he gave the right to become children of God" (John 1:12). Invite your teen to pray, and then follow his or her prayer with one of your own. You can turn that restaurant into a worship center for a few minutes.

You may feel more comfortable settling this matter outside in your car. If possible, I would do it before you get home, but most importantly, do it as the Spirit of God leads. Afterward, you will have to decide whether or not to go ahead with the presentation of the virtue ring. We suggest you treat your child as a newly made creature in Christ who is virtuous in His eyes. Another good way to cement his decision is to urge (not force) him to go forward the next time an invitation is given in your church. This provides him an opportunity to publicly testify to his faith before men as our Lord said, "Whoever acknowledges me before men, I will also acknowledge him before my Father in heaven" (Matt. 10:32).

Explain to your teen that the past is past and that he or she is now virtuous again in Christ Jesus. Since they have properly dealt with their sin, urge them to make the commitment to virtue until marriage, and give them the ring to wear from that day until their wedding day. Treat them as you would had they not had previous sexual experience.

My Friend Jim, The Virtuous-again Minister

One of the young men who came to Christ in our church in San Diego is a good example of becoming "virtuous again." I do not know where our youth pastor found Jim, but he was a mess! He had been strung out on drugs, had lived like an alley cat, and by most standards should have been dead. But God saved him and transformed him! When he first started attending our youth group, all the mothers were understandably overprotective of their virtuous daughters. The last boy on earth they wanted their daughters to go out with was Jim. Four years went by, and he grew by leaps and bounds. Finally, he surrendered to the call of God to the ministry (which he and his wife are in today).

Jim fell in love with one of the choicest girls in our church. When she walked down the aisle to become his wife, I looked over the audience and saw many of those same mothers (including the mother of the bride) who four years before anxiously protected their girls from Jim. On that day, their attitudes were different. Many of them thought, "Why didn't he pick my daughter?" or, "I hope my daughter marries a fine young man like Jim." Jesus does make a difference in our lifestyle!

CONCLUSION

Making a formal commitment to virtue may sound like a lot of fluff to those of us who had no such custom when we were teens. But we need to remember that we did not have the amount of sexual pressure on us that young people have today. This special night also sends two important messages to your teens that make it worth all the time, planning, and money: *Virtue is important, and so are they!*

You want to guide your children to lead a life of abstinence before marriage. The humanists in secular education want to give your children condoms in an attempt to have them practice "safe sex." You need to give them a challenge to be virtuous, which is truly the only way to be "safe."

Your child does not need unsafe condoms or birth control pills or any other unsafe means of encouraging promiscuity. He or she needs a virtue ring or key from you and a commitment to God to practice virtue until marriage.

---

[1] Richard Durfield, "A Promise with a Ring to It," *Focus on the Family Magazine*, April 1990.

Chapter Nine

GUIDELINES FOR DATING

Dating is an exciting experience, not only for a teenager but also for a father and mother. Some parents find it traumatic; others consider it an enjoyable part of raising their children.

The dating stage of life usually catches both teenagers and their parents unprepared. Young people have little idea what their parents expect of them, and parents are not always in agreement with each other. That's a formula for disaster. We prepare our children for school, Sunday school, birthdays, Christmas, swimming lessons, and almost every other event in life. Why do we fail to lay a proper foundation for dating? Beverly and I have discovered that if a strategic plan of action is instituted for the first child's dating life, it is relatively simple to get younger brothers and sisters to accept the same standards. But if parents strike out with the first, they may lose the ball game with the others.

Dating arouses fear in many parents for several reasons. First, it represents a giant step toward independence. Parents seldom accompany the dating couple; consequently, they lose a large measure of control when teens go out for several hours at a time. Second, some parents have not learned to trust their children, and dating accentuates that lack of trust. Third, some parents have not prepared guidelines in advance; thus, their fears become exaggerated.

Beverly and I have had the privilege of using our guidelines for dating on ten children—four of our own, plus six missionary children whose parents sent them to live with us for a time. Whenever we accepted teenagers of missionaries, it was on the condition that they accept our dating standards. Although we had confrontations at times with both the missionaries' children and our own, dating was a pleasurable time for all of us because we were genuinely concerned that these teens enjoy a good social life, and we gave them clearly defined guidelines.

STANDARDS FOR DATING

The following standards are those we developed through the years. They are not perfect, but they worked for us and for some of the thousands of families we shared them with at the over eight hundred Family Life Seminars we have conducted throughout the United States and Canada. At times, your popularity as a parent will drop to an all time low if you enforce standards such as these, but if you do not, both you and your teenagers may live to regret it. Popularity will be meaningless then.

1. *Dating is for fifteen-year-olds and over.* Reserving dating for this age bracket is no problem for boys. Many of them are not interested in girls until later, or could not afford to date even if they were. Girls mature earlier than boys, both physically and socially, and are often eager to start dating earlier, some as early as fourteen. Statistics indicate girls who begin dating at fourteen or younger have a 20 percent greater chance of becoming pregnant than those who wait until they are sixteen. Boys their own age are frequently disinterested in them or unappealing, so they often want to date older boys. That, of course, presents a special set of problems. It is usually best not to let ninth-grade girls date eleventh and twelfth-grade boys. They are too naive at this age to protect themselves from themselves much less from older, more experienced boys.

Although fifteen is the minimum recommended age for dating, this should not eliminate young people from enjoying each other's company in group activities—church youth outings, camp, sports events, or parties. But official dating, when a boy comes to a girl's home to take her out, should be reserved at least until the fifteenth birthday. We would not blame you for praying that they do not start dating until sixteen! Many parents set sixteen as the minimum age to commence dating.

2. *Date only Christians.* One cardinal principle clearly specified in the Word of God is: "Do not be yoked together with unbelievers" (2 Cor. 6:14). Dating is a yoke of fellowship that can eventually lead to marriage.

We can help our young people avoid the emotional trauma of ever having to decide, "Should I marry this unsaved person I am very much in love with or should we break up?" by refusing to let them go out in the first place. Remember, our sons and daughters will seldom get seriously involved with someone they do not date.

This standard may draw a few tears when a teenage girl is forbidden to keep company with the handsome high school quarterback, but it will forestall a calamity later. You will find that any young person who does not come from a home that shares your moral values will have a harmful and even "corrupting" influence on your son or daughter.

Through the years, we have watched fine, dedicated Christians lose their children, whom they dearly loved, because they did not establish this standard. We have recently prayed and cried with several who lived to regret it. Two daughters, married at eighteen and divorced at nineteen, broke the hearts of their parents and deeply troubled the waters of their early adulthood.

3. *Schedule a predating interview with Dad.* When a young man dates your daughter, it is serious business; he is going out with one of your most treasured possessions. If a person borrowed your car or boat, you would set some guidelines for its use. It is even more important when a young man "borrows" your daughter. This may frighten some prospects away, but they represent the group you want your daughter to avoid. Any boy who lacks the courage to look a girl's father in the eye when asking permission has no business dating her.

This interview gives Dad the opportunity to do four things. First, he can see for himself whether the young man is really a Christian (hearsay testimonies aren't always valid). Second, he can check the boy's motivation. Does he have goals or plans for his life according to his age level, or is your daughter his only immediate objective? Third, he can clearly lay down the guidelines they are to follow. Expecting your daughter to do this would be embarrassing for her, and something might be missed in the transmission. Fourth, he can size up the young man's home life. If the person loves and respects his parents, you can discern more readily what to expect in your relationships with him. The converse is also true.

A Suggested Predating Interview

Your daughter should prepare the boy who wants to take her out on a date by explaining that he needs first to meet you, her father, and get your permission. After your daughter introduces her prospective date to you, try to put the lad at ease by smiling, shaking hands with him, and welcoming him into your home. It is usually best for the daughter to become scarce for a few minutes. Here's how a typical conversation might go.

Father: "What can I do for you, Kevin?"

Kevin: "Mr. Petersen, I came over tonight to ask you if I can take your daughter out on a date."

Father: "I appreciate you taking the trouble to come by for a talk. There are a couple of questions I'd like to ask you, if I may. First, are you a born-again Christian?" If he says yes, you can follow that up with, "Where do you go to church and how active are you in the church?"

If you are not satisfied with his answers, ask, "What does your faith in Christ really mean to you? What influence does it have on your life?"

If the young man admits to not being saved, you can ask him if anyone has ever explained how he could receive Christ. If possible, you should share the gospel with him. If the boy will not receive Christ then, you should explain: "Julie's mother and I have raised her in a strong Christian home, and she has been a Christian for [however many] years. This is nothing personal against you Kevin, but we decided a long time ago that when Julie became old enough to start dating, we were going to limit her dates only to Christians. So as much as I do not like to disappoint you, I am afraid we cannot agree to let you date Julie."

If after your questions you believe he is a Christian, then you could say, "If Julie's mother and I agree that you and Julie can go out together, you should understand that we have several rules all of her dates must abide by." Then walk him through your requirements — double date to approved functions only, parking is forbidden, and making out is not an option. Then detail your time limits and explain the consequences if they are not respected.

At this point, it would be wise to ask, "Kevin, tell me something about yourself. What are your goals or ambitions in life?" (Even if he has no answer, it is good for him to have an adult ask such a question.) Then you can ask "What kind of a date do you have in mind?"

(Usually some event will have prompted the request.)

You can further add something like: "Kevin, Julie is one of the most precious gifts God has given to her mother and me. While we want her to have a good time during her dating years, there are certain limits we have placed on her for her own good. If you cooperate with our rules, you will find us easy to work with; if not, we will have to say you can no longer date her. Do you have any questions?"

There are two ways you can close the meeting. First, if you are convinced he is right for your daughter to date, say: "We would be happy to have you date Julie. Where would you like to go, who will be going with you, and what time can we expect you to bring her home?" If you're not sure about him, say, "Julie's mother and I will have a talk about this, and I will get back with you. Could I have your telephone number please?"

Then thank him for coming and stand up, which is a clear signal that the discussion is over.

Some parents may think such a talk is unreasonable. They are so interested in their daughter having a dating life, they let her date anyone who invites her out. That is not only unwise and dangerous, it shows less respect for your daughter than for your possessions. If a stranger asked to borrow your new car, you wouldn't turn over the keys without finding out something about him and setting strong guidelines. True enough, your daughter wouldn't bring over "just anyone." In fact, requiring such a meeting will force her to screen the candidates for her company. That alone makes such a session worthwhile.

What about Interviewing Your Son's Date? It is usually easier to interview prospective girls your son wants to date because he will have had to meet her parents' requirements already. This alone is a screening process. But sometimes he will want to date a girl whose parents have no dating requirements. If he dates the same girl two or three times and you do not know her personally, have him bring her along to a family outing or arrange an interview involving both you and your spouse. We suggest that Mom be involved in this interview because fathers can be misled. It takes a woman to evaluate a woman, particularly when her son is involved. Otherwise you should follow the same procedure with her as outlined above.

Some young people may grumble about having to meet you formally before dating your teen. However, most teens will respect you for your stand, and it will help them realize that "going out" is something special.

4. *All dating activities must be approved in advance.* Until young people get acquainted with you and your standards, do not let them manipulate you into quick approval of some type of activity that you do not favor. We made it clear to our teens that approved dating included all church activities and outings, chaperoned parties, sports events, and special occasions they wished to request. The don't-bother-to-ask list included movies, dances, unchaperoned private parties, and any activity where drinking took place.

5. *Until high school graduation, only double dating is permitted.* Probably the one requirement our teenagers objected to most was that they could only double date. There is safety in numbers—not much, but some. The main reason for this, however, is to force the teenagers to make plans in advance and to avoid long periods of time when they can drift into "heavy couple talk." Under the romance of the moment, young people can easily make premature love statements and commitments they do not really mean. The presence of another Christian couple greatly reduces this possibility, though it does not eliminate it altogether.

It is admittedly difficult at times to organize a double date, so to compensate for our stringent rules, we went out of our way to make the family car available to our son whenever his request was legitimate. If your son has wheels, it usually isn't difficult for him to find a friend to double date with, if he really wants to.

6. *Absolutely no parking.* Mount Helix (or the lover's vantage point in your community) may be an exciting place to "view the lights of the city," but it is not an ideal environment for avoiding youthful temptations. At this stage of life, touching the opposite sex is exciting, stimulating, and dangerous. We view dating as a time of fun and social fellowship, not a test of self-control.

You may ask, "Didn't your children ever park during their dating years?" We aren't so naive as to think they didn't, but if they did, we wanted it clearly understood that it violated our rules. One girl admitted, "Whenever I was tempted to park while on a date, I was always afraid my father might rise up out of the back seat."

My mentor in Christian counseling was the psychologist Dr. Henry Brandt. In Elisabeth Elliot's book, *The Shaping of a Christian Family*, she quotes Dr. Brandt's story about his children's dating years when they objected to his rules because he felt cars were for transportation not entertainment:

> He urged them to keep some daylight between bodies. His son's impassioned question was, "Don't you trust me?" His answer: "Absolutely not! When you are using one-third of the seat for both of you, touching that warm body with her blood running hot and your blood boiling, I should say I don't trust you. Put me in the same position with the girl's mother, I wouldn't trust me." In fact, he says now at the age of seventy-four, "Put me in the same position with the girl's grandmother, and I wouldn't trust me. Each caress, each kiss, has a cumulative effect. Kiss power is stronger than will power!"[1]

7. *Never go to a home or confined quarters without a responsible adult in attendance.* In a former time the automobile was the primary place where girls lost their virtue or became pregnant (particularly at drive-in theaters). That day is almost past because the automobile industry has miniaturized cars and popularized bucket seats; one would have to be a contortionist to have sex in today's most popular vehicles. So young people now look for more convenient quarters. Empty houses are ideal. A recent study found that one of the most popular places unmarried girls have sex is in their own bed at home.

Untended homes, due to both parents working, provide a dangerous environment that is much more conducive to "making out" and much more inciting to sexual relations than any car. Such places should be expressly off limits even for the most trustworthy teens. The Bible instructs us to "avoid every kind of evil" (1 Thess. 5:22). Two teens of the opposite sex in an empty house may not misbehave, but their unsupervised presence together could ruin their reputations and should be expressly forbidden.

8. No *undue public show of affection.* Love is beautiful to both teens and adults, but public demonstrations of affection that border on suggestiveness are harmful to a person's testimony and may imply moral license. The Christian community applauds teenagers who love each other but have enough self-respect not to maul one another in public. Proper dating should not detract from a young person's testimony or spiritual growth; besides, open expressions of affection today may prove embarrassing later should interest in that person evaporate. Public perception

generally assumes that private conduct is even more intimate, and this can tarnish a teen's reputation.

9. *Avoid all petting, caressing, or other physical expressions of affection that lead to sexual arousal.* This should be your toughest rule of all. Teens need to know that petting is adult behavior and should be reserved exclusively for marriage, where it is called "foreplay" and prepares a husband and wife for intercourse. Only the most naive fail to realize that the same preparations occur in the unmarried who engage in heavy petting. Almost all first-time sexual experiences before marriage occur as a result of heavy petting. Few, if any, of those who get pregnant before their wedding intended to do so. Petting took them over the edge.

The problem with sexual arousal is that most people, both men and women, experience a "point of no return." Sexual passions are not evil when reserved for the sanctity of marriage, but unmarried teenagers should avoid that kind of temptation. Since no one can predict where that point is, *the time to control it is before arousal.*

The following suggestions will help your teen say no should he or she be faced with temptation while on a date. This list is by no means complete. You and your teen should discuss this freely at an appropriate time and add your own ideas.

- *Make up your mind in advance you are not going to have sex.* Making the commitment to virtue will help. This resolve makes it easier to "just say no" at the very start of a relationship. Young people talk freely. You can be sure the word will get out that "she or he is not the kind who does it." (The opposite message also travels fast.)

- *Do not let yourself get into a compromising situation while alone on a date.* Getting out of the front seat of a parked car into the back seat is asking for trouble.

- *Do not trust your flesh.* Under certain tempting circumstances, anyone can fall. That is why temptation is best handled early (see 1 Cor. 10:13).

- *Draw a line in advance on what you will do on a date, and stick to it.* Light kissing is not required on the first few dates. It should be reserved for later and then in the safety of the front porch as a gesture of "thanks for a great time." Kissing communicates that someone is special to us, but it is also one of the first steps in foreplay. Long, passionate, and repeated kissing is exciting but rarely satisfies.

- *When you sense the other person is becoming emotionally worked up, it is time to say,* "I think I'd better be going home," *or* "Let's go get something to eat"—anything to break the spell.

- *Protect your erogenous zone* (the area from your neck to your knees). Affection can be expressed without touching in that sensitive area, which is territory that should be reserved for marriage.

- *Never French kiss!* Sooner or later, even among the most wholesome young people who indulge in kissing, one of them will resort to French kissing. This can be very stimulating and, therefore, should be saved for marriage. Rarely will a couple who does not French kiss indulge in sex.

- *Make no exceptions.* The first time your date puts his hand into the erogenous zone, remove his hand. Firmly make it clear that you do not do that! Touching in that area is not an expression of love but of passion. Movement into that erogenous zone should *always* be the signal to say, "I think it's time to go!" Then start moving. That sends a strong message that the territory between your neck and knees is off limits.

- *Plan in advance what to say.* Saying, "I'm not that kind of girl (or boy)," or "You should understand, I have made a commitment to God and my parents to be a virgin when I marry" is always appropriate. The sooner a date understands that, he will either stop dating you (which proves he is interested only in sex not love) or he will respect your vow. The best way for young people to guarantee they will maintain their virtue until marriage is to make the vow they will never engage in petting. Petting can be fun, but it is *dangerous.*

- *Never go to parties where you know they will serve alcohol, drugs, or some will have sex.* If you're not that kind of person, don't go to that kind of party.

Because sexual arousal is so exciting, the couple who indulge this pastime become dissatisfied with other worthwhile and meaningful dating activities. Once experienced, petting seems to take precedence over everything else and usually claims an increasing amount of their time. One reason for the high divorce rate today is that young people have engaged in such extensive petting that they know each other almost exclusively on the level of physical intimacy. This often blinds them to personal traits that might have discouraged matrimony had they not been so preoccupied. There is plenty of time for lovemaking after marriage. Until then, young people should be encouraged to participate in activities that will acquaint them with each other in various ways and provide them rich hours of pleasure.

Your teen may resent your intrusion into this area they usually think of as "private territory." It is not private to you, of course, for their abstinence or sexual activity has an effect on the entire family. Just as we provide them food, medicine, and protection even when they resent or reject it, we need to provide them all the tools they need in advance to maintain their virtue. Remember, there are members of the opposite sex out there who would love to take your child's virtue away from them— and your son or daughter may not recognize that. Besides, the day will come when they will be grateful for what today they may call "overprotective parents." Just make sure the spirit with which you convey these things is always one of concern for their well being. They understand that even when they will not admit it.

At sweet sixteen one of our daughters said testily, "Dad, I get the feeling you don't trust us!" To which I replied, "Honey, I don't! I don't trust you, or boys, or myself under the wrong circumstances." She went away mumbling to herself, but years later she admitted, down in her heart, she understood.

10. *Curfew is at* 11:00 P.M. *for girls,* 11:30 *for boys* (with approved exceptions). Aside from certain well-chaperoned functions we knew in advance would last later than 10:30 P.M., we expected our girls home at 11:00 and our boys at 11:30 (the extra thirty minutes allowed time for our sons to escort two girls and another guy home without missing the curfew). If supervised youth activities lasted until 11:00, then the curfew was thirty minutes after they left the party. These deadlines were universally resisted at first and were earlier than those set by most parents, but we reasoned that little wholesome activity occurred in our city after eleven o'clock.

The good snack shops are closed by then, and we think teenagers should be home by that time. Admittedly, most parents are more lenient, but do not let your resistive teen intimidate you out of holding to what you know is best for them. Unless conditions today are different than they seem, our curfew times would be the same.

Our son remarked after marriage, "One thing I found embarrassing about our family's dating rules was that all the girls I dated had a later curfew than I did." One girl asked him, "Larry, why are your bringing me home at eleven? I don't have to be in until twelve." Despite the embarrassment and minor problems it caused our teens, we have no regrets. One daughter who often chafed under the curfew commented four months after the birth of her daughter, "Remember those dating rules? We're planning to use the same ones for Jenny when she's old enough to date." Parents have a different perspective than teenagers.

Some parents may not know how to enforce the curfew. Whatever hour you set will usually be considered too early and may even be ignored. This will only create conflict and stress between parents and teens. We solved that problem simply by stating that every minute they were late coming home would cost them a fifteen-minute penalty on the next date. One boy brought our daughter home so late that their next date was only one-and-a-half hours long. They had to cut short their miniature golfing on the seventh hole to make it home on time. But in four years of dating after that, they were late only once, when they had a flat tire on the freeway. Young people need to know that parents will keep their word. When they test your rules, be sure you don't flunk their examination.

Parental Guidance Required

Many parents consider these guidelines too stringent and decide to "massage the rules." Too often parents decide, "I can trust my children," so they let them establish their own dating standards or give them too much flexibility. In some cases it has worked very well, but in many others we have seen the quality training of early childhood and early adolescence tragically marred by excessive dating freedom. Such parents have forgotten the powerful influence of teenage peer pressure and the power of the normal teenage libido.

It is tragic when the self-control lessons of childhood are overpowered by these new and exciting drives, confronted when teens are least able of coping with them. These are the years of greatest emotional instability; decisions will often be made on the basis of emotion rather than mind and will. Someone has said, "When the emotions and will conflict, the emotions invariably win." This is dangerous, because emotion-based decisions are almost always wrong. It takes a good deal of maturity for anyone to learn that only when the mind and emotions agree is it right to proceed with anything. Even then, the mind should be guided by the Word of God. Solomon counseled, "A wise son brings joy to his father, but a foolish son grief to his mother" (Prov. 10:1). What is true of sons holds true for daughters also.[2]

Whenever you have to be inflexible in the application of a dating rule, take pains to be friendly, loving, and sometimes compensatory. But don't be too lenient. Parents must not leave to teenagers whose reasoning is at best immature such decisions as, "Who can I date?" or "What can I do on a date?" or "Where can I go?" or "How late can I stay out?" Those decisions, leading to adult responsibilities, are made by teens at their peril. This is one matter that can rightly be labeled "parental guidance required."

Dating can be a delightful experience for both teenagers and their parents. But it will be enjoyed best and longest when we safeguard our teenagers' futures by providing clear guidelines and lovingly seeing to it that they are maintained. Your children may never thank you, though some do after marriage. Presenting a normal and sexually volatile son or daughter as a virgin on their wedding day makes all the effort worthwhile.

---

[1] Elisabeth Elliot, *The Shaping of a Christian Family* (Thomas Nelson Publishers), 193.

[2] For further discussion of this matter, see Beverly LaHaye, *How to Develop Your Child's Temperament* (Eugene, Ore.: Harvest House Publishers, 1977), 108-144.

Chapter Ten

WHAT GIRLS NEED TO KNOW BEFORE THEY START DATING

T he differences between boys and girls physically are obvious and stand as visible symbols that their psychological and emotional differences are equally varied. Most young girls don't have a clue about that difference and what makes boys tick sexually. As we have seen, girls are romantics. From early childhood, their fantasies are of prince charming and motherhood, not sex. Ask a five-year-old girl playing with her dolls what she wants to be when she grows up and she will probably say, "a mommy." She automatically thinks of family and childhood. Ask a five-year-old boy, and his answer will almost never be "a father." He thinks in vocational terms of being a fireman, a policeman, or a ball player.

By the time he is in high school, a boy's sex drive has kicked in and may be the strongest driving force in his mind. While girls may have an increase in libido, their thoughts are about nonsexual socialization, dating, fun, parties, holding hands, and maybe kissing. If she does not understand that her feminine characteristics and particularly her body are to a boy's desires what gasoline is to fire, she may get into trouble without even looking for it. Every mother (or if she is not available, every father) should teach her daughter what boys are like. The following points describe those traits and also offer your daughter some basic guidelines for her relationships with boys.

What Boys Are Like

1. Boys are high-octane sexual creatures.

Somewhere between fifteen and sixteen most boys, even the best of them, become extremely sex driven. Even when boys are taught by their parents to keep that drive under control and reserve its expression until later, it is difficult for them to do. A boy's sex drive can affect virtually everything about him. This drive does not decrease as they mature, but it builds until it leads them to get married—unless they find a girl or several girls with whom they can have sex prematurely. In that case, they often delay marriage or get out of the mood altogether.

Boys are not evil because they have this strong sex drive, but if they cultivate it by looking at pornographic magazines or movies and indulging in immoral fantasies, they can become aroused at the slightest provocation. Girls need to realize that boys have this strong sex drive at a time of immature self-control. You cannot always tell by looking at them which boys are obsessed by sex and which ones have their desires under control. Their speech and the way they treat girls will often give them away. It does not take long for the word to get out that they are "interested in only one thing." Smart girls will avoid such boys like the plague, even if they are the captain of the football team or the most popular boy in school. The boy who does not treat girls with respect can't be trusted. However, all sex-driven boys do not let it show. Some are smart enough to know they can get "branded" and nice girls will not like them. And "nice girls" are always in demand.

Romance versus passion. The difference between a young person who enjoys romance and one who is interested in passion is usually timing and body contact. Teens enjoy being with the opposite sex. That is why boys ask girls on dates—they are inspired by being in their company. It is exciting to go on a date with someone you like, who treats you special, is fun to be with, and likes you as a person, not just your body. The boy who wants to park and pet is not interested in the girl; he simply wants to use her body.

Your daughter needs to understand the difference and realize at the outset that petting is sexual foreplay and should have no place in teen dating. She needs to get the long-range view of dating that leads to courtship and eventually marriage. The demand for instant gratification is a sign of immaturity. The boy who wants her body right now is not in love, he is in heat. Bill Gothard says, "Love can't wait to give, but lust can't wait to get."

2. Boys are great talkers, especially about their sexual escapades.

The "macho image"—how both other boys and girls think of him—is very important to a boy. When it comes to sex, you can almost count on him bragging to his friends about what a girl lets him get away with. It doesn't matter that he tells her he loves her and vows to keep it secret. Many guys tell that to every girl they go out with; it's just part of the line they give girls to get what they want from them. Even if he does "love" her, it will likely last only so long, particularly if she gives in to him sexually. Boys often tire of getting what they want too easily. Then after they have broken up with a girl, they can ruin her reputation by bragging. Girls, on the other hand, are prone to keep their sexual escapades secret to protect their reputation. Boys brag about theirs to boost their reputation.

Better that the locker-room conversation about your daughter is that she will not give in to sex than that she is an easy mark. The nice guys are impressed with girls who still have a good reputation.

3. Boys are easily excited sexually.

Your daughter needs to understand that a boy's high-octane sex drive can be excited in a second. All she has to do is dress provocatively for a date, or brush against him with her breasts, or lead him on with her talk. Boys often interpret a long or passionate kiss as license to let their hands start roaming. Some girls think it is cute to tease a boy, only to find she has a 175-pound gorilla on her hands. If she made the mistake of getting into the back seat of his car, she may get more than she bargained for. Make sure your daughter understands the law of progression and that she has the capacity to ignite a boy's sexual passions very easily.

Most boys will treat a girl the way she acts. If she is always a lady, he will treat her that way. If she acts like a tramp (as some younger girls do just to impress older boys), that is the way she will be treated. Try to get your daughter to understand that by refusing to get sexually involved with a boy, she increases his respect for her. The result of giving in to his sexual desires produces both a loss of respect and reputation. For when the boy gets home and begins thinking about her, he may conclude that what she lets him do with her, she will let others do. When she loses the boy's respect, she soon loses the boy.

4. Boys can have sex without love.

A nice girl would probably never have sex with a boy she does not love. A boy only has to be aroused to have sex, and almost any girl can arouse him. When aroused even he cannot tell the difference between feelings of passion and love. If a boy does not love a girl enough to marry her, he doesn't love her enough to have sex with her. Sex bears responsibility—adult responsibility. Until a couple is ready to accept the responsibility of sex—and marriage is proof they are ready—they should not have it.

Some Basic Guidelines for Your Daughter's Relationships with Boys

1. *Your daughter should choose only boys who have a good reputation.*

Your daughter often knows something about a boy before she goes out with him. He may be inexperienced or he may be popular with the girls. She should not look at the boy's popularity but at the kind of girls he is popular with. The way he treats other girls is the way he will treat her. A Christian girl should never date anyone but another Christian. Even then she should not forget he is a boy trying to be a man.

2. *Your daughter needs to realize she will probably "love" several boys before she gets married.*

Most young people mistake having a crush on a person as being in love. The truth is, your daughter will probably have that feeling for several boys before she graduates from high school. Somehow you must get her to understand that love feelings are transitory at her age, and that dating should be for fun and friendship.

Sexual activity can become an end in itself and make a person blind to what another person is really like. It is always best for couples to get to know each other over time without sexual involvement.

3. *Premarital sex often destroys immature love.*

A sixteen-year-old girl wrote to "Dear Abby" to ask why the neat boy (two years older) dropped her like a hot potato after their first date. He pressed her for sex and she confessed, "I don't know what came over me, but I was putty in his hands and gave in." She thought he would love her if she gave him her virtue. Just the opposite happened. Abby said it was his guilt at seeing her the next day that caused him to turn away and ignore her. He never dated her again and she felt "used."

A fundamental principle of life is "a realized need is a demotivator." Your daughter should learn that principle. Sixteen-year-olds do not usually discover it by themselves.

4. *Your daughter should not fall for a boy's lies or lines.*

Many boys want instant gratification and will tell a girl anything to get sex. They may even tell a girl "I love you" on the first date. The girl thinks he means it, but he says it to get sex. Afterward, he considers her an easy mark.

Another tactic boys use after heavy petting is to say he has "a stone ache" that needs release and having sex is the only way to relieve it. That approach should tell the girl she has already gone too far, for that "ache" is nature's way of preparing him for sex. If she believes this line she may give in, and it is a lie. No man has ever been injured by not having sex! Your daughter needs to know that and tell a boy so if he ever brings it up. One of the oldest lines in the book is, "If you love me, you will prove it by making love to me." Premarital sex is so dangerous to both young people she can reverse the statement and say, "If you love me, you will not want me to endanger my future and yours." A rule of thumb is that boys will do whatever girls let them do.

5. *Your daughter should make her dates respect her no man's zone.*

Until marriage, all girls should consider the area from her neck to her knees as "no man's land." All sensory feelings between those spots of the body point to sexual arousal. Fondling of that area can heighten her emotions and, at certain times of her monthly cycle (particularly the seventy hours of highest fertility), make her so passionate she could lose control of her will. Only one man should ever have access to that area: her husband.

6. *Your daughter should not be afraid to tell any boy she gets serious about that she has made a commitment to virginity.*

If your daughter has made a vow of chastity, as we outline in chapter 8, she should not be timid about telling any boy she is close to. He needs to know her standards, and if he really loves her he will help her keep that vow. If he is the right kind of boy, he will have already made the same commitment.

7. *Premarital sex will end a relationship; it will also end the freedom of youth.*

There is a joyous and contagious freedom to a nonsexual relationship. Premarital sex changes that. It is almost impossible to back up and return to a nonsexual relationship. Once a couple has been intimate, they either want to be intimate again each time they are together or their intimacy creates such guilt they break up. Once virginity has been broken, it is easier to have sex with the next person. These are the first steps to promiscuity. All promiscuous girls once were virgins.

8. *Your daughter needs to set her goal to always conduct herself on a date in such a manner that if she breaks up with the boy they can remain friends.*

Nonsexual dating can be fun, exciting, and positive for both parties. A girl should realize that the boy she dates will someday be some girl's husband and some child's father. She should always conduct herself as a Christian woman so that if they meet years later, she will be proud to have him introduce her to his wife and children as "a special friend from high school." If they were sexually involved, such a meeting would produce guilt, shame, and embarrassment.

It takes a mature Christian girl to realize when she dates a boy, she is going to make a contribution to his development into manhood. She will either help him to set high standards or she will lower his standards of how to treat a Christian girl. You hope your daughter will make a positive contribution to her boyfriend's Christian development. He will definitely not grow spiritually if they carry on a sexual relationship.

9. *Public demonstrations of affection will destroy a couple's reputation.*

Some couples cling so closely together you could not slide a sheet of paper between them. Many girls think this denotes possession and tells their friends the couple loves each other. In reality it makes people think, "If that is what they do in public, what do they do in private?" Because of too much body contact in public, some girls who have not been sexually active have the reputation of those who are.

10. *Your daughter does not have to be sexually active to be popular.*

Every teen wants to be popular. Most fledgling daters worry that they are not attractive to the opposite sex, and some think giving sexual favors will make them popular. They may be right for a while, but it will be with the wrong kind of guys. In addition, a girl who gives sexual favors may end up pregnant or with a disease that makes her very unpopular and lonely and could change her life forever. What most teens do not realize is that anyone can become popular. One popular youth speaker wrote the following in his book to teens:

HOW TO RATE WITH THE GUYS...

According to a survey, the guys mentioned 10 things most often in describing a good date:

1. Good conversationalist	6. Prompt
2. Attractive	7. A good personality
3. Ladylike in behavior	8. Friendly
4. Neat	9. A good sense of humor
5. Not too demanding	10. Maturity in attitude and behavior (not the giggly type)

Note that all of these "good date" characteristics can be developed. Conversational skills can be improved.... Attractiveness can be developed by any clean, wholesome girl, regardless of whether she is "beautiful" or not. Ladylike behavior can be learned, as can neatness, promptness, a good personality, friendliness and a sense of humor.

When you are on a date, let the guy know that you are interested in him. If you are in a crowd, concentrate on HIM. Look him straight in the eye when you talk to him. Learn to listen Anybody can talk, but there are not many good listeners. Talk about his interests. Do not talk about your other dates and avoid gossiping. Relax and be yourself.[1]

11. *Your daughter has the right to demand respect.*

As a virtuous young lady, your daughter has the right to have her values respected. Some boys do not respect women. Their relationship to their mother or sisters is poor; they have never learned that good men respect good women. Teach your daughter that if a boy does not respect her and her values, he has two-and-a-half strikes against him already. She should start by making it clear that she expects him to treat her like a lady. She should make him open doors for her, make him call her on the telephone, make him come to her house to meet her parents and pick her up. She should insist that he bring her home on time and refuse to do anything with him that compromises her standards. In short, she should make him respect her. If he does not respect her, he will never really love her. If he does not respect her, he will use her and discard her as he does a car when he has gotten the good out of it.

Girls have the right to be respected, but in today's society they have to demand it. Most boys will admire a girl who demands respect for herself, her values, and her virginity. The good ones will come back; the others she does not need. If the price of popularity comes at the cost of respect, it is too expensive. She may pay that price the rest of her life.

12. *Someday your daughter may be asked by her daughter if she was a virgin when she married.*

One of your dreams for your daughter is that someday she will marry and become a mother herself. Just sixteen short years after your daughter's first baby girl is born, she will be telling these same things to her. Your daughter needs to know in advance that her teenage daughter is likely to ask "Mom, were you a virgin when you married Dad?" She needs your help now so that when that day comes, she can look your future granddaughter in the eye and say, "Yes, I was!" and in her heart say, "Thank God for a mother who loved me enough to prepare me for the most important and dangerous part of my life."

13. *Girls have the most to lose.*

Life is not always fair. That is true in the differences between boys and girls. Boys never experience a period; girls have one every month. Boys never have labor pains; women have lots of them in order to have babies. This does not mean boys get all the breaks. They have the responsibility of learning a vocation and earning a living for their family, sometimes at a job they hate. Life is not fair, but it does seem to balance out.

One of the things that is not fair is that girls pay a higher price for premarital sex than do most boys. Many a boy has gotten a girl pregnant and walked away to a carefree life with other girls. One boy in Maryland bragged that he has impregnated seven girls and walked away from them all. Girls, on the other hand, are often left with the shame that is still very real with unwed pregnancy. A girl's life is changed forever. She may not be able to finish high school; he may go off to college as if nothing ever happened. She may bear his child; two years later, he may not recognize her on the street. Girls need to know they have the most to lose. Therefore, they must be taught that they are the moral cop in their relationship. She must know when to say *no!* and to insist he take her home *right now!* Until the day she marries, she must always remember that she has the most to lose.

Summary

Your daughter needs to know these things before she starts dating, not to destroy her fun but to prolong it. The ideal relationship to cultivate with your daughter is one in which she will feel comfortable sharing with you some of the things she did on her date. Much of this will depend on her temperament. Some people are just more talkative than others. But you can be certain that if your daughter does anything she feels guilty about, she will not share it with the adults who love her.

---

[1] George B. Eager, *Love, Dating, and Sex: What Teens Want to Know* (Valdosta, Ga.: Mailbox Club Books, 1989), 113.

Chapter Eleven

WHAT BOYS NEED TO KNOW BEFORE THEY START DATING

Most boys do not know much about girls. In fact, most men do not either, for girls and women are often more complex than men. This is particularly true in the emotional area. Girls tend to be more emotional than boys. They cry easier and more often and tend to be more trusting than boys. They also are more impacted by their families at an early age. For example, if they are not given the love and affection they need early in life, they may be so starved for love that they make sexual compromises to get that needed love. For this reason, some very nice girls have exchanged sex for love when all they really wanted was affection.

Most girls have no idea how sexually stimulating what they wear, how they act, and the closeness of their body is to a boy. I know a minister's son and a missionary's daughter who fell in love at sixteen. They made a striking couple. Both loved the Lord and wanted to serve him. When they were seniors in high school, the boy broke off their relationship because he could not handle his emotions. Her spiritual life was not affected by their affectionate kisses after a date. But affection almost never stops at a safe point—it always craves more. The boy could not handle his high-octane emotions when she nestled her body against his. She seemed to find it a way of saying "I love you," but he was ignited with passion. Although they never did anything they were ashamed of, he knew they eventually would if he could not control his thoughts. After confessing his out-of-control thought-life to the Lord, he decided "it was time to cool it." They had another year of high school and two to three years of college ahead of them before they could think about marriage, and he knew they would never make it. So they broke up. The night he told her, they both cried. The girl never really understood. She still thinks he broke up because he did not love her. In truth, he broke up because he did. Neither of them has had a date since.

Both parents can be proud of those young people because they have their priorities right. Both have made a commitment to virtue and are saving themselves for their wedding night. For now, they had to break up to preserve that vow. I have a hunch, after counseling the boy, that if that beautiful and virtuous girl had known how explosive her body was to him, she would have conducted herself differently, and they would probably still be together.

Some Basic Guidelines for Your Son's Relationships with Girls

A whole book could be written about the differences between the sexes. Your son does not need to know all of them—save some for him to discover after he is married. He will have a lifetime to learn them! But for now, he should know at least the following before he starts dating.

1. Your son should take the lead.

God's plan is for men to be leaders. We hear many shrill voices to the contrary today, but one of the main causes for heartache in marriage is the failure of many men to take the initiative to lead. Teach your son that he should always be in charge. He lines up the transportation, he plans the activity, he calls the girl, he meets the conditions set down by her parents, he gets her home on time after the date, and he should set out to make the girl feel good about herself.

2. Your son should plan all dates carefully.

Dating should be fun. But it is so much fun just being with someone you love that it becomes a date any time you are together. If your son and his date do not have a special place to go or activity to attend, then gradually they will do what all human beings find exciting: show affection for the opposite sex. As we have already seen, that can be extremely dangerous. If they do not have a project, they will become each others' project. It is reassuring to the girl's parents if your son can tell them what their plans are in advance—particularly, who they will be going with and what they will be doing. Not only is this good policy, but her parents will be more likely to let them go out together again.

3. *Your son needs to avoid getting serious too soon.*

We hope you insist that he can only double date through all or most of his high school years. Two young people alone will naturally become serious long before they should. It is his job to line up the other couple.

One of the boys who dated one of our girls used to try to get around that rule by saying, "All my friends are busy tonight. Can we go out alone?" Obviously, he needed more friends, and he was not going to find them just going out with our daughter. It was amazing to me how soon after we said no that he called back and said he had found a couple to go with them.

Most parents get suspicious when teens try to bend the rules. Teach your son to respect and cooperate with the rules set down by the girl's parents. A fine young man who dated one of our daughters felt we were particularly unreasonable on a rule. He sounded off at home, and his wise father said, "Son, I don't agree with that rule either, but you have to realize, Linda is Pastor LaHaye's daughter, and he can set any rules he wants to. You have two choices: either put up with the rules cheerfully so you can date her, or go with someone else." Eventually they married and are currently serving the Lord together. Today, I do not think any of us can remember what that rule was.

You may have to make positive suggestions of places they can go and things they can do. Your son may ridicule your ideas, but do not be surprised if he picks up on some of them.

4. *Treat all dates politely and with respect.*

You have probably taught your son already that it is polite for men to treat women with special respect. Men should open doors for women, introduce them to friends, and go out of their way to publicly indicate they are special. Just this morning, Bev and I attended a presidential prayer breakfast in Washington, D.C. When a charming lady came to our table, I pushed my chair back and stood to my feet. She graciously said, "Oh, you shouldn't stand up." I replied, "My mother taught me to always stand up for a lady!" Obviously she was pleased. As the father of two lovely daughters, I can tell you that one of the things I rated their dates on was politeness. Boys that did not know how to treat a girl like a lady were "oncers."

Someday your son may take a girl out who has never been taught manners. He is in a good position to set a new standard for her when it comes to picking dates. If he treats her like a lady, she will be more likely to act like one, not only in his company but for her future. Treating her with respect will make any girl feel good about herself. Your son needs to be challenged to realize that no matter how much he loves the girl he dates in high school, he will probably not marry her. After their break up, he does not want her to be ashamed to look at him afterward or acknowledge she went with him, learn habits from him that may get her into trouble with other boys, or say things about him that would tarnish his reputation.

A woman at one of my seminars asked what she could do about getting her children in a good youth group. "In this small town, this is the only church that has a dynamic program for young people." Naturally I asked why she and her husband didn't bring the family to church there. She replied, "Oh, I couldn't come here regularly. I used to go with one of the deacons when we were in high school, and every time I see him, I am reminded that we were sexually intimate back then." Guilt kept her teens from a positive youth experience when they needed it most.

5. *Dating is not for petting, making out, or body contact.*

Another thing your son needs you to tell him is that dating is for fun and getting to know girls his own age. Dating is not for petting. The first date or two should have almost no body contact. Hand holding comes first; then, eventually, a good night kiss in a well-lighted place may be appropriate. Young people need to understand that people bent on sinning "[love] darkness instead of light because their deeds [are] evil" (John 3:19).

6. *Your son needs to know the Law of Progression.*

It is possible for even the best of boys or young men to let their passions run away with them. Make sure you go over the Law of Progression with your son so he understands that most of the Christian young people who got into trouble or "went all the way" never intended to do so. But the chart in chapter 2 reveals how his—and a girl's—emotions can be gradually ignited. In addition, sexual activity is never satisfied; it always craves more. What a couple does on one date is exceeded in the next date or two unless they mutually draw a line and say "no further." This is particularly true of young people who genuinely care for each other.

One Christian couple was so right for each other, all four parents, who happened to be good friends, gave them too much freedom to spend long periods of time together without supervision. They would sit together on the couch and watch TV, holding hands, then kissing, and then more. Those naive parents became early grandparents and created heartaches and hardships for themselves and their children. One youth authority said couples who spend three hundred hours together alone will become sexually involved, even if at first they do not intend to.[1]

How far is too far? An automobile is equipped with warning signals to let you know when you are in danger of ruining the engine. When the engine is running hot, a red light flashes, telling you something is wrong. You need to stop immediately and find out what it is. Here are some "warning lights" to let you know when you are going too far in your displays of affection:

- You are going too far when a guy's (or girl's) hands start roaming.

- You are going too far when either of you starts removing clothing. Keep *all* of your clothing on all the time.

- You are going too far when you arouse genital feelings.

- You are going too far when you are doing something you would not want to be doing around someone you really respect.

- You are going too far when you cannot make an intelligent decision as to what you should or should not do and carry out that decision.

Before you start dating, you need to set your guidelines as to how far to go. The only guideline that is 100% safe is: Keep your hands off and your clothes on![2]

7. Your son should set a spiritual tone for all dates.

God holds men accountable to be the spiritual leader in all couple relationships, both before and after marriage. Wise parents will urge their son to make it a practice to pray with every girl he dates. The scripture teaches, "whatever you do, do it all for the glory of God" (1 Cor. 10:31). He can pray a short prayer when they first get into the car to go out, asking God's blessing on their time together. Then take a few moments to thank God for the good time just before he walks his date to the door. True, not many kids do that today, but it would certainly be a safeguard to their conduct. God is with them wherever they go and sees whatever they do. Praying together will make them more conscious of His presence.

8. Dating should not interfere with your son's spiritual growth.

Some young people can be a spiritual blessing to each other while dating, but only if they observe a pure relationship. The moment they start taking sexual license with each other, their spiritual life goes down the tube. Your son should set as one of his goals to be a spiritual blessing to any girl he goes with, particularly one he dates seriously. The likelihood is she will be someone's wife and mother someday, and God may have brought them together to make a positive contribution to each others' lives.

One of my favorite pictures is of our youngest daughter on her graduation day from a Christian college. Dressed in cap and gown, she gave a warm embrace to the young man she dated her freshman and sophomore years. He too had his graduating regalia on. They were saying goodbye and have not seen each other since. They were both also saying, without words, thank you for two fun-filled years that made a positive impact on my life. When they met he was a dedicated Christian and 4.0 student. She was a fun-loving cheerleader type who had never learned how to study. Because of his influence, she got better grades in college than she did in high school and went on to become a credentialed Christian school teacher. She taught him to loosen up, not take life and himself so seriously, and enjoy preparing to serve the Lord. They broke up after two years, and he found the girl that became his wife, went on to graduate school, and is now a Christian counselor. Even though they did not go together their last two years, their relationship had been so positive they could still be good friends. We could wish that for all young couples no matter how old they are.

9. Your son needs to guard his mind.

Because boys are so visually stimulated, your son needs to learn to guard his mind during the dating years. Most red-blooded boys start fantasizing about girls when they are only fourteen. Because they have no regular release for their sex drive until marriage, it is not uncommon for them to develop thought patterns that destroy their spiritual life and intensify their already explosive emotions. In such a condition, a young man is a danger to himself as well as the girl he dates. This is particularly true if he indulges in pornography or watches lewd TV shows or movies.

Mothers are often naive about such things. They can put mental pictures out of their minds almost as fast as they come in. Their sons can't! If your son is healthy and normal, he needs to know the dangers of indulging fantasies and to do what scripture says: "Avoid every kind of evil" (1 Thess. 5:22) and to "take captive every thought to make it obedient to Christ" (2 Cor. 10:5). The young man who does not learn to control his thoughts will never become strong spiritually and is a moral threat to himself and his family.

I have been called into several cases of serious juvenile sex crimes perpetuated by boys from active Christian homes. Their first offense was totally out of character and unexpected. In each of these cases, the boy acknowledged losing the battle in his thought-life long before committing the actual crime. One college sophomore from a good Christian home committed a "date rape" while away at school. He admitted to a pattern of sexual fantasies starting in early high school, which led to indulgence in pornography and, eventually, to committing a terrible crime. This type of moral decay could affect and enslave any young man.

10. *Your son must be the moral cop!*

Most boys grow up thinking they can go as far as a girl will let them on a date. Consequently, their subconscious purpose for dating can be "more, more, more." Such a false notion will ruin what could be a good relationship, destroy his reputation, or get them both into a sexual practice that will either destroy their lives or someone else's later.

Your son needs to know that he is responsible to God to set a standard for his behavior that he will follow no matter what girls want to do. He may date a girl sometime who is far more experienced than he, who may urge him to go to a remote place to "make out." He can be polite yet firm only if he has established in advance principles that he will not violate under any circumstances. He needs to be reminded that an aggressive girl or woman is almost impossible for the average man to resist unless he is deeply committed to purity. He alone is responsible for his behavior, and he will bear the responsibility. Girls cannot rape unwilling men; they can seduce them, which only proves that a man who allows himself to get into a bad situation is unwise (Prov. 5).

11. *Your son needs to understand the pattern of a girl's monthly cycle.*

By the time a boy begins dating, he should know how his body functions and also how a young woman functions. He should learn that from his parents, his church, and at youth camp in "boys only" classes. Before he dates, he should be taught by his parents that girls are not only highly emotional, but their mood swings often follow their monthly menstrual cycle. That accounts for why his girlfriend may cry more easily at times and possibly spend much of a date close to tears. She may be embarrassed and frustrated for not being able to control her feelings. Therefore, he should never tease her but should be understanding and kind.

He should also know that for four to eight days a month, a girl may have a higher intensity of passion than at other times. During such times, she may want to be more physical than usual. Her emotions can turn to passion, and she can act out of character for her values. At such a time, most girls are extremely fertile. Unless your son is the moral cop on duty, he could lead a girl into an activity they both will regret the rest of their lives. Teach your son to respect and protect his date on such occasions. He can express his love without being passionate. Passion usually beclouds good judgment.

12. Sexual activity destroys relationships, it does not strengthen them.

One of the most surprising discoveries that has come out of our research on premarital sex is that it is almost always engaged in by two people who sincerely believe they love each other and think having sex will strengthen their relationship. Most women who were sexually active in their late teens know better. Premarital sex demotivates men from marriage, or it creates such pressure on the couple, because of guilt and fear of exposure, that it causes them to break up. Some never recover spiritually. Some women get pregnant, and that changes their entire lives. Once a couple has been sexually intimate, their relationship is usually changed by either an unwanted pregnancy or an early break up.

13. It does not take a "man" to get a girl pregnant.

A social worker asked a boy who was accused of getting five girls pregnant why he did it. "To prove my manhood," he admitted. The boy was fourteen! Every day in this country, four thousand women have abortions; many of them are unmarried and still in their teens. Many of them were impregnated by a boy their own age (some by boys only thirteen years old).

Your son needs to know that the male macho lie that sexual intercourse proves manhood is a devilish deception. It takes a man to control himself. Anyone can let his glands takeover and follow the path of least resistance. Humans were not designed just for sexual expression. That is a small part of life, even for those who marry. According to surveys, the average couple makes love only two to three times a week. Obviously, there are many other things in life of more importance. Though good love-making enriches all of marriage, it should be kept in perspective. It is not a sign of manhood. Teach your son that until he is ready for father-hood (and he won't be ready for that until he is married), he should not have sex. It is a true sign of manhood for him to wait until he can respon-sibly care for the child he and his wife create.

14. *Girls need to be protected.*

When a young man takes a young woman on a date, he is taking out her parents' most precious possession. She must be protected at all costs. Your son needs to understand that it is an act of trust on her par-ents' part to put their daughter in his care for an evening. He should value and preserve that trust, not betray it. Just because he can "get away" with something does not mean it is right.

Many years ago, a minister friend confided a heavy load of guilt he carried all through his adult life. It seems that he went with a beautiful girl all through high school and had sex with her many times during their senior year. They were both unsaved at the time and justified it because they were in love and planned to get married when they graduated. He had a hard time getting into college so he joined the Navy. The girl's par-ents sent her to college, and after a few months they drifted apart emo-tionally. The girl got swept up in the college social whirl and became very loose in her morals, dropped out of college, and became a prostitute. The young man was converted to Christ in the service and dedicated him-self to God for the gospel ministry, got married, had three children, and is a successful pastor. But he confided to me, "God has forgiven me for my teenage sin—I have no problem with that. What I do have problems with is that I helped to destroy her life. Prostitutes have an average life span of thirty-three years. Here I am at forty-five. I have two teenage daughters and can hardly look at them without wondering where that poor soul is and whether God will 'visit the sin of the father on the next generation.'"

You do not want your son to spend his adult life living under that kind of guilt. You need to warn him that his primary duty in life right now is to develop maturity and character. Much of that will come as he learns to control his sexual desires by avoiding passions that should be reserved for marriage.

15. *Men have a long, hard road to vocational preparedness; premature sexual activity can destroy your son's potential.*

Modern technology has all but rendered the self-made man obso-lete. Whether your son hates school or loves it, he needs to thoroughly understand that any vocation he goes into will take four to eight years of preparation after he finishes high school. The more technical the vocation, the more time and work it will take to prepare for it. Your son has a long, hard road ahead of him if he is to make the best use of the talents God has given him.

Unfortunately, the sex drive of young men and women has not lessened just because technology has increased. As we have seen, the society your children are being raised in promotes sexual promiscuity and self-satisfaction as though there were no responsibilities to such actions. Your son needs to weigh the fact that premature sex is a serious threat to long-term educational endeavors.

When young men sacrifice long-range educational goals for premature sexual satisfaction, they are setting themselves up for enormous frustration later in life. Many men turn this into anger at their wives, which becomes fatal to their marriage.

One TV repairman who was a wizard with electronics followed this pattern. When he and his wife came in for counseling, it all tumbled out. He felt he was more capable than many of his supervisors, but he did not have the education to qualify him for the promotions he sought. Instead, he was so good at what he did they gave him all the hard jobs no one else could solve. If it were not for his basic spiritual resources, their marriage would not have lasted. Those frustrations were unnecessarily caused by an unplanned pregnancy and a premature marriage his sophomore year in college.

Summary

Consultations with thousands of young people and with other counselors have convinced us that there is not one positive benefit to premarital sexual activity. There are many disadvantages, many of which we have listed. Your son needs to know them before he starts dating, and from time to time he needs a refresher talk. When you see him becoming "too serious" with a girl, you should lovingly sit down with him and review some of these subjects. He may not welcome such a talk at the time, but he will appreciate your love and concern someday—particularly, if you save him from a tragic experience.

Parents have a right to ask their teenage son if he is indulging in adult sexual behavior. Though he may resent your "intruding" on his privacy, the thought that you might intrude again some day may cool his youthful passions some night before he destroys himself and the nice girl he thinks he is in love with. You must protect him from himself and from those who would ruin his health and mind and harm even his person.

---

[1] George B. Eager, *Love, Dating, and Sex: What Teens Want to Know* (Valdosta, Ga.: Mailbox Club Books, 1989), 127.

[2] Ibid., 128.

Chapter Twelve

WHAT CHRISTIAN TEENS SAY ABOUT SEX THAT THEIR PARENTS NEED TO HEAR

 e wish every parent of eleven- to twenty-year-old young people could have attended the discussion groups we had with active church youth about sex. The sessions were lively and extremely revealing.

Most of these young people were a bit scared and intimidated by the much publicized sexually transmitted diseases, the AIDS epidemic, and the high teenage pregnancy rate. Almost all of them knew some girl who had gotten pregnant out of wedlock. This concern may signal a slowing of the sexual activity rate of today's young. If parents move gently but aggressively into this area, with the kind of training we have outlined in this book, many children can be saved the traumas that almost inevitably confront sexually active teens.

How the Sessions Were Conducted

The teen opinions we have accumulated do not represent the population at large. All our sessions were pulled together by church youth leaders and involved active church young people; only a few of them betrayed a spirit of rebellion. The sessions were held in Virginia, Maryland, California, and Oregon. The latter was held in a small town and is representative of young people living in a rural community. The other three were held in large cities. Yet their responses showed very little difference. All the participating teens said they attended Bible-believing churches with a good youth program. We were reminded again that parents should keep their teens in a good church where the teens' peers are more apt to share their moral values.

We began by telling them that many of the couples who had read our book, *The Act of Marriage*, had children their age and were concerned that they be able to maintain their virtue in the face of one of the most aggressive attacks ever on moral values. We soon found out that they knew exactly who the culprits were: the media, movie and TV makers, and what one teen called "rabid sex educators." Even he sensed that one of his instructors was "obsessed with sex." We explained that we believe most parents want to talk to their young people about sex, but that it was hard for them to do. We also said that we wanted to write a book that would provide them the necessary material and motivation to do so.

Then we explained that we wanted to see where today's Christian young people were coming from by having them fill out a questionnaire and then opening the meeting for a free and open discussion. Almost every teen was vitally interested and none of them seemed embarrassed. We were impressed that they all had strong opinions on the subject. It would be impossible to list all their answers here. What follows is a summary or compilation of their responses by topic.

Parents as Sex Educators

Approximately 70 percent of the teens had already talked to one or both of their parents about sex and said they felt comfortable discussing it. While a few indicated their parents were nervous or embarrassed, they had prepared them well. The only problem was that most parents started too late. Much of what their parents talked to them about, the young people had already learned in school or from their friends. Most of the teens said they felt free to discuss the subject with their parents, and about 60 percent said they wish their parents would bring up the subject more often. Almost all felt it was the parents' responsibility to bring up the topic.

One of the surprising things we discovered was that most of these teens, well over 90 percent, would rather learn about sex from their parents than from any other person. Those whose parents did not talk to them about sex still wished they had and said they would be more aggressive about talking to their own children about it.

Sex Education in School

Virtually all the young people had attended sex education classes, both those who attended Christian schools and those who did not. The most usual grade-levels for instruction seemed to be third grade, fifth and sixth grades, again in eighth or ninth grade, and again in twelfth grade. Some of the teens had sex education almost every year, either in sex education classes or in child development classes.

Most complained that their classes were to explicit. Some of the students were embarrassed by what they learned in class and most indicated that it was "just assumed that everyone was having sex." As we discussed this, one of the boys said he thought his friends who bragged about having sex were lying. Most of the students thought that sexual activity was not as universal as both the kids and teachers would have them believe.

Most of the young people who attended public school had seen condoms, handled them, seen demonstrations on how to apply them, and were told where they could get them free. One student said his ninth grade teacher introduced them by blowing one up and letting the class bat it around. One senior said, "In tenth grade the teacher played with condoms and other birth control devises to make us comfortable with them." Several other young people agreed to having had the same exposure to contraceptives. As expected, those students attending a Christian school said they had never seen a condom in class.

It came as no surprise that much of their public school sex education classes were devoid of moral values. The great concern seemed to be "protect yourself from pregnancy and disease by using a condom." Very few of the teens were aware of how unsafe condoms are, and they were surprised to hear that even the manufacturers of condoms do not claim that they are totally dependable.

One charming girl said her eleventh-grade teacher was "a Roman Catholic and clearly taught abstinence," and was the favorite teacher of the girls in school. For the most part, these young people felt that abstinence was not presented very well and that it was stated or implied that "graduating from high school as a virgin was not realistic." According to some of the students, it is considered "impractical" to expect today's youth to be virtuous. Several said their sex education teachers "didn't seem to think there was anything wrong with premarital sex."

The discussion on homosexuality was enlightening. Almost all the public school teens had heard it presented as "an optional lifestyle" with little emphasis on how dangerous that lifestyle is. They seemed surprised to learn that AIDS is overwhelmingly a homosexually transmitted disease. They know about "dirty or contaminated needles" being dangerous, but almost all of the teens had been presented with the idea that AIDS was transmitted among heterosexuals just as much and easily as it was transmitted among homosexuals. Obviously, someone is not teaching these young people the truth about AIDS and homosexuality. That should be illegal.

One of the girls identified a danger of sex education that few people mention: "I don't agree with sex education. After I had it, for awhile I wasn't able to control my thoughts because of what I knew." The last thing a young person needs is to have external stimulus to his or her sexually inspired thought life. Can you imagine what could have happened if this girl and her boyfriend had gone out on a date when her thought life was not pure and her hormones were stimulated? Some sex education classes actually inspire the very thing they are supposed to control.

One junior, who would make any parent proud, wrote, "I feel sex education should come from the home. My parents have done an excellent job in raising my sisters and me. I just hope I have kids who have as good of morals as we do—and as high of goals." Almost all these young people said they intended to teach their children about sex and to start early. Some thought they would start teaching their child "by nine years of age"; others said, "at least when the girls started having periods." Not one of the kids said they would wait longer than thirteen to arm their kids with this information so that the public school would not beat them to it.

Sexual Activity

Estimates of sexual activity among their peers fluctuated wildly. The figures went from "50 percent to virtually 100 percent" for public high school kids. Christian school estimates were much lower: they varied from 0 to 30 percent. Most Christian school students felt that about 15 percent of their peers might be sexually active, which is close to the percentage given by the Association of Christian Schools International survey. As mentioned, the young people felt excessive sexual activity is starting to slacken due to the fear of disease, pregnancy, and loss of reputation. Girls are beginning to realize that boys brag about what they do with them on dates, and most girls do not want to be considered morally loose, even if they are. Who knows, we might be on the verge of seeing moral self-respect and a desire to avoid fatal sexually transmitted diseases return large numbers of people to a new quest for morality. If so, it will not be due to what most public school educators are doing.

Dating

Almost all young people are interested in dating. The Christian young people we met with were no exception. Some of them started dating as early as eleven years old (believe it or not), but many of them were not permitted to date until they were sixteen. As we have seen, the dangers of sexual activity increase in direct proportion to the early commencement of dating. These teens seemed to understand that, for many indicated they would have a higher standard for their own children than their parents had for them. The consensus was that group dating at church and other activities was okay until fifteen or sixteen, and then double dating was acceptable. While there was disagreement among them on whether single dating should be permitted before graduation or during their senior year, all the students said that high school was no time to be thinking about marriage. They understood that for most of them, college or other vocational training was required before they could become "too serious."

Those who did not have a steady date felt it was best to "date around," but those who felt they were in love thought it was all right to have a steady. Several said that those who obeyed their parents' dating rules should be given more freedom than those who did not. Even they knew that a spirit of rebellion was dangerous.

Teens on "Making Out"

Most young people have no idea how stimulating kissing and caressing can be until they experience it. While virtually all the young people we met with claimed they opposed petting or making out, they did not see anything wrong with kissing. Anyone would admit it is exciting and stimulating, but these young people thought kissing could be controlled. They had no idea of the Law of Progression until I shared it with them. Even then some did not agree. I have a hunch they did not want to give up that experience; however, almost all said that expressions of affection should stop there. Somehow, we have to do a better job of getting them to realize kissing is a dangerous pastime.

As one girl said, "My parents don't want me to kiss the boys I date, but they don't tell me why. I think it is a lot of fun." She's right. Kissing is fun. It is exciting and stirs the emotions like few things in life. Young people need to be convinced that it is an adults-only pastime and should be reserved for engagement and marriage.

Dating Rules Teens Want to Set for Their Children

We were surprised to find that only about half of these teens had dating rules, but almost all of them said that when they are parents they will have rules for their teens. We got the impression that those who did not have rules wished their parents would establish some. The following rules were suggested without much negative response:

- "Date only Christians" (or at least someone who goes to church, some said).
- "Make your dates meet your parents."
- "Always date in a group or go to well-lighted places."
- "Don't go to places where you will be tempted to have sex."
- "Choose an environment that glorifies God."
- "Be home on time." (There was little agreement on what time that was. However, none thought midnight was right. Most fluctuated between 11:00 and 11:30 P.M.)

Random Teen Comments

One-and-a-half-hour discussions did not provide sufficient time to talk about everything the teens wanted to share with us. However, the following are some of the comments we think parents should read:

From a twelfth-grade girl: "My parents are so naive when it comes to what their children are facing. Most parents, particularly Christian parents, think 'My child would never engage in sex.' They should talk about abstinence."

Another twelfth-grade girl: "Sex before marriage is an absolute disaster and leaves terrible scares emotionally because it leaves you feeling impure and like a failure. Virginity is something you can never get back. I have had to learn the hard way. If it weren't for Jesus in my life to forgive me and lead me to a better path, to show me what's right, I don't know where I'd be."

From a twelfth-grade boy: "It is really difficult to date only Christians because in a public school it is sometimes hard to find a Christian girlfriend. But don't settle for second best even if they seem like the right one. If they are not Christians, don't date them."

An *eleventh-grade girl said*: "I plan to give my children the same rules my parents gave me, except I would add, 'Always think Jesus is sitting next to you on a date.' That should keep them good."

A *twelfth-grade boy responded*: "Please don't make parents feel that all teenagers want to go out and have sex. There are a lot of us that do know our limits and do know what's right!"

Teens on the Commitment to Virtue

Almost half of the teens we talked with had made a commitment to virtue, but not one of them had been led to that decision by their parents. Either their pastor, youth pastor, or a camp speaker had challenged them somewhere between the ages of thirteen and seventeen to make such a commitment. Several said their commitment helped on dates and planning for dates because it gave them a goal for their conduct. We realize that these were special young people who, for the most part, are committed to serving Christ. None of them ridiculed the idea or indicated it had no merit.

We believe this commitment to virtue is the sleeping giant that would help save your children from this permissive society. Every parent with whom we share this idea thinks it is great, and many parents said they wish they had challenged their son or daughter to make such a commitment. Please reread that chapter and take our advice, the advice of parents who have done it, and the advice of the youth we met with, and lead your teen at age thirteen or fourteen to make such a commitment.

Millions of idealistic young people are being destroyed by lack of a vision of themselves as a virgin when they marry. This permissive society implants a vision of sexual activity. You should give your children's idealism a challenge for which they and their future lifetime partner will be eternally grateful.

Recently I was snow skiing with a handsome sixteen-year-old who is extremely popular in school, a tennis star, and an all-around athlete. He is a Christian but does not attend church regularly. His parents are divorced and he gets little spiritual encouragement from his father, with whom he lives. As we talked, he asked what I was writing on now, so I explained the heart of this book to him. Then I described the commitment to virtue many Christian parents are encouraging their teens to make. He had never heard of such a thing before. I did not even have to ask his impression, for he volunteered, "That's a neat idea! If I ever have any kids I would like to get them to make such a commitment. God knows we need all the help we can get today to do the right thing."

Most Christian young people would welcome such a challenge to virtue by their parents. Try it! Someday your son or daughter will "rise up to call you blessed" and just may pass the same challenge on to your grandchildren.

Part Four

SOME SPECIAL CONCERNS

PROTECT YOUR CHILDREN FROM SEXUAL ABUSE

Great numbers of children are being sexually molested today. Every responsible sex counselor I know is amazed at the frequency with which it occurs in our society. The sordid details of tragic scandals hit the front pages of newspapers with mind-boggling regularity, and no group is immune. In the early nineties, thirty-seven adults filed a lawsuit against a Catholic priest they claimed sexually molested them as children. In San Diego, a large evangelical church made the news as the mothers of seventeen children, who were in the church's day-care program, reported that their children had been sexually molested. Child molestation is a sin-sick disease that, unfortunately, continues to grow.

According to one government authority, current statistics suggest that one-fourth of all adult women were molested by the time they were thirteen years old; one-third by the time they were seventeen. Never has there been a more urgent need for parents to guard their children from sexual abuse.

Pedophilia is indeed on the increase and even more dangerous because it is not always practiced by strangers. Unfortunately, outsiders are not the only ones children must fear; often they are abused by members of their own families. The widespread breakdown of the family in American society and the delaying of marriage, which accounts for the present generation having more single men than any other generation in history, aggravates the situation. An especially vulnerable circumstance occurs in families where a stepfather (or stepbrother) is sexually attracted to a blossoming teenage stepdaughter.

A girl in one of our discussion groups had trouble looking at me when I challenged the young people to a commitment to virtue. During the prayer time, when I gave them a few moments to make their commitment, she began to sob softly. The youth pastor's wife took her out and counseled her. This young girl was molested by her stepfather when she was nine years old and felt she could not make such a commitment. We shared with her that she was not to blame for her stepfather's sins. God had cleansed her and made her a "new creature." She could and did commit herself to being virtuous.

Girls the Principal Victims

Girls are victims of sexual abuse in much greater numbers than boys mainly because men are often more sex-driven than women. Depression-producing guilt and the loss of self-respect are frequently the result of teenage girls and young women being sexually molested as children. In addition, they often become angry, frigid, or promiscuous; some resort to lesbianism. Many molested girls marry beneath their potential because of their guilt and shame, thus making their entire lives miserable as a result of someone else's sin.

I become angry just thinking of a man sexually violating a child, particularly when the perpetrator is the girl's father. I am almost embarrassed to recount the first such case I faced in the counseling room many years ago. A beautiful fifteen-year-old girl came to ask how she could make her father stop demanding sex from her without letting him know she had confided her dilemma to me. "If he knew I told you, he would kill me," she said. When I suggested she tell her mother, she replied, "I already did, but she is afraid she will lose him if she doesn't let him."

These people were not pagans; they were members of my congregation. I was able to stop this molestation, but two years later the girl became promiscuous and pregnant. She felt she had no virtue to protect because of her father. Years later this man died a long and painful death. I could not help thinking that he may have suffered the just reward of his deeds.

Small girls and early teenagers are especially vulnerable to sexual abuse. Usually they are physically forced or seduced, then threatened with revenge if they tell anyone. Sometimes, when a victim is driven by guilt or anger to disclose the situation, the mother doesn't believe the sordid tale or refuses to face the truth.

The home environment, however, is not the only place where child sexual abuse occurs. In recent years, the national media has focused attention on widespread exploitation outside the home. Numerous revelations of child pornography rings operating in certified day-care centers suddenly hit the headlines and TV talk shows.

Kee MacFarlane, director of the Child Sexual Abuse Diagnostic and Treatment Center of the Children's Institute International in Los Angeles, believes there is a nationwide network of "child predators" who have opened day-care centers so they will have access to young children. In her testimony before a congressional committee, Miss MacFarlane made this statement:

> I believe that we're dealing with a conspiracy, an organized operation of child predators designed to prevent detection. The preschool, in such a case, serves as a ruse for a larger unthinkable network of crimes against children. If such an operation involves child pornography or the selling of children, as is frequently alleged, it may have greater financial, legal and community resources at its disposal than those attempting to expose it.[1]

It is feared by many responsible observers that the problem of day-care abuse is far more prevalent than most people believe. Parents must be more careful whom they permit to care for their children.

The testimonies of women indicate that sexual abuse has existed for years and will continue to accelerate as long as corrupt minds have easy access to pornography. The $10 billion pornography business and the filthy movies shown on cable television have inspired sex perversion and molestation in many homes. Pornography is to the mind and emotions of men what gasoline is to fire; it has become the single most inflammatory force for evil in our society. Until judges stop heeding the cry of attorneys who appeal to the First Amendment as their defense and start protecting our children, the problem will remain an unquenchable inferno. Pornography is not protected by the First Amendment.

As long as these and other causes of child molestation remain, we can expect a steady increase in the problem. If we do not confront the problem through legislation or experience a moral and spiritual revival, I predict that by the twenty-first century the number of female victims of sexual molestation under age seventeen will increase to more than 50 percent in the United States.

The Damage to Children

Children who are sexually abused often suffer irreparable emotional, physical, and spiritual damage. They may suffer lacerated genitals and rectal damage; they face a higher than normal risk of cervical cancer in later years.

The emotional damage caused by child abuse is almost irreversible. Cliff Linedecker, author of *Children in Chains*, an exposé of child pornography, prostitution, and sexual abuse, has observed, "Children who are used sexually by adults or who are seduced, enticed, or forced to pose for pornography are left almost inevitably with severe psychological scarring that can never be erased."[2] Some of these emotional scars are feelings of worthlessness, guilt, betrayal, rage, powerlessness, and distrust. As adults, victims of child sexual abuse are often unable to maintain normal relationships with other people. They feel unwanted, dirty, and useless.

The Texas Department of Human Resources (Select Committee on Child Pornography) listed seventeen short-term side effects of child sexual abuse: 1) Regressive behavior; 2) delinquent behavior; 3) sexual promiscuity; 4) poor peer relationships; 5) unwillingness to participate in physical and/or recreational activities; 6) running away; 7) drug or alcohol abuse; 8) confusion; 9) depression; 10) anxiety; 11) suspicion; 12) bad dreams; 13) restlessness; 14) personal behavior inconsistent with prior behavioral patterns; 15) unexplained medical problems; 16) learning disabilities; and 17) self-mutilation.[3]

A PROFILE OF CHILD MOLESTERS

What does a sex molester look like? Dr. Bruce Gross, acting director of the USG Institute of Psychiatry, Law, and Behavioral Science, has seen more than a thousand child molesters in the last twelve years. His description: "It's impossible to identify them. They look like the typical person in the community." A youth pastor, boys club director, airport executive, priest, security officer, boy scout leader, elementary school-teacher—all these kinds of people have been convicted of child molestation in recent years.

Molesters do not fit the stereotypical image of the "dirty old man" (although 90 percent of the people arrested for molestation are men).

They are vastly different. They do not fit into any narrow ethnic, social, or economic categories, although patterns can be discerned among other characteristics. It is known that the majority of molesters are not strangers to the children they molest—they are trusted friends, relatives, community leaders, and other authority figures.

The Marks of a Molester

What kind of man or boy would sexually molest a helpless child? Though molesters are difficult to identify, there are certain marks or characteristics a parent should be alert for:

- A sexually obsessed male who reads pornographic literature or views sexually explicit movies;

- An adult who was molested or abused as a child, particularly one who does not relate well with adults of the opposite sex;

- An alcoholic or heavy drinker who loses his self-control but not his sex drive when drinking;

- An insecure man who is afraid of being rejected by a woman his own age and thus picks on a child;

- An infantile man who cannot relate to adults but spends much time with children;

- Men married to overpowering and dominating women who stifle them sexually so that they turn to their own children or stepchildren, who are more submissive;

- Undisciplined men who fail at all they set out to do but find the sexual conquest of a child gives them a much-needed feeling of power;

- Brainwashed victims of our humanistic society who actually talk themselves into thinking that it is good for children to become sexually active early in life and that adult-child sex is a "loving experience" beneficial to the child.

Such individuals are sin-sick. Our children must be protected from them. Linedecker cautions,

The child pornographer or panderer of today is more likely to be sophisticated, mobile, educated, and wealthy. Often he is a pillar of his community and is respected for his involvement in youth-oriented activities such as scouting for boys and girls, church-sponsored programs, summer camps, and other accepted activities for building character in the young. Several men connected to child pornography and child prostitution rings are millionaires.[4]

The molester who is known to a child is seldom bent on violence. Stunted emotionally, he is simply displaying childlike feelings and attitudes. Dr. Shirley O'Brien, writing in *Child Pornography*, describes the pedophile as someone who is emotionally immature.

> Some men with pedophiliac tendencies do marry and have children. Even so, they may still exhibit these immature characteristics and remain sexually inadequate. If pressured or rejected by his spouse, he may seek gratification with a child. He will seek someone who is accepting, someone who will do his bidding and not make fun of him.[5]

The pedophile actually believes that he "loves" the child with whom he has sexual relations. He woos the youngster much as a man courts a woman, and he photographs the child because he knows the relationship cannot last forever. Frequently he trades pictures with his friends, who operate in an informal network; some of the photographs eventually end up in pornographic magazines.

Molesters as Victims of Abuse

There is considerable evidence that adult molesters of children were themselves victims of sexual abuse as youngsters. A. Nicholas Groth, a clinical psychologist and director of the sex-offender program at the Connecticut Correctional Institution, has worked with molesters for eighteen years. He has identified a consistent pattern: unstable, unsettled families; lack of consistent or fair discipline in the home; and abuse or neglect at home. Groth found "evidence of some form of sexual trauma in the life histories of one-third of the offenders he worked with. This statistic was significant when compared with the finding that only about one-tenth of adult male non-offenders report similar victimization in their lives."[6]

A Dangerous New Breed of Molester

Dr. Bruce Gross is alarmed about what he calls a new breed of child molester—those men who have been convicted of child molestation and are now out of jail. According to Gross, if such people continue to molest children, "the likelihood of them killing their victim is extremely high."[7] With a conviction already behind them, these men fear they will face longer jail sentences if they are arrested again and therefore can rationalize killing children to destroy potential witnesses.

PROTECTING OUR CHILDREN

The following list enumerates methods commonly used by child molesters, especially men who are strangers to the victim. This list was developed by Kenneth Wooden, executive director of the National Coalition for Children's Justice. It is good for us as parents to discuss these with our children.

- *Affection/love.* Most child molestations and murders are committed by someone who is known by the child or is a member of the family.

- *Assistance.* Molesters often approach a child asking for help of some kind: directions to a popular landmark, nearby restaurant, or school; assistance in finding a lost puppy; aid in carrying an armload of packages to a car.

- *Authority.* Because children have respect for authority, some molesters take advantage of them by dressing as police officers, clergy, or firemen.

- *Bribery.* This is one of the oldest ruses. Children may be offered toys, candy, or other rewards.

- *Ego/fame.* Sometimes children are promised a modeling job, the chance to compete in a beauty contest, or the opportunity to star in a television commercial.

- *Emergency.* The emergency lure is designed to disarm, confuse, and worry a child.

- *Games and fun.* With this enticement, seemingly innocent play often leads to intimate bodily contact.

- *Jobs.* Older children can be attracted by an offer of high-paying or interesting jobs.

- *Threats or fear.* Some molesters use threats of violence, flashing guns or knives before the victim.

By discussing these tactics with our children, we can reduce the risks of their falling victim to sexual abuse. Because as many as 100,000 to 500,000 children are molested each year, it is essential that we provide our children with the information they need to avoid becoming victims.

One of the most sensitive approaches to child abuse has been produced by William Katz, head of the Christian Society for the Prevention of Cruelty to Children. The "Little Ones" educational program includes *Protecting Your Child From Sexual Assault*, which is a parent teaching guide, and *Little Ones Activity Book*, a coloring book for children. By leading children through the activity book, we can provide them with a thorough understanding of God's love, the importance of privacy, and their right to say no to someone who attempts to touch them. The activity book takes children through a series of lessons on "yes" and "no" touching. It shows them when it is appropriate for someone to hug or show affection. Then it teaches them to resist the kind of touching that violates their privacy. (Information on the "Little Ones" materials can be obtained from the Christian Society for the Prevention of Cruelty to Children, 8200 Grand Avenue South, Bloomington, MN 55420.)

Keeping Alert to Signs

We must keep alert for signs of possible child molestation. What do we look for?

- *Unusual marks*, bruises, or reddening around the anus or genitals.

- *Personality changes*. Abrupt changes in behavior may indicate sexual problems. Dr. Shirley O'Brien warns, "If a child's personality seems to change overnight and the pattern persists, it is a signal that something is wrong."[8]

- *Depression*. Has the child suddenly become chronically depressed for no apparent reason?

- *Secretiveness*. Has the child suddenly become sneaky about his activities? Has he been caught lying about where he spends his time?

- *Language*. Is the child demonstrating a sophisticated knowledge of sexual terms or activities?

- *Material goods*. Has the child recently acquired toys, clothing, or money whose source cannot be accounted for? Bribery could be the cause.

Teaching your children about sexual abuse should become an important feature of your sex education program. To ignore the dangers posed by child molesters is to leave your children vulnerable to abuse and exploitation. You should encourage them to tell you whenever they encounter a situation they do not understand. As the rate of child molestation continues to rise, it becomes essential that we safeguard our children by opening the conversational door to the subject. It may be difficult for a small child to talk to his or her parents about this delicate subject, but you should make sure your child knows that if anyone ever touches his or her private parts, he or she must come and tell you. This communication removes the guilt feelings so common in children and will help you to preserve your children's innocence. A child's assurance of freedom to open a conversation about this subject at any time is your best means of protection.

HOW TO REACT IF YOUR CHILD HAS BEEN MOLESTED

If one of your children has been molested, you must first realize that he or she needs your reassurance that you will take care of him and continue to love him. Often a child who has been victimized will feel like the guilty party. You must let the victim know that everything will be all right and that no one will blame him or her for what has happened.

Extreme tact, calmness, and gentleness should be maintained in finding out exactly what happened and who did it. Do not rush the child. He or she will be experiencing conflicting emotions and desperately needs your love and respect. Also, your child may feel she is betraying a "friend" by divulging details, for it is standard procedure for a pedophile to swear a child to secrecy. Because you train your children to keep promises, they may become confused when you ask them to break a promise.

If there is physical evidence on the child's clothing or body, let it stand. You should not wash the child's genitals or underwear until he or she has had a medical examination. Once you have determined to your satisfaction that the child has indeed been molested, you should contact the local police department. You will be directed by them to an appropriate medical facility.

Be careful to keep channels of communication open. All children need love, particularly those who have been traumatized. Pay close attention to them, and continually emphasize your willingness to discuss sexual matters with them. Because memories are most acute when combined with emotion, it is best for you to be as relaxed as possible in handling such a trauma. As a Christian parent there is one other thing you can do: pray daily for your child's protection.

The apostle Paul describes further means for protection in Ephesians 6:13-18.

Therefore put on the full armor of God, so that when the day of evil comes, you may stand your ground, and after you have done everything, to stand. Stand firm then, with the belt of truth buckled around your waist, with the breastplate of righteousness in place, and with your feet fitted with the readiness that comes from the gospel of peace. In addition to all this, take up the shield of faith, with which you can extinguish all the flaming arrows of the evil one. Take the helmet of salvation and the sword of the Spirit, which is the word of God. And pray in the Spirit on all occasions with all kinds of prayers and requests. With this in mind, be alert and always keep on praying for all the saints.

---

[1] Nadine Broznan, "Witness Says She Fears 'Child Predator' Network," *New York Times*, 18 September 1984, A21.

[2] Clifford Linedecker, *Children in Chains* (New York: Everest House, 1981), 119.

[3] Interim Report, Sixty-sixth Legislative Session, Select Committee on Child Pornography: Its Related Causes and Control (Washington), 21-22.

[4] Linedecker, *Children in Chains*, 32.

[5] Shirley O'Brien, *Child Pornography* (Dubuque, Ia.: Kendal/Hunt Publishing Co., 1983), 9.

[6] Ibid., 83.

[7] Joan Sweeney, "The Child Molester: No Profile," *Los Angeles Times*, 25 April 1984, 1.

[8] O'Brien, *Child Pornography*, 139.

Chapter Fourteen

THE MYTH OF SAFE SEX

T he grave consequence of America's sexual revolution, started by the entertainment industry, explicit sex education teachers, and pornographers, is the ever-increasing problem of sexually transmitted diseases (STDs) that are infecting large numbers of people. It is estimated that as many as twenty-one million Americans now suffer from incurable genital herpes (Herpes Simplex II); approximately one million men and women contract gonorrhea each year; and more than 100,000 cases of syphilis are recorded annually. These are the *reported cases*. In addition, we are now facing one of the most serious threats of all: the AIDS epidemic. The disease is now spreading into the heterosexual community, and among hemophiliacs and others who receive contaminated blood transfusions.

On April 1, 1993, the *New York Times* carried on its front page the results of the latest Guttmacher Institute Report that "56 million people in the United States are infected with a sexually transmitted disease." More than half of these infections are incurable. That means that one out of five Americans has a STD! Those who engage in casual sex, which is a euphemism for promiscuity, are playing sexual roulette with their bodies. Every fourth person with whom they have sex could be a carrier of an incurable disease. If one in ten airplane flights crashed, no one would be flying today. Yet high risk sex is being engaged in thousands of times every night. We have only begun to see the tragic results of our modern sexual revolution. Obviously, with as many as 56 million carriers of sexually transmitted diseases in our country, this epidemic is beginning to resemble the end-time plagues described in the Book of Revelation.

According to King Holmes, former president of the American Venereal Disease Association, "There are twenty or more genital infections known to be spread by sexual intercourse, and the incidence of several has been increasing at epidemic rates during the last decade."[1] The most dangerous, of course, are gonorrhea, syphilis, genital herpes, and AIDS.

> Each year, an estimated 12 million cases of STDs occur in the United States. The exact number is not known, because many infections are not routinely reported to health authorities, and many asymptomatic infections are not readily diagnosed. In recent years, the spectrum of STDs has broadened substantially to include infections caused by more than 20 pathogens including bacteria, viruses, and parasites.... Syphilis has risen dramatically during the past three years.[2]

There is no such thing as "safe sex" outside of marriage. Even then safe sex within marriage requires that your child's spouse be a virgin, which is what this book is really all about. Sexual abstinence before marriage is not just our idea or the Bible's. It is the position of most responsible medical experts. The deputy assistant secretary for population affairs in Washington, a medical doctor, said, "Abstinence is the only sure way our young people can be protected from pregnancy and the ravages of AIDS and other sexually transmitted diseases."[3]

Josh McDowell, after reporting on the alarming rise in STDs and AIDS, said, "At this rate one in every four Americans between the ages of 15 and 55 eventually will get a sexually transmitted disease."[4] Then he quoted a University of California medical doctor who said, "Teenagers have more STDs than any other group in the United States." Some of these diseases, particularly AIDS, have an incubation period of three to thirteen years. Some of the teens your child goes to school with may be carriers and not know it.

A girl who attended one of our discussion groups for high schoolers said she had been sexually active since she was fourteen. She had sex with so many boys—"at least twenty!"—she had lost count. At sixteen, she received Christ and became active in the youth group and was living a chaste life. Such a girl may not know whether she is carrying an STD virus or not and may fall in love with your virtuous son. Now you see why blood tests are often required for marriage. Such tests should be taken several months before the wedding invitations are sent out, particularly in cases where infection is a serious possibility.

No Safe Sex Apart from Virtue

Young people today need to be taught that premarital sex is risky business. The public school and media campaign urging young people to use condoms to have safe sex (even giving them out freely in school, which gives school sanction to sexual activity) is a big lie! As Dr. Robert C. Noble, professor of medicine at University of Kentucky College of Medicine, said in an article in Newsweek magazine, "There is no safe sex" (meaning outside of marriage). He was reacting to a TV show that ridiculed the "prudish woman who advocated abstinence among teenagers" with whom he agreed. He said, "What do I know about all this? I'm an infectious-diseases physician and an AIDS doctor to the poor. Passing out condoms to teenagers is like issuing them squirt guns for a four-alarm blaze. Condoms just don't hack it; we should stop kidding ourselves." Then Dr. Noble told the story of a twenty-one-year-old boy he was taking care of who was dying of AIDS. "He could have been the model for Donatello's David...long blond hair, deep blue eyes, as sweet as he could be. His mom is in shock. He called her the other day and told her two things: 'I'm gay and I've got AIDS.' His lover looks like a fellow you would see in Sunday school. He has had sex with only one person!" And that is all it takes.[5]

There are two principles that all young people need to know: 1) Whenever you have sex with a person it is the same health risk as having sex with all the people that person has had sex with during the past ten years, and 2) condoms are not safe! Even the manufacturers do not claim condoms are safe but admit to a failure or breakage rate of anywhere from 4 to 14 percent. Besides, most people do not use condoms when having sex. As Dr. Noble said, "In the heat of passion, the brain shuts down. You have to use a condom every time. Every time. That is 'hard to do.'" Then he pointed out that after fifteen years of education on STDs in school and college, only "41 percent of college women surveyed in '89 said they used them every time."

Even when condoms are used every time, they are not safe. That is why the new commissioner of the Federal Drug Administration, Dr.

David Kessler, has announced that all condom manufacturers must state on their packaging that their products do not protect against sexually transmitted diseases. Their products just aren't safe. In one test of married couples that used condoms every time they had sex, 10 percent of the women got pregnant. Evidently the sperm were able to penetrate the pores of the condom. That is a scary fact, for the germs that cause STDs are even smaller than sperm.

When I asked the high school students in our discussion groups why they thought their friends were ignoring the well-advertised dangers of promiscuous sex, their response was, "They don't think they'll get caught." Most young people have an immortality complex—bad things just will not happen to them. Our eighteen-year-old grandson recently cartwheeled off his motorcycle at sixty miles an hour and broke his neck. He had six-hour surgery to fuse three vertebrae together and was in an uncomfortable body cast for three months. He came within an eyelash of being paralyzed for life. I asked him, "Josh, are you going to sell your motorcycle?" He replied "Not on your life. I'm looking forward to riding as soon as the doctor gives his okay." (He has decided to give up competitive racing.) Adults read stories like that and say, "They're crazy!" No, they're just young. I can think of some pretty dumb things I did at that age too, can't you?

You cannot make choices for your children. You can only give them sufficient information in the hopes that in those crucial situations in life—even those mad moments of passion—they will make the right choices. But they cannot do that without the right information. They need to know about these contagious diseases before they venture out into today's dangerous social world. Included in the glossary to this book are brief descriptions of some of the most common diseases you should be familiar with. This listing will help you properly instruct your teen about the dangers of illicit sex. We suggest you take an hour sometime and go over these diseases with your teen and discuss this important subject with them.

Your teenagers or young adults need never fear any form of sexually transmitted disease if they obey the Word of God concerning sexual conduct. Only those who are sexually promiscuous and immoral risk getting STDs and causing harm to many other people by spreading the disease through sexual intercourse. I wonder how many unfaithful husbands have given their wives incurable herpes? Or how many unfaithful women have infected their unborn babies with venereal disease? My counseling experience suggests there are far more than most people realize.

The spread of STDs in our society is the penalty for discarding God's clear teachings on sexual matters. Perhaps the most frightening STD is AIDS, which is reaching out to destroy not only the sexually promiscuous but the innocent as well.

The world's answer to these dangerous diseases is more government-funded research or condom distribution and the well-advertised "safe sex." But, as we have already seen, condoms do not make for safe sex, a fact now so commonly known, educators are calling the use of condoms "safer sex."

God has given young people a better model: it is called virtue. Former Surgeon General C. Everett Koop said at a school administrators conference, "Sexual abstinence is a very good idea for youngsters of school age. Today—in the presence of the deadly AIDS epidemic—I think we, as adults, must step forward and help our children address the phenomenon of their own sexuality in a caring, developmental way." Part of the caring way he had in mind is to confront them with the dangers of promiscuity.

With fifty-six million carriers of STDs in our society and with as many as twelve million new cases springing up each year, someone should warn these children about the extremely high risk these diseases pose to young developing bodies. Who better than the people who love them most: their moms and dads. When your virgin son or virtuous daughter walks down the aisle to marry Mr. or Miss Right, you will have no regrets that you sounded that warning, for abstinence before marriage and fidelity afterward is the only way to assure "safe sex."

---

[1] Eric W. Johnson, V.D. (Philadelphia: J.B. Lippincott, 1978), 7.

[2] Katherine M. Stone, "Avoiding Sexually Transmitted Diseases," *Obstetrics and Gynecology Clinics of North America*, 17 (1990).

[3] Private letter, 17 January 1992.

[4] Josh McDowell, *The Myth of Sex Education* (San Bernardino, Calif.: Here's Life Publishers, 1987), 159.

[5] *Newsweek*, 1 April 1991.

Chapter Fifteen

WHAT TO DO IF YOUR WORST NIGHTMARE COMES TRUE

Can you visualize coming down to breakfast some morning to find this note on the kitchen table?

> *Daddy, I'm pregnant. I'm sorry—I'm so sorry. Please don't hate me!*

A pastor named Bill had an experience like that. His fourteen-year-old daughter burst into his bedroom at 2:00 A.M. and sobbed out those very words. The good news is that God faithfully guided this pastor and his family through that traumatic and enormously painful experience.

Imagine their hurt as they stood with their daughter in front of the whole church as she voluntarily confessed her sin and told how she had repented and sought God's gracious forgiveness. We were moved by his testimony that the leaders of the church came forward after her plea for their forgiveness to stand with them and express their love for the girl and her family. We had a church with that kind of grace; would to God all pastors did.

In spite of being engulfed in her parents' love and that of the church, that young girl's life was changed forever. Her education was disrupted, her body began to change, her relationships were different, she was bothered by shame, and for nine months she and her parents were forced to face that awful decision: "What do we do with the baby?"

Pastor Bill kept a journal throughout his daughter's pregnancy and later had it published under the title, *Daddy, I'm Pregnant* (Multnomah Press). If you know anyone who is going through such an experience, I suggest you give them a copy of the book. The Bible tells us that we can "comfort those in any trouble with the comfort we ourselves have received from God" (2 Cor 1:4). I also encourage you to read the book for yourself. It will inspire you to be gently aggressive about instructing your children early, enforcing their dating rules, and helping them make a commitment to virtue. You can be sure Pastor Bill and his wife never believed their child would have sex so young, much less get pregnant.

That Girl Is Not Alone

Over 1.1 million teenagers will get pregnant this year, many of them younger than the child mentioned above. Some of these girls will come from the finest Christian families. As pastor of a large church with a strong youth ministry to help young people develop their spiritual lives, I still saw such tragedies happen.

A lovely Christian girl from one of the finest families in our church came to see me one afternoon and said, "Pastor, I'm pregnant! I only had sex with my boyfriend one time. This is going to kill my parents. Will you come with me when I tell them?"

"My daughter is pregnant and she is only seventeen!" wept a broken-hearted mother. "What should I do?"

"My son just got his girlfriend pregnant and they are both still in high school. What should we do?" mourned another parent.

These cries for help are real, and they are not uncommon. Almost every pastor has heard them several times. Many parents fear an unwed pregnancy. When it happens, one of their first reactions is to place blame. "Where did we go wrong?" or "Why did the church fail us?" But it is a waste of time to fix blame. A parent can do everything right and still be faced with moral tragedy.

Preventing Pregnancy Out of Wedlock

There is no foolproof way for parents to prevent a teen pregnancy, for everything still depends on our children's exercise of their free will. Many Christians have done everything right in raising their children only to see them rebel—even for a moment. Sometimes that is all it takes to steal their virtue and plunge them into the world of adult problems.

No one can watch over his teen twenty-four hours a day. However, the percentage of teen pregnancies is much lower in families in which parents have properly prepared their children for this tempestuous phase of life. In addition to such careful teaching, here are some qualities that we believe will help teens resist the temptations of promiscuity and avoid unwanted pregnancies:

- A warm, loving relationship between parents;
- Strong Christian beliefs that are practiced in the home;
- The parental sex training we have presented in this book that treats sexuality as normal and beautiful and provides relaxed communication on the subject between children and parents;
- Thorough instruction from the Word of God that makes God's moral standards clear;
- A consistent avoidance of sexually debasing TV programs, movies, magazines, or conversation in or out of the home;
- Close surveillance of a teen's friends that prohibits fellowship with those who do not share your values;
- Adherence to rules for dating;
- Active participation in church and youth group activities;
- The commitment to virtue described in chapter 8;
- A consistent teaching of responsibility in all areas of life;
- An abundance of parental prayer.

Following these guidelines will reduce the likelihood of your teens becoming sexually active before marriage. But remember, these guidelines do not guarantee that your teen will abstain from sexual activity; they still have a free will.

"It's the Nice Girls Who Get Pregnant"

A disconsolate father called and identified himself as a supporter of our ministry. He said he was a medical doctor and an active member of his church. Then he said, "My oldest daughter will be seventeen next month and she is pregnant. She is a straight-A student with only one year of high school left. Would it be possible for you to let her come to San Diego and attend your Christian high school? I will be happy to pay for her board and room with a Christian family. She said it was the first and only time she ever had sex...and I believe her." I told her father that it is usually the nice girls who get pregnant. Permissive girls go on dates equipped to avoid pregnancy.

This fine Christian girl committed a sin of passion that almost ruined her life. Like thousands of other teenagers, she and her steady boyfriend began making out one night during the most fertile part of her monthly cycle. At that time a young woman's emotions are often highly combustible, and hers got out of control. One kiss led to another, and she did what she never dreamed she would do. Kissing led to petting, petting led to intercourse (the Law of Progression), and she came home feeling very guilty. Five weeks later, she discovered she was pregnant.

It was this unfortunate girl's lot to commit a sin that carries with it the heaviest consequences. In her case it was "8 pounds, 7 ounces" and much heartache for her and every member of her family. The girl stayed in her parents' home until she was four months along. By that time she could no longer keep her condition secret, so she came to San Diego to live with a Christian family in our church. We arranged private tutoring so she could finish the eleventh grade in time to return home and graduate with her class after the birth of her child.

This Christian girl had made a dreadful mistake that was entirely out of character for her. She was a spiritual girl with a sincere desire to serve the Lord. Her loving, supportive parents testified, "She has never been a rebellious daughter and has never given us a moment of trouble before." Fortunately, she repented of her sin, sought God's direction in her life, and today is a well-adjusted Christian wife and mother.

Could this ever happen to your daughter? Given the right circumstances, a Christian is vulnerable to any sin if he or she makes the first compromise. That is why the Bible teaches that playing with sin is extremely dangerous. Teens need to be taught to avoid sin rather than try to get as close to it as possible without getting burned. Those who take the risks usually get burned.

What Should a Parent Do?

We have counseled many Christian families through teenage pregnancies and have made some observations on how to handle the situation. First and foremost, face the problem head-on without recriminations and accusations. "How could you do such a thing?" is no way to greet a daughter when she makes that tragic announcement. If ever she needed love and acceptance, it is at that moment. She is terrified and guilt-stricken enough. She needs to know that God forgives her (if she repents), and she needs her parents' forgiveness. It may be difficult for her to understand and accept God's forgiveness if she does not receive forgiveness from her parents.

One of the saddest cases we have dealt with concerned an eighteen-year-old girl in the youth group of our church. The girl's father was so angry and humiliated that he kicked her out of the house and never let her return. She became angry and rebellious toward her father and toward God. The situation eventually destroyed her life and her parents' marriage.

True love is unconditional. At a time like this, a girl needs to know that, like the Prodigal Son, she is continually loved by her parents. We love our children because they are our children, not because they do everything right. It is important that parents show that although this was their daughter's sin, they will help her through this trial. As tragic as it is, this is not the end of her life. Thousands of young women have risen above this kind of crisis to live effective and useful lives. But this is much easier when she has loving, supportive parents.

Should She Marry the Father?

Should a pregnant girl marry the father of her unborn child? In some cases she should. But not in every instance. If the father is unsaved, she definitely should not marry him. That would violate Scripture (2 Cor. 6:14) and may well sentence her to a lifetime of marital misery. If the couple are both Christians and had been engaged or were talking about marriage, and if both parents concur, it may be wise to speed up their wedding plans.

Most of the time, however, a decision to marry because of pregnancy only means following one giant mistake with an even bigger one. The divorce rate is catastrophic among young people who decided to marry due to pregnancy. Marriage interferes with their educational and vocational potential. It usually thrusts the young man into the marketplace without adequate skills or the opportunity to develop them; it forces him to try to support a family on minimum wages that will barely sustain one life. Such a couple have two strikes against them before they even begin to live as a family.

It is far better for the couple to deal with the consequences of the unplanned pregnancy as best they can and seek as much as possible to resume normal lives. Although pregnancy without marriage is a tragedy for all concerned, it is not the end of the world. Placing the responsibilities of marriage and parenting on teenagers is rarely the best solution.

What about the Father?

Occasionally I have counseled young women who were so promiscuous that they did not know who had fathered their child. That is not usually the case. Most girls have no problem identifying the father of their child. So what about the father? It is very important that he not abdicate his responsibility for this new life.

We recommend that the father of the girl arrange a meeting with all the people concerned—the two young people and their parents. At that meeting the boy and his parents need to be confronted with his sin, though not in a judgmental way, like the Pharisees who wanted to stone only the woman taken in adultery. (Obviously two people are involved in this sin.) The boy's parents must know what he has done; if he is a minor, they are responsible for him.

The boy needs first of all to recognize his actions as sinful and repent of them. Shame and guilt often encourage repentance and turning to the Lord. If the boy is saved, this should cause him to turn back to Christ; if he is unsaved, he needs to accept the Savior. He and his parents also need to acknowledge the lack of moral standards. If properly counseled, this young man can become motivated to live a productive life with a new respect for the sanctity of sex and the importance of self-control. If he rejects the offers to repent, he is likely to continue to misuse his sexuality.

Is Abortion an Option?

The standard argument for those who allow abortion is that it can be performed legally and safely in a hospital. In one month's time the whole crisis of a pregnancy out of wedlock would be over.

Abortion may be legal, but it is not morally right. Regardless of what the justices of the U.S. Supreme Court decided in 1973, abortion is murder. It is not an option for the Christian family.

An unmarried couple dealing with pregnancy desperately need the blessing and guidance of God. The last thing they should do is add murder to fornication. Besides, the crisis wouldn't be over in a month. Abortion advocates do not warn women that post-abortion depression is very common. I have conducted funeral services for women who have committed suicide after having abortions. Moreover, women who have had abortions tend to have more difficulty sustaining a pregnancy later on; some have to forego motherhood altogether. Many women carry their guilt to the grave. As difficult as it is to carry an unwanted pregnancy to full term, it is far better than suffering the weight of abortion guilt for a lifetime.

At the first Washington conference of Concerned Women for America (CWA), Beverly, the president of CWA, presented a graphic prolife film that showed an actual abortion being performed. Before the showing to the twenty-one hundred women was completed, twenty-seven of them left the room, weeping. One fled screaming, "They lied to me! They didn't tell me it was like that!" All twenty-seven of these women had had abortions, some of them many years before. None of them could handle the guilt of knowing they had killed another human being. Only by asking God's forgiveness through His Son's death on the cross is there cleansing for their sin and peace with God (see 1 John 1:7,9).

Who Should Pay?

We believe the boy and his parents should pay *all* the medical and preliminary expenses of his child. This should include the cost of prenatal care, hospital delivery, doctor's fees, board and room for the girl if she goes to another city to have the child, and travel costs. The total expense may reach $2,500 or more, but we consider it imperative that the young man assume full responsibility for them.

A girl pays a price in nine months of carrying the child, the shame, pain, and estrangement from her family, and in postnatal care. The least the boy should pay are the expenses. He may have to borrow the money from his parents until he can earn it. It will do him no good to avoid his responsibility by ignoring the girl's plight or by letting his parents bear the financial consequences of his actions.

If he and his parents refuse to bear this responsibility, the girls' parents have two options. If he is unsaved and refuses, they should hire a good attorney and force him to bear the expenses. If the boy's family are Christians and refuse, then they should be taken before the church. A group of church leaders of his congregation and the girl's church (if they attend different churches) should sit in counsel and make a binding declaration. It is not in the boy's best interest to let him avoid financial responsibility for what he has done.

Should She Adopt Out or Keep the Child?

The big question my broken-hearted doctor friend had to face was should his daughter offer the baby for adoption by a Christian couple, or should she raise the child herself? Since I first began counseling people in this kind of situation, there has been a complete reversal in social practice. Thirty years ago a single woman almost never kept her child. Today many of them do. A recent survey indicated that 90 percent of unwed mothers keep their children. Some unwed mothers do so to increase their welfare payments. Others are so love-starved that they keep the baby because they need to love and to feel loved. We believe it is in the best interest of the child to find a Christian couple who is praying for a child and allow them to adopt the child. At this point, the child's concerns are the most important.

In the case of the doctor's daughter, I urged her to keep her local friends from knowing anything about her condition, to have her baby miles away from home, and to let us help her find a Christian couple who would seek adoption. When she asked, "Why shouldn't I keep my baby?" I offered the following reasons:

1. *Single parenthood is not the biblical model.* Ideally, all children need two Christian parents to love them and give them a balanced home, training, and example. When the time comes for the youngster to marry and raise a family, he will have been exposed to a biblical role model. God will provide for the widow or unwillingly divorced mother who is left to raise children alone, but we are not certain He will make up the difference when a young woman deliberately chooses that lifestyle to satisfy her own desire to have a child.

2. *Difficult to provide basic needs.* An unwed mother will probably have a difficult time providing even the basic essentials of life for her baby. In all probability, she will not be able to support her child's needs for a higher education and adequate training to reach his potential. Her decision could seriously limit the vocational potential of her child.

3. *Marriage opportunities are limited.* The mother's opportunities for finding a Christian husband are sharply reduced. I know of several happy cases where a Christian man has married a single mother and adopted her child. But this is the exception, not the rule. Usually her motherhood would be a hindrance to her meeting and getting to know eligible men so that a love relationship could develop.

4. *Best for the fulfillment of God's purposes.* Motherhood will probably limit a single woman's finding "the perfect will of God" for her life. Placing the child for adoption has traditionally served the best interests of the baby and provided a means for the mother to pick up the pieces of her life, resume her education, and prepare herself as "an instrument for noble

purposes, made holy, useful to the Master" (2 Tim. 2:21). In the long run, it is usually best for the fulfillment of God's purposes in both the mother's and child's lives to allow a Christian couple to adopt the child.

5. *Best for child's psychological development.* Most of a woman's reasons for keeping the child are selfish. Many unwed mothers who kept their children have told me, "I need someone to love." Many young women grow up today starved for love and turn to their fatherless children to fill that need. This kind of love can lead to a "smother" kind of love that often has a harmful effect on a child's psychological development.

Probably the hardest thing for a young mother to do is to place her child for adoption. But when all the facts are considered, most Christian young women decide that it is the best course of action. It is certainly better for a woman to go into her marriageable years unencumbered by children. Her life will go on, and her natural yearnings to share her life with someone else will grow. Besides, in a real sense, all parents raise their children for someone else. For a mother of sixteen or seventeen to decide to keep her child may someday prove to be costly. Even if she has the best of intentions, she may find herself alone again while she is still in her thirties.

One word of caution: *Make sure* the children are adopted into Christian families that will raise them with the same spiritual values you hold. Once assured of that, you can commit the children to God and get on with the rest of life.

My doctor friend's daughter took that advice. We found her son a fine Christian family, and she went back home and finished high school and college. Giving her son up for adoption was a heartrending decision, but she did it, and most of the time she knows in her heart it was the right choice.

Should She Tell Her Prospective Husband?

Should a single mother who adopts out her child tell her prospective husband about her past? There is no universal answer to that question. Some young men are mature enough to handle that knowledge, and some are not. If the woman has successfully kept her experience a secret and there is little likelihood it will ever be revealed, it is probably best not to tell him. In most cases, however, someone could inadvertently let the truth out.

For this reason, we usually suggest that the woman tell her suitor the truth but only after he asks for her hand in marriage. She should *not* reveal it to just any man with whom she gets serious. If a Christian man falls in love with her and proposes marriage, she owes him the truth. Indeed, this disclosure can be a good test of how much he truly loves her. He will feel disappointed and disillusioned when she first tells him, but if he really loves her, he will realize that, by God's grace, she is not the same person today that she was as a teenager. He needs to see her as the godly woman she has become. If he rejects her because of this knowledge, she can reasonably conclude that his legalistic rigidity would have made him difficult to live with anyway.

Guilt and the Loss of Self-esteem

Guilt seriously weakens self-esteem, particularly for the Christian woman who has made the mistake of having sex out of wedlock. This sin, like any other, can be forgiven, but two conditions accentuate the problem of guilt: The church's standards of virtue and morality, and the highly public aspect of pregnancy. We have indicated a way for unwed girls to maintain secrecy during pregnancy, but even at best this is difficult.

For these and other reasons, a Christian unwed mother is likely to have a difficult time regaining her self-respect and rebuilding a strong self-image. She is confronted with the fact of her sin every day for at least nine months. By the time her baby is born, her self-image may be at an all time low. That is one reason why her family should not condemn her once she has acknowledged her sin and received God's forgiveness. She needs their reassurance that making the youthful mistake of engaging in premarital sex does not indicate a permanent character flaw. Who of us as adults would like to be judged on the basis of our behavior as teenagers?

Many young people have let God use the experience of parenthood out of wedlock to prove their dependence on Him for grace and power to become godly adults. This tragic experience is not the end of a person's life. With God's help and adherence to His principles for living, they can become strong in the Lord and in the power of His might.

A Change in Dating Policy

After the unwed parenthood is dealt with as suggested, one more thing must be considered: prevention against reoccurrence. This experience should teach both the boy and girl about the weakness of the flesh and the high cost of sin. Such a lesson should warn them and their parents that new standards of behavior must be followed carefully, and neither person should ever again get physically involved with the opposite sex before marriage. True love never requires sex in order to develop. Lust demands sex. A relationship built on physical attraction will cloud the other attributes and confuse even the most mature judgment. Sin is always avoided best by reducing the opportunities for temptation.

A Beautiful Story

As a woman spoke to me between sessions at a Family Life Seminar in Virginia, I had the feeling I had seen her before. She assured me we had never met. Then she asked if I recalled a handsome young man from my former pastorate in San Diego. Yes, I did. I even remembered when he was a baby and had watched him grow to be a fine young man. I expected that one day he might go into the ministry.

The woman shocked me by saying, "I am his mother!"

"How could that be?" I asked. I knew his parents well, for they were active members in my congregation. But as I looked into her face, it was almost like looking at the young man she claimed was her son.

Then she told me her story. When she was a young, single girl, she got pregnant and placed her son for adoption. Later she married and had three other children, but she never forgot her son. About fifteen years after the adoption, she received Christ and was totally transformed. A year later her husband was saved. One night she had a dream that so disturbed her, both she and her husband woke up. She was so distraught, her husband urged her to talk about it. So she told him about her teenage pregnancy and confessed her great concern that her son become a Christian.

At the urging of her understanding and loving husband, she began a vigorous search for her son and somehow traced him to San Diego. Imagine how thrilled she was to discover that in the providence of God, her son had been adopted by Christian parents who had known Christ longer than she had! Since their reunion the young man has spent half of one summer getting acquainted with his natural mother and half-brothers and sisters. Both sets of parents became good friends though they live three thousand miles apart. At last, that mother's heart was at peace.

All parents of unwed mothers, as well as the mothers themselves, should remember an important principle when contemplating placing their children for adoption by Christian parents. Jesus said, "Let the little children come to me, and do not hinder them, for the kingdom of heaven belongs to such as these" (Matt. 19:14). Jesus is more interested in bringing these children to Himself than we are. Do the best you can to select the best Christian home, and then leave the rest up to God.

Chapter Sixteen

SINGLE PARENTS WANT VIRTUOUS CHILDREN, TOO

One of the phenomena of our times is the rise in single-parent families. The reasons are legion, from death to divorce to irresponsibility. Eight out of ten single parents are women; the others are fathers or grandparents. Most of these have the same dreams for their young as the couples we address in this book. The women may or may not receive financial support, but most have to go out into the marketplace to work. That almost always puts a greater strain on child raising, including promoting sexual purity.

Both of us were raised by single parents for part of our lives; our fathers died when we were both young. Bev's father died when she was two, leaving her mother with Bev and Bev's four-year-old sister. Years later her mother married again, giving her the experience of being raised by a mother and stepfather and sharing her growing up years with a half-brother and sister. My father died when I was nine, leaving my mother with me, a five-year-old daughter, and a seven-week-old son. Mother was twenty-eight years old at the time of my father's death. She never married again, but by trusting God and working hard she gave us as great a childhood as she could.

Both Bev and I thank our parents for giving us the greatest of all gifts. Early in life, they led us to Christ and involved us in the church. For this and other blessings we are eternally grateful. We know what love and sacrifice on the part of parents is all about—we saw it in our mothers. Neither of them taught us about sex. It wasn't fashionable in those days, but neither was it as necessary as it is today. Both, however, taught us about virtue. We were Christians and sexual purity was the standard; nothing else was acceptable. They paid the price to keep us active in Bible-believing churches where their values could be fortified by other adult figures.

Our single mothers did a good job in their day, but that is not enough today. Single parents must accept the challenge to be the primary teachers of sexuality to their children. We are confident they too can raise sexually pure children in this sex-obsessed age.

God Is the Father of the Fatherless

One of the treasured promises in the Bible to single parents is Psalm 68:5, where we are commanded to praise God for he is "a father to the fatherless, a defender of widows." Men can take comfort from this verse too, for scripture teaches that "God is no respecter of persons." He doesn't protect just the widow, but will help the godly single father who wants to raise his children to love and serve God, too. But let's face it, most single men marry again. They seem to have a harder time coping with loneliness and can, more easily than women, seek out another companion. Besides, there do not seem to be as many godly men available as there are godly women, and no woman who wants to raise virtuous children who grow up to love and serve God should settle for anything less.

It should be a comfort to all single parents that God will be there for their children to provide the emotional and spiritual support they need. Instead of letting the feelings of hopelessness overcome them, they need to seek God's help in the raising of their children and trust Him to provide what they lack. That is His promise. We have a hunch that when single parents pray for their children, they are doubly effective.

In this day of well-advertised sexual perversion, it is important for single mothers to understand that they can raise "sexually straight" sons. When single mothers see a boy raised by one parent become a homosexual, they often fear that will happen to their child. They forget that most homosexuals were raised by two parents. Children can understand when Dad or Mom are not in the home; what fouls them up sexually is lack of love from a parent who *is* in the home. While it is ideal for a boy to have a father in the home or for a girl to experience being "a daddy's girl," life is not always ideal. God will make up for the lack of the ideal, so trust Him to do so.

Your Attitude Is the Principal Thing

Parents set the pace in the home by their attitude. If you let the loss of a partner or the rejection of a mate through divorce make you bitter, you can destroy your children. If you gripe and indulge in self-pity, you will raise bitter, griping, and rebellious kids. That is why the Bible challenges us to a life of thanksgiving (1 Thess. 5:18). Teach your children to be praisers and thankers for the good things of God.

We have worked with young people long enough to know that they reflect the attitude of their parents. (Any experienced youth pastor can tell the attitude of the parents in the home by observing the attitude of their kids.) This is particularly true of divorced single parents. Usually there is a degree of hostility at being rejected, but hostility is a very expensive emotion. If a parent tries to turn her children against the former spouse, she will negate all the good things she does for them. Angry children do not make obedient children. If you are a single parent as the result of a divorce, you must come to grips with forgiving your former mate to adequately convey love to your children.

If we could say only one thing to all divorced single parents it is this: Try to make friends with your former partner for your children's sake. Divorce is always hard on children. It may even propel some into early sexual activity out of rebellion or because they are love-starved and think sex will provide love. This usually ends up making them bitter when they wake up to the fact that they have been used. Friendly relations between former partners will reduce (not eliminate) the harmful effects of a tragic divorce. The bottom line is forgiveness. The best thing a divorced single parent can do for her children and herself is to forgive the former spouse, even when he does not deserve it.

Ephesians 4:32 teaches that we are to forgive others "just as in Christ God forgave [us]." Our Lord even tied our own forgiveness to our ability to forgive others by saying that if we do not forgive others, we will not be forgiven (Matt. 6:14-15). So be sure you win the battle of forgiveness. Then teach the principles from chapter 2 on how to raise virtuous children, just as you would if both parents were in the home.

Remember, while the ideal may be two parents united on the teaching of their children about sex, love, and dating, most people are not experiencing the ideal. At best only half the homes have two natural parents to do the teaching, and many of these do not agree on the standards, dating age, church attendance, and many of the other things covered in that chapter. Single parents do have one advantage, even though they have to do all the teaching—they don't have someone else in the home to undermine or disagree with their teaching and standards.

So be as aggressive as any couple in teaching your children early. Work at being shockproof and always open to discuss the subject, even with your children of the opposite sex. Also remember that just because your children may appear embarrassed or noncommittal or even secretive, couples have those same problems with their children. Single parents sometimes assume that any adverse reactions to their teaching about sex or discipline of their teen is because they are a single parent. If they would look around, they would find that couples often have some of the same problems.

Take Time to Love Them

The greatest gift single parents can give their children is love, and that is well within the capability of every parent. Too many parents think they must work hard to provide the things of this world, but love is the greatest thing they can provide their children.

Naturally, children benefit from the love of two parents, but if it is impossible to receive the love of both a mother and father, children understand that as they mature. Your love, as long as they get it, is enough for their emotional development.

My personal sense of security has come from the love of my godly mother. Because of her, I cannot remember not being loved. We were poor, but I do not remember that. I enjoyed childhood because I knew the love of a parent. Even though my brother, sister, and I have different temperaments, we all have the same sense of self-acceptance. Our mother's love made us feel good about ourselves. We did not have to engage in premarital sex in a misguided search for love and self-acceptance.

Our friend Dr. William Bennett, former secretary of education, and his brother were raised by a single mother because of an unfortunate divorce. He has said of his childhood, "I'm sure there were times my mother wished she had help in raising us, particularly as we grew older and bigger. But she gave us plenty of love and taught us family values that prepared us for life." He and his brother are just two more testimonies to the fact that one loving parent can do the job with God's help.

Children do not automatically obey and respect their parents; they must be taught respect and obedience when they are young. Single parents need to start early and be aggressive. Teach them to live by your values and give them lots of love. With God's help you will make the difference in their life.

Teach Them by Example

Just like married couples, single parents need to back up what they teach and what they expect of their children by the example of their lifestyle. You cannot teach your children to be virtuous unless you practice virtue yourself. This is particularly important if after an appropriate time you begin dating again. Make sure your conduct is "above reproach." Your children can learn to accept your dating. Even when they rail against it, they can understand your need to have companionship with the opposite sex. But be sure of this—they will watch your every move. You need to be able at all times to look them in the eye and show them that you have a "conscience void of offense." If you do not, all your training will be for naught, and you will end up with an even greater load of guilt if they use your behavior as an excuse to break their virtue vow.

What to do if you've already blown it. What is a parent to do if in a mad moment of passion, he violated God's law and his marital commitment? I asked that question of a dear friend whose wife divorced him four years ago when he admitted to infidelity. The day came when his handsome sixteen-year-old son told him that a cute girl at school had approached him and said, "I would like to have sex with you." So this loving father, now fully repentant and living a "straight arrow life," challenged his son to be a virgin when he got married. The boy angrily turned on his dad and accused him of his former sin. He said to his son, "Son, what I did was 100 percent wrong. God has forgiven me, but as you know, your mother can't. I have regretted that sin every day since then. But that is no excuse for you to follow my bad example. If anyone should know the tragic consequences of that sin it is you. You can remember when we had a loving family, and you can remember that my sin destroyed our home, separated us, and has brought nothing but heartache and tragedy. I don't want that kind of life for you. I pray to God that you will be a virgin when you marry and that you will be faithful to each other all your lives so you can avoid the suffering we have all experienced."

It's better never to have to make such a soul-wrenching confession to your children. To avoid that, set an example of how a single parent should live in relation to all others. Be sure of this, they will be watching!

Many people have been raised by a single parent for most of their childhood. I have found them in almost every walk of life. Many of those I have met are very successful and have happy homes. The one common denominator for those who seem most well adjusted is that they did not lack for love during their impressionable, growing-up years.

With God's help, you too can raise virtuous children who will grow to love and serve God. It will take eighteen to twenty years of your life, but it takes two parents the same investment of time. You will be glad someday that you spent your time wisely.

YOU
CAN
DO IT

Sexual purity has always been the "perfect will of God" for our children, but never has it been more important to raise children to be virgins when they marry. Today, almost everyone knows about the deadly disease of AIDS and many of the other sexually transmitted diseases. In addition, just this week, USA *Today* and other media released reports that cancer increases alarmingly among women who have had abortions, one of the unfortunate consequences of promiscuity. Furthermore, there is no way a young person can be sexually permissive and spiritual at the same time—and spiritual sensitivity is especially crucial when our sons and daughters are making the major decisions that will chart the course of their lives. These are just some of the reasons why raising our children virtuous is worth the effort.

Yes, raising virtuous children most definitely requires effort. Thanks to the media, the entertainment industry, public school sex educators, and a government policy that finances abortions for any reason, often without parental consent, parents are left to pick up the pieces and pay the runaway bills sexual promiscuity creates.

Raising virtuous children is harder today, but it can still be done by loving, determined parents. These parents arm their children with the facts of their sexuality early, protect them from the wrong kind of peers, set clear guidelines for dating, and keep them out of public school sex education classes taught by adults who hold anti-Christian values so destructive to society.

There are signs that virtue is slowly being reconsidered as a viable alternative to the "anything goes" mentality of the world. That mentality has bred not only disease and illegitimate babies by the millions, but has also brought unbelievable amounts of heartache and suffering to young people who were cheated out of their childhood. "Children having children," is more than a cover story for *Newsweek* magazine. It is a tragedy of life for millions of girls and their unfortunate children. Last year alone 1,165,000 unwed teenagers became pregnant, an all-time record.

Recently a baby-faced girl of sixteen, who admitted to having sex occasionally with her boyfriend, lamented to the *Washington Post*: "Everything you see is sex, sex, sex…. You turn on the TV and see somebody having sex. It's in music videos and every movie…it's like not having sex isn't even a possibility." Our culture claims to be "sophisticated about sex," (we think "obsessed" is more accurate), but such "sophistication" has consequences—unwed pregnancies and STDs, heartache and sorrow, broken dreams and psychological scars that may last a lifetime.

The consequences of sex before marriage put sex into the "high risk behavior" category today; we want better for our children. For that reason, we teach them the merits of virtue, which has no adverse consequences. Among the thousands I have counseled through the years, many about sexual dysfunction, never have I heard a person complain about being a virgin when they marry. As we have seen, virtue is its own reward.

Aggressive Parenting for the Twenty-first Century

We are confident that you want your children to be virgins when they marry. If that is already impossible, you want them to be virtuous from this day on until they marry. But we have to be more aggressive about preparing them to live in this sexually obsessed age than our parents were with us. The reason is very simple: our parents lived in a culture that was at least neutral in its effect on their values, and in some cases, was actually supportive. That is no longer true! Today our post-Christian culture is rapaciously destructive of the family and its values. Consequently, we have to be more aggressive about protecting our family from the adverse values of the world while carefully inserting our own.

Thank God for the Local Church. We expect that the liberal and antimoral domination of our media, government, and educational system is not going to go away any time soon. In fact, it has a stranglehold right now on every family value we hold dear. But God has given you a special friend in the raising of your children — your local church. You have spiritual resources available to you that can protect your children from the moral holocaust going on all around them. See to it that your small children regularly attend Sunday school and church and that your teens are active in a good youth program. By regular church attendance and participation, by prayer and regular devotions in the home, by the establishment of sound rules for dating which are lovingly enforced, and by your positive moral example, you can still expect your children to walk down the aisle as virgins.

At the end of this book, we list additional helps provided by our Family Life Ministries, as well as other ministries we recommend. You may find something there that will be a good supplement to what you are teaching at home. The cost is small, but the results could be very effective. You invest in health care, education, and the spiritual development of your child; don't hesitate to invest in the "virtue protection" of your most precious possession.

Don't Forget the Challenge to Virtue. Young people are still idealists in search of a challenge. Why not challenge them to virtue? The world appeals to them to engage in "free sex," which turns out to be mighty expensive. Why not appeal to their youthful idealism and challenge them early to make a commitment to virtue. That will guarantee that they will take an AIDS-free and a STD-free body into their marriage. The children you help preserve may be your own grandchildren. (You might want to go back and reread chapter 8.)

Every Parent's Dream

It is natural for parents to look forward to their children's wedding day. Deep in the heart of every loving parent is the dream that when their son, dressed in his rented best, steps forward to take his bride's hand from her father, he will be a virgin. And every mother and father dreams that the beautiful white dress their daughter wears down the church aisle will be a true symbol of virtue. When the father takes his seat next to his wife, they will look into each other's smiling face and tear-filled eyes and say without words, "It was worth it all! It was worth all that instruction and those efforts to guard them against the bad influences of our culture, including the influence of some of their peers. It was worth it to oppose them when their temporary periods of rebellion could have destroyed them. It was worth it all to give them the gift of a sexually pure body to present to their partner for life."

You can see that dream fulfilled, but you are going to have to work at it. With God's help, you can still "do everything through him who gives [you] strength" (Phil. 4:13).

Our Dream

Bev and I were privileged to have that dream fulfilled in all three of our children's marriages (one of our sons is still single). We have also been privileged to have many of the two million or more who have read our book *The Act of Marriage* write to thank us for such a clear but discreet description of that intimate area of marriage and tell us how meaningful it was for them. Many wrote that it was helpful "because we were virgins when we married, and we really didn't know anything about sex until we read your book."

Today, as we send out *Against the Tide*, we have still another dream. We dream that our challenge to virtue and the giving of a virtue ring will become so popular among Christian families that someday, two newly married lovers will write to tell us that one of the delights they experienced on their wedding night was the exchange of their virtue rings.

What a marvelous pair of keepsakes!

SEX INFORMATION PARENTS NEED SO THEY KNOW MORE THAN THEIR CHILDREN

T his book would not be complete without an alphabetical list of every imaginable subject parents will be confronted with by inquisitive children, including sexually transmitted diseases. When children ask their endless stream of questions, it is a healthy sign to us parents. It means we have a good relationship with them and can be their teachers instead of someone else who doesn't share our values.

Whenever your child asks a question you do not know the answer to, do not panic. Just look him in the eye and say, "I'm not sure myself. Give me some time and I'll find an answer." Or you might say, "Let's look that up in this family book."

No one knows all the answers on the subject of sex, so we need never feel threatened if we come up blank. However, there is good material available today in Christian bookstores. If you don't find the answer under one of the following headings, please consult our book *The Act of Marriage*, or Dr. Ed Wheat's book, *Intended for Pleasure*[1] (particularly for people who are contemplating marriage).

ABORTION. The ending of a pregnancy before the fertilized egg or embryo or fetus has developed sufficiently to survive by itself outside the mother's womb. There are two kinds of abortion, *spontaneous* abortion (or *miscarriage*, as it is commonly called) and *induced* abortion (when the fetus is deliberately or artificially removed.)

Not all miscarriages can be explained. Some women seem to have a difficult time sustaining a pregnancy, particularly during the first trimester. In some cases it seems to be nature's way of eliminating a life with potential birth defects. A miscarriage is an act of God and should not leave the mother with a sense of guilt over the death of her child.

Induced abortion is quite another matter. It is performed deliberately by forcibly extracting the fetus from the uterus. Such abortions are an inhumane procedure that inflict torture upon an unborn child.

Abortion is murder and should not be considered an option by a Christian family. Admittedly, nine months of pregnancy and an unwed mother present many problems and heartaches for any Christian family. But they are not nearly so serious as carrying the burden of murder. I have known cases where authoritarian Christian parents insisted that their teenagers have abortions and came to regret it. They destroyed their testimony and moral credibility in the eyes of the most important people in those situations—their pregnant daughters. By contrast, I have seen several families trust God and stand up with their teens in that hour of crisis and have it change the course of their lives.

Prochoice advocates do not mention the guilt women often carry after an abortion. Dr. Grace Ketterman, a psychiatrist, told about her work as the director of a maternity home where more than nine hundred pregnant young women came under her care and how the Supreme Court's decision in 1973 made abortion a promising means of instantly solving their problems. She said, however, that after some time, "I began to be consulted by a pitiful parade of girls needing help. They had had abortions; sometimes more than one. They were full of remorse for their irresponsible taking of human life—unborn to be sure, but life nevertheless."[2]

We wonder how much the high suicide rate among teenagers today is affected by depression caused by the guilt that follows abortion.

ADOLESCENCE. The time in a person's life that generally parallels the teenage years. Beginning with puberty, when the sexual organs mature, this is a time of transition from childhood to adulthood.

ADULTERY. Sexual intercourse between two people who are not married to each other. God expressly forbids adultery. Exodus 20:14 states, "You shall not commit adultery." In Matthew 5:27-28 Jesus reaffirms this prohibition and extends it even to lustful thoughts. The words *adultery* and *fornication* are used in the Old and New Testaments to refer to a person having sexual intercourse with someone to whom he or she is not married. Fornication includes other sinful acts such as incest, sodomy, and homosexuality.

Sexual intercourse is to be reserved *only* for a man and woman who have been joined together in marriage. All other sexual intercourse is considered adultery or fornication in the eyes of God and is condemned as sin.

All sexual sin begins in the mind. The man who commits adultery does not suddenly decide to have an "affair." There is a time of incubation long before he finally betrays his wife. Lustful thoughts planted by pornographic magazines and films; watching scantily clad women at the beach; reading sexually arousing novels—all these and more gradually lead a man into sexual sin. Paul says flee from any temptation to engage in immorality. The person who continues to leave himself open to sexually stimulating materials is eventually going to fall.

AIDS. See SEXUALLY TRANSMITTED DISEASES (STDS).

AMNIOTIC FLUID. The watery fluid that surrounds and protects the fetus as it grows in the mother's womb.

AMNIOTIC SAC. The tough, elastic bag that holds the growing fetus and the amniotic fluid. When the baby is ready to be born, this sac breaks open and the amniotic fluid flows out of the uterus and vagina. When this happens, the mother's "water has broken."

AMPULLA CHAMBER. The storage chamber for sperm that have left the epididymis and traveled through the vas deferens.

ANDROGEN. The hormone that produces sexual changes in a boy, including the growth of the sex drive, body hair, and a deepened voice.

BIRTH CONTROL. The use of various means to prevent pregnancy. There are no specific references to birth control in Scripture, so in our opinion it is a morally neutral subject. We believe that Christians should seek to bear children. That is a primary purpose of love, marriage, and sex. Our generation is the first to have the scientific ability to avoid having children. This circumvents the purpose of God. If two young lovers marry and do not use contraceptives, they will probably become parents the way the Creator intended. Today, however, it is difficult to impossible to support all the children we could have. So we suggest that couples prayerfully decide on how many children they can raise. For some that is one or two; for others it is six or more. This is a private decision each couple must make.

Young people do not need to know about the various methods of birth control; that is like giving them a license to be promiscuous prior to marriage. Let them study the methods of birth control in *The Act of Marriage* just before their wedding. In the meantime, they need to practice abstinence.

CERVIX. The small opening at the bottom of the uterus that connects with the birth canal, or vagina. This opening is usually only the size of pencil lead but expands many times when the baby is ready to be born.

CHASTITY. Abstinence from premarital or extramarital sexual intercourse. Purity in conduct and intention.

CHROMOSOMES. Tiny thread-like bodies in each cell that contain the genetic blueprints for each person. Sperm cells and ova both contain twenty-three chromosomes. When an egg is fertilized, the combined forty-six chromosomes determine the hair color, temperament, facial features, body build, and hundreds of other characteristics of the developing child.

CIRCUMCISION. The surgical removal of the loose skin (foreskin) covering the end of the penis, usually performed for hygienic or religious reasons within a few days after a boy is born. With the foreskin removed, it is easier to keep the penis clean from possible infections, inflammations, and glandular secretions that might cause physical problems. In more primitive areas of the world, circumcision is still a religious rite or a rite of passage, indicating that a young man has entered adulthood.

In Old Testament times the Jews performed circumcision as a religious rite eight days after the boy was born. This was performed in obedience to the Lord's covenant with Abraham (Gen. 17:9-14).

Circumcision was not an option to the ancient Hebrews. It was a specific command of God that had to be obeyed. An uncircumcised man was to be cut off from his people.

Under the new covenant, instituted by Jesus Christ, Christians are free from this commandment. Circumcision is still routinely performed, but now there is new spiritual significance to this Old Testament custom. To a Christian, it does not matter whether or not a man's penis is circumcised. What does matter is that the person's heart is circumcised by removing the old sin nature (Col. 2:9-12).

Paul and Barnabas faced problems with the issue of circumcision among the Gentile and Hebrew converts. The Jewish Christians still believed that circumcision was mandatory, but Paul argued before the Jerusalem Council and convinced the leadership that the ceremonial laws had been superseded by the new covenant under Jesus Christ (Acts 15).

CLIMAX. See ORGASM.

CONCEPTION. The moment when a sperm cell burrows its way into and fertilizes an egg, creating a new life.

CONTRACEPTION. See Birth control.

COWPER'S GLAND. The first sexual gland to function when a man is sexually aroused. It sends a slippery fluid through the urethra to neutralize the acids of the urine and to provide lubrication for intercourse. Once the acid is neutralized, the sperm can pass through the urethra unharmed.

EJACULATION. During intercourse, the friction caused by the inward and outward thrusts of the penis in the vagina build up sexual energy in the man until there is an expulsion of sperm from the urethra. This is known as ejaculation. It occurs from friction during masturbation as well. In every ejaculation, the average male discharges about a half-million sperm cells. Yet it requires only one cell to fertilize an egg during intercourse; the rest are discarded. Ejaculation in the male is also called an orgasm.

EMBRYO. The unborn baby during the first eight weeks of development. After the eighth week, the baby is called a fetus.

ENDOCRINE SYSTEM. Glands in the male and female that secrete powerful hormones into the bloodstream, controlling the activity of organs or tissues in another part of the body.

ENDOMETRIUM. The soft, fur-like lining that develops on the wall of the uterus. During a woman's menstrual period, this lining fills with blood in preparation to receive a fertilized egg. When no egg is fertilized, the lining dissolves and is discharged through the vagina. If a fertilized egg embeds itself in the lining, the endometrium becomes part of the placenta.

EPIDIDYMIS. A mass of small coiled tubes just above the testicles. Inside, the sperm cells mature before passing through the spermatic duct (vas deferens) into the ampulla chamber and seminal vesicles.

ERECTION. The state of sexual arousal in which the penis fills with blood and becomes stiff and ready for intercourse and ejaculation.

ESTROGEN. A powerful female hormone that is secreted by the ovary and placenta during puberty, the menstrual cycle, and pregnancy. It stimulates secondary female characteristics such as breast development.

EXTERNAL ORGASM. The external orgasm, or *coitus interruptus*, is an unreliable and dissatisfying means of preventing conception. A man would need an extraordinary amount of self-discipline to withdraw from his wife just at the moment when his sexual passion is at its height. Intercourse is a time for mutual surrender to fully enjoy lovemaking, not a time for "self-discipline." That is why all sexual activity should be reserved for marriage. Coitus interruptus is unreliable for reasons other than passion. When the Cowper's gland begins secreting its lubricating fluid through the urethra, sperm cells often accompany it *before* ejaculation. Therefore, it is possible for a wife to get pregnant even without ejaculation into her vagina.

FALLOPIAN TUBE. The two tubes (also called oviducts) that lead from the ovaries into the uterus, or womb. Each month an egg, released from one of the ovaries, makes its way through the Fallopian tube, where fertilization can take place. The egg proceeds to the uterus either fertilized or unfertilized.

FANTASY. To fantasize or to think about having sexual relations with someone you are not married to is a sin condemned in Scripture. In Matthew 5:28 Jesus speaks of the sin of adultery in terms that no one had heard before. He reaffirms the Old

Testament teaching that it was sinful to commit the act of adultery, but He says that it is just as bad to *think* unchaste thoughts about another person. These evil thoughts or imaginations are what we call "fantasy" today. In Philippians 4:8 Paul discusses the importance of keeping our minds focused on the good and the true. He encourages the Philippian Christians, "Finally, brothers, whatever is true, whatever is noble, whatever is right, whatever is pure, whatever is lovely, whatever is admirable—if anything is excellent or praiseworthy—think about such things."

It is a sin for a married person to think about having sexual relations with another; it is just as much a sin for an unmarried person to have fantasies about having sexual intercourse with another. (In *The Act of Marriage* we list several steps for overcoming this temptation.)

FERTILIZATION. See CONCEPTION.

FETUS. A developing life in the womb after the eighth week. The word means "young one."

FOREPLAY. The activity of kissing, hugging, and caressing as a man and woman prepare for intercourse. It is a time of closeness, warmth, and sharing in the most intimate expression of love between husband and wife.

Many people do not realize that men and women have different levels of arousal. A man can be sexually aroused and ready for intercourse within minutes, but a woman's desire is slowly intensified during foreplay until she is ready to give herself totally in sexual intercourse. Foreplay should be an unhurried time of relaxation, gentleness, and caring. Both husband and wife should be more concerned about making one's partner happy than about one's own desires. Only with this selfless attitude can the act of marriage truly be mutually satisfying.

FORESKIN. Loose skin that covers the head of the penis (glans penis). This foreskin is normally removed by circumcision shortly after a boy's birth.

FORNICATION. Sexual intercourse between an unmarried man and woman.

FREQUENCY. There is no "correct" number of times that a husband and wife should have sexual intercourse each month or week. The frequency is a matter of personal preference mutually agreed upon by husband and wife. In the surveys we have seen, the average is from two to three times a week. That does not mean a husband and wife are "abnormal" if their lovemaking is more or less. We would question the health of a marriage, however, if a husband and wife seldom or never make love. The act of marriage is a good indicator of the love a man and woman have for each other. The desire to "become one" in sexual intercourse should be frequently present in a good marriage.

GENE. A unit in a chromosome that carries a particular physical characteristic.

GENITALS. The reproductive or sexual organs of a man or woman.

GLANS PENIS. The head of the penis. Containing densely packed nerves, this is one of the most sensitive areas of a man's body and when stimulated will promote ejaculation.

HEREDITY. The transmission of physical and emotional traits to children through the combination of the father's and mother's chromosomes.

HETEROSEXUAL. A man or woman who is sexually attracted to members of the opposite sex. Heterosexuality is evidence of normal sexuality in men and women.

HOMOSEXUALITY/LESBIANISM. A person who is sexually attracted to members of his or her own sex. There is no reliable scientific evidence that people are born as homosexuals. It is a learned behavior. There are certain factors that *predispose* some people toward homosexuality, but there is no genetic or hormonal cause for it.

Until 1973 the *Diagnostic and Statistical Manual* of the American Psychiatric Association listed homosexuality as a sexual abnormality, a deviation that needed to be treated or cured. But under pressure from an increasingly radicalized homosexual movement, the APA removed homosexuality from its abnormal listing in 1973. In humanistic circles, homosexuality is now viewed as an alternate lifestyle, not as a sin or sexual perversion. Changing the definitions of words, however, does not change the reality.

Homosexual behavior is one of the most difficult perversions to cure. But there is hope. Homosexuals need, first of all, a changed inner nature that can come only from repentance for sins and acceptance of salvation in Jesus Christ. If you know someone struggling with homosexuality, you might consult your church for the names and addresses of organizations that can help him or her.

HORMONE. A chemical produced by an endocrine gland that affects other organs or tissues within the body. Certain hormones promote male or female characteristics.

HYMEN. A membrane that partially covers the opening to the vagina. The opening of the hymen (also called the *maidenhead*) of a virgin is about one inch in diameter.

IMPOTENCE. The inability to achieve or maintain an erection. During the last twenty years, more and more men have experienced difficulties in completing the act of marriage. Impotence frequently is not due to physical problems, but to thought patterns and stress factors that hinder a good sexual relationship. Most doctors I have talked with believe that impotence is caused by the intense emotional and career pressures of our present culture. Our world is far more insecure than it was twenty to thirty years ago. Men are less sure of themselves in their traditional role as head of the household. This self-doubt has led several writers to analyze the phenomenon of the "feminized male." With the women's liberation movement still generating sex-role confusion, we may expect even more sexual dysfunction among men in the years ahead.

INTERCOURSE. The insertion of the erect penis into the vagina during lovemaking. It is called sexual intercourse or the "act of marriage," which when confined to marriage is approved and even encouraged by God. All sexual activity outside of marriage is forbidden and called "fornication" or "adultery" in the Bible.

LESBIAN. A female homosexual.

LIBIDO. The desire for sexual activity present in males and females; also known as the sex drive.

MASTURBATION. Self-stimulation of the sexual organs. A man rubs his penis until he ejaculates; the woman manipulates her clitoris until she has an orgasm.

Modern sex educators encourage masturbation. They even recommend what they call "outercourse" or mutual masturbation for couples, calling it a form of abstinence. This is a line of reasoning that Christians and most other parents consider repugnant. One of the popular sex education books states that children should be encouraged from the moment of birth to fondle their genitals and to masturbate or engage in "self-pleasuring." The authors also say that "it has become clear to us that society must cease trying to interfere with the child's natural discovery and enjoyment of self-pleasuring."[3] We strongly disagree with such humanistic nonsense.

Masturbation is one of the most controversial sexual subjects in the Christian community. The various opinions range from the viewpoint that masturbation is a marvelous gift of God to the view that it is a sin to be conquered by a Spirit-controlled believer. The Bible is silent on the subject, but we can draw certain principles from Scripture that might give us guidance. (See the discussion in chapter 6.)

MENOPAUSE. Menopause is also called the "change of life" in women and usually occurs over a five-year period from around ages forty-five to fifty. During this time a woman's menstrual cycle and monthly period become irregular and eventually stop. A woman in her forties will begin to notice increasing irregularity in her cycle. This comes from a gradual decrease in the estrogen produced by her ovaries. Once menopause is complete, no more eggs are released for fertilization and a woman can bear no more children.

The irregularities in the cycle result from the changes in the lining of the uterus. Some women experience fatigue, headaches, mood swings, and "hot flashes." There may be a noticeable sagging of the breasts, broadening of the hips, and an increasing weight problem. The emotional problems that may accompany menopause can be controlled by taking estrogen as prescribed by a physician. This allows a woman to go through menopause with a minimum of discomfort or extreme mood swings.

Men also experience a "menopause" of sorts, but it is usually not as difficult for them as for women. Usually in their late fifties men experience hormone changes that result in headaches, nervousness, fatigue, and other symptoms.

MENSTRUATION. Menstruation is the monthly discharge of a bloody fluid from a woman's uterus. It is the first visible sign that a girl is becoming sexually mature, capable of conceiving a child. The monthly menstrual cycle is also called a *period* and is usually completed in twenty-eight days.

The onset of the menstrual cycle, called *menarche*, is part of the body's maturation in changing a child into an adult over a four- or five-year period known as *adolescence*. A girl's first period can begin anywhere between the ages nine and seventeen. Adolescence and the accompanying sex changes are all triggered by the master gland, the pituitary, that begins secreting hormones into other organs.

The menstrual cycle is a woman's monthly preparation for child bearing. The ovaries begin manufacturing estrogen, which is one of the primary hormones involved in maturing physically. Estrogen also causes a rapid development of the lining of the uterus in preparation for a fertilized egg. The lining fills with blood, waiting for the egg to implant itself to the wall, the placenta develops, and the blood begins supplying the needed nourishment to the human embryo. If the egg is not fertilized, the blood supply diminishes and millions of cells in the uterine wall die and are soon discarded in the menstrual flow. The fluid discarded from the uterus is actually half blood and half mucus and pieces of the uterine wall that are not needed.

The menstrual cycle lasts for thirty to thirty-five years until menopause.

NOCTURNAL EMISSION. A nocturnal emission, or "wet dream," refers to the ejaculation of sperm while a male is asleep. Every day the testicles manufacture sperm that accumulate in tubes and small storage areas in the body. When these storage spaces are filled, the male experiences a need for sexual release. In a uniquely designed system, God has made an escape valve for the sperm through wet dreams. The male who experiences a nocturnal emission usually has a sexually oriented dream, but this should be no cause for guilt feelings; no one can control the content of his dreams. Wet dreams are usually disturbing to boys in puberty unless their parents have prepared them properly so they know in advance what to expect.

NUDITY. While many humanistic psychologists and psychiatrists promote nudity in families, we believe the Scriptures and common sense make it obvious that parents should not allow themselves to be seen in the nude by their children.

Many parents mistakenly believe they will create wholesome attitudes toward sex in their children if they openly display their sex organs. But what usually happens is that the child becomes morbidly obsessed with sexual matters and may develop voyeuristic tendencies or begin fantasizing about having sexual relations with his or her parent. This may also lead to sexual experimentation with playmates. One psychoanalyst observed that parents who walk around in the nude in front of their children are unconsciously seducing their own children.

Before the Fall in the Garden of Eden, Adam and Eve were naked and felt no shame. No sin was connected with their nudity; they were pure in the sight of God. But when they sinned, they immediately clothed themselves because they felt ashamed and fearful. Since the Fall, the Bible condemns physical nakedness, especially among family members. In Genesis 9 we are told that Noah planted a vineyard, got drunk, and lay in his tent naked. One of his sons, Ham, discovered his nakedness and told Japheth and Shem about it. Shem and Japheth put a garment on their shoulders, *backed* into the tent so as to avoid seeing their father in such a condition, and covered him. They turned their faces away in respect to their father.

Wise parents should teach their children to be modest in their dress and behavior. Nudity outside the bedroom should have no place in a Christian home. We realize that occasionally a parent will be caught off guard and be seen in the nude, but when that happens, the reaction should be calmness and discretion with a move to covering as soon as possible.

ORAL SEX. This subject, like masturbation, is controversial in the Christian community. What is oral sex? One term, *fellatio*, refers to the act of a woman receiving the penis in her mouth to sexually stimulate the male. In *cunnilingus*, the male stimulates the woman with his mouth over her vulva, often with his tongue on her clitoris. Both acts can bring orgasm if prolonged.

I do not recommend the practice of oral sex, but admittedly there are no biblical grounds for forbidding it. It appears to be a matter of personal preference. There is one major consequence if it is practiced promiscuously. Herpes Simplex II is a sexually transmitted disease caused by a cold-sore virus that has become a national epidemic during recent years. One college counselor has observed that this disease is widely spread through oral-genital encounters. Oral sex has been popularized through a variety of men's and women's magazines, and it seems to have been the sexual "fad" of the last ten years. More than twenty million Americans now have this incurable "genital herpes."

ORGASM. The climax of sexual intercourse. In males it occurs when semen is forcefully ejaculated from the penis (see EJACULATION). In females, orgasm results from the clitoris and vulva being manipulated during foreplay. These external sexual organs undergo physical changes. The clitoris enlarges and becomes more sensitive in much the same way as a man's penis becomes erect. As the clitoris is continually manipulated, the woman moves toward orgasm. The clitoris has been described as the "sexual trigger" of a woman. Sometimes a woman does not learn to experience orgasm through intercourse until she has once achieved orgasm through manipulation by her husband's fingers. While some women feel uncomfortable at the suggestion of manual manipulation, most Christians agree that it is a legitimate part of lovemaking between a husband and wife.

ORGASMIC FAILURE. Dr. David Reuben, author of *Everything You Always Wanted to Know about Sex*, uses the term "orgasmic impairment" to describe a woman's inability to achieve an orgasm during lovemaking.[4] The woman's clitoris, as explained earlier, is her sexual trigger. If this organ is tenderly manipulated by the husband with his finger or his penis, his wife will usually experience orgasm.

Unfortunately, some men and women still suffer from lack of information regarding the mechanics of sexual love. I believe misconception and misinformation about orgasm are the main causes of sexual malfunction among women. It was once thought that a woman should not have an orgasm and that it was only the privilege of a husband to experience sexual release. Fortunately our ideas have changed, but guilt feelings remain for some women. These feelings can significantly impair a woman's enjoyment of sex.

Fear is another cause of orgasmic failure. Sometimes a woman is afraid she will not perform as well as she should, and as a result she doesn't.

In counseling engaged or married couples, I try to allay whatever guilt or fear they may have regarding sexual intercourse. I tell them that the act of marriage is God-ordained and God-blessed and the highest physical expression of love between a husband and wife. The marriage bed is to be a place of joy, free from inhibitions—the one place where modesty is to be shunned if a man and woman are to experience the full blessings of sexual love (see Heb. 13:4).

OVARY. Either of two female organs near the kidneys that produce ova (eggs) and the hormone estrogen, which governs feminine characteristics. Each month a mature egg cell is released from one ovary and passes through a Fallopian tube to await fertilization.

OVULATION. The process of discharging an egg from the ovary.

OVUM. An egg cell.

PENIS. The spongy, tube-like male sex organ that serves a dual purpose in at times eliminating waste water and at times ejaculating sperm.

PERIOD. The three to five days during the month when a woman is experiencing *menstruation*.

PETTING. Kissing, hugging, and caressing that take place between a boy and girl on a date. Petting is actually foreplay, or the activity that prepares a couple for sexual intercourse. During petting, a boy will usually massage a girl's breasts and genitals; a girl will rub his sex organs. This is risky, because it leads both the girl and boy toward sexual intercourse. Pregnancy, sexually transmitted diseases, guilt, fear, and loss of respect or self-respect are all potential consequences of unrestrained petting.

PITUITARY. The master gland at the base of the brain that secretes hormones affecting growth, sexual development, and the functioning of other glands: the adrenals, sex glands, and thyroid.

PLACENTA. A spongy organ attached to the wall of the uterus and connected to a fetus by an umbilical cord. Filled with blood veins, this organ filters food and oxygen through the umbilical cord and disposes waste products from the fetus. (Also called the *afterbirth*.)

PORNOGRAPHY. Material that is sexually explicit, erotic, and offensive—whether it be movies, magazines, TV programs, books, videotapes, or other forms of communication.

Pornography is one of the most serious social scourges of our nation and is currently an $8-billion-a-year industry. We have seen rising levels of sexually transmitted diseases, child sexual abuse, homosexuality, divorce, rape, and social deterioration in America because of the spread of pornography. Only tough, consistent law enforcement, citizen action, and prayer will rid our country of this psychological disease.

PREGNANCY. The period of time, roughly nine months, between conception and the birth of a child.

PROGESTERONE. A chemical, often referred to as the "pregnancy hormone," that is secreted by the ovaries and prepares the lining of the uterus for the placenta and fetus. It also prevents further menstruation and ovulation during pregnancy.

PROSTATE. A gland located near the urethra and bladder that secretes part of a male's seminal fluid. It is not uncommon in old age for the prostate to enlarge, impede urination, and require surgical removal.

PROSTITUTION. Prostitutes are people who provide sexual services for money or other material gain.

PUBERTY. The period of time in a child's life (beginning anytime between age nine and seventeen) when he or she begins to mature sexually.

RAPE. Rape is a violent sexual act usually perpetrated against women by men. In rape, a man forces a woman to have sexual intercourse with him. In many cases he also brutalizes or kills her. The man who rapes is usually an angry person who has a poor self-image. He rapes in order to feel a sense of power or revenge against those he believes have hurt him in the past. Rape is not so much an act of self-gratification as a psychological weapon. It is probably the most physically and emotionally traumatic experience a woman can ever endure.

Women who have been raped need spiritual counsel to overcome their feelings of guilt and uncleanness. Often rape victims blame themselves for being raped instead of placing the blame where it rightfully belongs—on the cruel rapist and the greedy pornography industry whose products often stimulate the rapist toward his crime.

SCROTUM. The sac of skin that hangs behind the man's penis and contains the testicles, which produce male hormones and sperm cells.

SEMEN. The fluid that contains the sperm cells. Semen is ejaculated from the penis when the male reaches orgasm. It contains secretions from the testicles, prostate, seminal vesicles, and Cowper's glands.

SEMINAL VESICLES. Two storage areas for sperm, located on either side of the prostate, that are connected to the sperm duct, or vas deferens.

SEX DRIVE. We are sexual creatures with an innate desire to procreate. This desire is properly fulfilled only within the bonds of marriage. The God-given sex drive in men and women is a blessing as long as it is kept under control. For the unmarried, the sex drive must be sublimated, or rechanneled into constructive pursuits.

The sex drive within marriage is a variable thing, depending on people's temperament, background, and general energy level. Some mates seem to lack any sex drive; others are seemingly never satisfied. The frequency of sexual relations between a husband and wife should be mutually agreed upon.

SEXUAL INTERCOURSE. Sexual intercourse is the act of marriage. During this union, a man places his penis inside a woman's vagina. Using his pelvic muscles, he thrusts in and out until semen ejaculates from the penis into the vagina. Sexual intercourse is God's design for the reproduction of the species. It is also a way for a husband and wife to express their love toward each other; it is designed for their enjoyment.

SEX SLANG. Some people have a habit of using vulgar words to describe the beautiful union God has given to a husband and wife. Sexual slang words are used as curses or statements of violence against others. I do not believe any Spirit-filled Christian should use these terms.

SEXUALLY TRANSMITTED DISEASES (STDs). Any variety of contagious diseases normally transmitted by intimate sexual contact, especially promiscuous activity. Some STDs are medically treatable and some are not. We discuss here some of the more common diseases:

AIDS. AIDS (Acquired Immune Deficiency Syndrome) is the most frightening disease to come along in the past century, and in spite of millions of dollars spent on research, there is no cure. Some doctors say there never will be. Because AIDS is 100 percent fatal, "probably no other disease in recent times has caused as much fear or drawn as much of the public's attention as AIDS."[5] Because so many homosexuals and liberals hold high office in government, we have an unscientific policy of keeping the carriers of AIDS secret, which is unlike the treatment of any other contagious disease. Consequently, it is claiming tens of thousands of victims. Unless a cure is found, it may claim thousands of lives each year before the turn of the century.

The number of teens who have AIDS has increased by more than 70 percent since 1989 making it the sixth leading cause of death among youth ages fifteen to twenty-four. Josh McDowell says, "One-fifth of all people with AIDS are in their 20s. Many of them were infected when they were in their teens. One study revealed that three out of every 1,000 college students are infected with HIV."[6]

On April 10, 1992, I received a publication from the U.S. Department of Health and Human Services (#231) that expressed alarm at the rapid increase of AIDS among high school young people. Their conclusion was, "The most effective means of preventing HIV infection are refraining from sexual intercourse, maintaining a monogamous sexual relationship with an uninfected sex partner."

AIDS is a disease believed to be caused by a virus, HTLV-III, that attacks the body's immune system, destroying the ability of the body to fight off sickness. When this happens, any simple problem can quickly become a life or death matter. Many AIDS victims die from pneumonia or develop rare forms of cancer. The number of AIDS victims may be greater in number than reported, for many diseases caused by a weakened immune system are recorded as the actual cause of death when AIDS is the real culprit.

How does a person contract the disease? Homosexuals get it through intimate contact—the exchange of blood and semen during anal intercourse or oral sex. Drug users get it through contaminated needles. Innocent victims have been subjected to it through blood transfusions. Currently, one out of fifty thousand blood transfusions is contaminated.

America is facing one of the most serious epidemics in history. Only God knows where this new epidemic will end, but unless medical science finds a cure or unless our nation's sexual habits change, this disease could take the lives of a large portion of this nation's population by the year 2000.

It would be tragic to wait until enough people have died before our society decides to take action against the conditions that allow this disease to spread. It is amazing that everyone does not see that our country is desperately in need of moral and spiritual revival.

For a thorough look at this disease and its ramifications for the church, read *The AIDS Epidemic: Balancing Compassion and Justice* by Dr. Glenn Wood and Dr. John Dietrich (Multnomah Press).

Gonorrhea. One of the nation's health authorities said, "Gonorrhea has become the most common reportable disease in school-age children, surpassing chicken pox, measles, mumps and rubella combined."[7] The Centers for Disease Control indicated that "adolescents 15-19 actually have the highest rates of gonorrhea of any age group." Once known as "the Clap" and thought to have been cured by penicillin, it has returned stronger than ever due to sexual promiscuity; some strains are no longer responsive to penicillin.

The gonococcus germ that causes this disease incubates in two to ten days, causing painful urination and a discharge of pus from the penis. In "asymptomatic gonorrhea" there are no symptoms in males. This means that an infected man can unknowingly transmit the disease to others.

Women commonly show no visible symptoms of gonorrhea, which makes the disease very dangerous. When a woman is infected, the gonococcus germs multiply around the cervix, causing a thick pus discharge. In addition, they often move up into the Fallopian tubes, which can cause pelvic inflammatory disease (PID). This can be treated, but scar tissue may block the Fallopian tubes, causing sterility. If the tubes are only partially blocked, there is a danger of tubal pregnancies. Gonorrhea poses a risk to unborn babies. If the mother has contracted gonorrhea, the baby can be infected as it passes through the birth canal. A baby's eyes are particularly vulnerable. Once infected, blindness often results. Doctors now routinely put silver nitrate drops or penicillin ointments in a newborn's eyes to avoid venereal infection. Nevertheless, a baby can be infected at birth through his nose, mouth, or rectum.

Gonorrhea can cause inflammation of the testicles in men and sterility, arthritis, and heart disease in both men and women.

Syphilis. This disease is caused by spirochetes, which multiply rapidly in the body and attack normal tissues—especially the bones, joints, liver, heart, large blood vessels, eyes, spinal cord, and brain. Four stages characterize the disease. In the primary stage, the person develops a "chancre" or sore, either on his lips, inside his mouth, or on the genitals. In the second stage, he develops a rash and loses hair. In the third stage, called the "latent period," no symptoms are visible and a person can unknowingly pass the disease on to others. During the late stage, a person may suffer heart disease, brain damage, paralysis, and blindness.

Syphilid infection increases the likelihood that a person could contract AIDS. In a pregnant woman, syphilis can have disastrous effects on her unborn child. One fourth of the children born to mothers with the disease are born dead and others have very serious birth defects. In some cases children are born with a syphilitic infection that does not appear until later in life.

Herpes simplex II. Thirty million Americans (nearly 15 percent of the population) now suffer from the incurable venereal disease Herpes Simplex II, and approximately 500,000 more contract the disease each year. During the first week after infection, clusters of blisters develop on the penis, labia, thighs, lower abdomen, buttocks, and anus. These blisters often break, causing excruciating pain. The person with herpes also experiences tenderness in the groin, a sick stomach, and fever. The medicine Acyclovir (trade name Zovirax) helps to relieve the pain caused by blisters, but it is not a cure. Many carriers find that the blisters flare up again in response to stress or to emotional disturbance. This sexually transmitted disease, which can be contracted by one sexual contact with an infected partner, often spoils the very thing that caused it, for it makes sexual activity extremely painful. That is a high price to pay for promiscuity. Our children need to know how dangerous herpes is because it is highly contagious and many who carry it may not know at first or may not admit it.

Nongonococcal urethritis. Nongonococcal urethritis (NGU), is caused by a strain of bacteria known as *Chlamydia trachomatia*. These bacteria incubate after about five days and infect the urethra, causing painful urination. This STD reflects the same general symptoms as gonorrhea. There are an estimated four to nine million new cases each year.

Trichomoniasis. Trichomoniasis is caused by protozoa called *Trichomonas vaginalis*. It incubates after four to twenty days, usually in seven days. In women it produces a vaginal itch, pain in the pelvic area, and a yellowish-green discharge. Men seldom have any symptoms, though some experience itching and a whitish discharge from the penis in the morning, or less commonly in the evening.

Chlamydia trachomatous. In the last decade chlamydia has become a well-known venereal disease. It is related to several sexually transmitted diseases and is a major cause of pelvic inflammatory disease (PID), which is very painful and dangerous. In women it can produce a nagging infection that usually robs her of ever being a mother. In some cases the infection remains so small she is unaware of its presence, but it scars her Fallopian tubes and makes pregnancy impossible. Sometimes it explodes in sudden infection causing great pain and requiring the removal of female child-bearing organs. If an infected woman does have children, they may be born with eye deformities or pneumonia. In men chlamydia attacks the genitals with infection which can render him sterile. It can make sexual intercourse very painful for both men and women, again destroying the very activity that transmits it.

SPERM. The mature male reproductive cells that fertilize the female ovum.

SYPHILIS. See SEXUALLY TRANSMITTED DISEASES.

TESTICLES. Two oval-shaped organs inside the scrotum that manufacture millions of sperm cells and produce testosterone, the male hormone responsible for secondary sex characteristics in males (such as voice change and body hair).

TESTOSTERONE. A male sex hormone produced in the testicles that produces secondary sex characteristics during puberty.

TRANSVESTISM/TRANSSEXUALITY. A *transvestite* is a person, usually a man, who dresses and behaves like the opposite sex. Because he feels he should have been born the other gender, he is uncomfortable with his sexuality and begins to wear women's clothing and assume female mannerisms. These people are not homosexuals, and many of them are married with children, but they secretly wish to be women.

Some transvestites decide to have sex-change operations to make them into females. Thus they become *transsexuals*. Through hormonal therapy and operations, they eventually look like females, but are obviously unable to bear children.

UMBILICAL CORD. The cord that connects the fetus to the placenta in the mother's uterus. Through the cord, which contains two arteries and a vein, the baby receives nourishment and oxygen and expels waste material through the mother's system.

URETHRA. In both males and females, the tube used to eliminate urine or waste water from the body. In the male, it is also the passageway through which sperm cells are ejaculated during intercourse.

VAGINA. A woman's birth canal, the passageway from the cervix (the opening to the uterus) to the vulva (the external sex organs). During intercourse, the man's penis is placed inside the vagina.

VENEREAL DISEASE. See SEXUALLY TRANSMITTED DISEASES.

VIRGIN. A male or female who has never experienced sexual intercourse.

VULVA. The external female sex organs, including the clitoris, labia majora, and labia minora.

UTERUS. The pear-shaped organ in the mother's body that holds the developing embryo and fetus. It is one of the largest muscles in the body.

WET DREAM. See NOCTURNAL EMISSION.

WOMB. See UTERUS.

X CHROMOSOME. A sex-determining chromosome found in both males and females. A female's eggs contain only X chromosomes; half of a male's sperm contain X chromosomes and the other half have Y. When an X chromosome sperm fertilizes an egg, the child becomes a female

Y CHROMOSOME. A sex-determining chromosome found only in the male sperm. If a Y chromosome sperm fertilizes an X chromosome egg, the child becomes a male.

---

[1] Dr. Ed. Wheat, *Intended for Pleasure* (Old Tappan, N.J.: Fleming H. Revell Co., 1981).

[2] Grace H. Ketterman, *How to Teach Your Children about Sex* (Old Tappan, N.J.: Fleming H. Revell Co., 1981), 153.

[3] Mary Calderone and James Ramey, *Talking with Your Child about Sex* (New York: Ballantine, 1982), xv.

[4] David Reuben, *Everything You Always Wanted to Know about Sex But Were Afraid to Ask* (New York: Bantam Books, 1971).

[5] Josh McDowell, *The Myth of Sex Education* (San Bernardino, Calif.: Here's Life Publishers, 1987), 159.

[6] Ibid., 160.

[7] Ibid., 173.

A p p e n d i x   A

SEICUS
FAMILY FRIEND
OR FOE?

he following is taken from the article "They Call This Abstinence?" by Tom Hess, which was published in the May 18, 1992 issue of *Citizen* magazine (used by permission):

Add "abstinence" to the growing list of words, such as "safe," "values" and "family," that some school and health officials use to describe programs that teach heterosexual and homosexual practices to teen-agers.

"When they say 'abstinence-based,' they also teach foreplay, or what they call 'outercourse,'" said W. Reyn Archer, M.D., deputy assistant secretary for population affairs for the U. S. Department of Health and Human Services in Washington, D.C. "They say intercourse is not a good behavior for adolescents, but they're willing to heat up the kids to the moment of passion, and then suggest that they just say 'no.' It doesn't work."

The nation's leading advocate of "outercourse" education is Debra Haffner, executive director of the Sex Information and Education Council of the United States (SIECUS), a privately funded organization in New York City.

"Outercourse is a concept that sexuality educators use among themselves to describe alternatives to sexual intercourse," Haffner said in a speech to parents in Greenwich, Conn., last year. "What our children need to understand is that they can give and receive pleasure without putting themselves at risk of pregnancy and disease."

Archer, of HHS, and other critics of "outercourse" say Haffner's rhetoric isn't as innocent as it seems. They point to an article in the September/October 1988 SIECUS *Report*, "Safe Sex and Teens," in which Haffner lists "safe sex" practices for teens:

"Flirting, dancing...undressing each other, masturbation alone, masturbation in front of a partner, mutual masturbation....Teens could surely come up with their own list of activities."

In an interview with *Citizen*, Haffner said the article was written for "sex education professionals," and that the above is "taken out of context...."

Taken out of context? She is the head of the most powerful sex education teachers' group in the country and was teaching sex educators how to teach "abstinence" to teens. Such teaching won't cool youthful ardor, but rather heat them up. Besides, no responsible parent would want their child to be taught "outercourse" as if it were a form of abstinence.

We have seen that sexual activity is never satisfied until it culminates in intercourse—such "teaching" would only increase sexual activity among teens. No wonder parent groups around the country are rising up to oppose the latest SIECUS brainstorm.

Appendix B

BIBLICAL PASSAGES FORBIDDING ADULTERY AND FORNICATION

dultery and fornication—indeed any form of sexual relationship outside of marriage—is always prohibited in the Bible. Consider the following passages:

Old Testament

"You shall not commit adultery" (Exod. 20:14; Deut. 5:18).

"Consecrate yourselves and be holy, because I am the LORD your God....

"If a man commits adultery with another man's wife—with the wife of his neighbor—both the adulterer and adulteress must be put to death.

"If a man sleeps with his father's wife, he has dishonored his father. Both the man and the woman must be put to death; their blood will be on their own heads.

"If a man lies with a man as one lies with a woman, both of them have done what is detestable. They must be put to death; their blood will be on their heads" (Lev. 20:7, 10-13).

These moral laws were given to Israel as they entered the land of Palestine "to preserve life." While we do not advocate putting people to death for adultery today, the penalty does indicate the rigor of God's moral laws. Obviously, God was serious when He commanded men and women not to use their sexuality outside of marriage. The following proverbs were given after Israel had been in the Promised Land for several hundred years:

> My son, pay attention to my wisdom,
>> listen well to my words of insight,
> that you may maintain discretion
>> and your lips may preserve knowledge.
> For the lips of an adulteress drip honey,
>> and her speech is smoother than oil;
> but in the end she is bitter as gall;
>> sharp as a double-edged sword.
> Her feet go down to death;
>> her steps lead straight to the grave.
> She gives no thought to the way of life;
>> her paths are crooked, but she knows it not
>> (Prov. 5:1-6).

> My son, keep your father's commands
>> and do not forsake your mother's teaching.
> Bind them upon your heart forever;
>> fasten them around your neck.
> When you walk, they will guide you;
>> when you sleep, they will watch over you;
>> when you awake, they will speak to you.
> For these commands are a lamp,
>> this teaching is a light,
> and the corrections of discipline
>> are the way of life,
> keeping you from the immoral woman,
>> from the smooth tongue of the wayward wife.
> Do not lust in your heart after her beauty
>> or let her captivate you with her eyes,
> for the prostitute reduces you to a loaf of bread,
>> and the adulteress preys upon your very life.
> Can a man scoop fire into his lap
>> without his clothes being burned?

Can a man walk on hot coals
　　without his feet being scorched?
So is he who sleeps with another man's wife;
　　no one who touches her will go unpunished
　　(Prov. 6:20-29; see also Prov. 7.)

Our Lord on Adultery

The Lord Jesus often spoke out on this subject, raising its sinfulness from the physical act to the lustful thought. While he was quick to forgive repentant adulterers, He always condemned the practice as sin. Consider these statements:

"You have heard that it was said, 'Do not commit adultery.' But I tell you that anyone who looks at a woman lustfully has already committed adultery with her in his heart. If your right eye causes you to sin, gouge it out and throw it away. It is better for you to lose one part of your body than for your whole body to go into hell. And if your right hand causes you to sin, cut it off and throw it away. It is better for you to lose one part of your body than for your whole body to go into hell.

"It has been said, 'Anyone who divorces his wife must give her a certificate of divorce.' But I tell you that anyone who divorces his wife, except for marital unfaithfulness, causes her to become an adulteress, and anyone who marries the divorced woman commits adultery" (Matt. 5:27-32).

"I tell you that anyone who divorces his wife, except for marital unfaithfulness, and marries another woman commits adultery" (Matt. 19:9).

Now a man came up to Jesus and asked, "Teacher, what good thing must I do to get eternal life?"

"Why do you ask me about what is good?" Jesus replied. "There is only One who is good. If you want to enter life, obey the commandments."

"Which ones?" the man inquired.

Jesus replied, " 'Do not murder, do not commit adultery, do not steal, do not give false testimony, honor your

father and mother,' and 'love your neighbor as yourself'"
(Matt. 19:16-19).

Other New Testament Passages

Adultery and *fornication* seem to be used interchangeably in some places in the New Testament. *Fornication*, which comes from the Greek word *porneia*, literally means any sexual violation ranging from adultery to homosexuality, and it is always forbidden. The new Gentile converts from paganism were given the following mandate by the early church elders:

"It seemed good to the Holy Spirit and to us not to burden you with anything beyond the following requirements: You are to abstain from food sacrificed to idols, from blood, from the meat of strangled animals and from sexual immorality. You will do well to avoid these things" (Acts 15:28-29).

Do you not know that the wicked will not inherit the kingdom of God? Do not be deceived: Neither the sexually immoral nor idolaters nor adulterers nor male prostitutes nor homosexual offenders nor thieves nor the greedy nor drunkards nor slanderers nor swindlers will inherit the kingdom of God (1 Cor. 6:9-10).

The body is not meant for sexual immorality, but for the Lord, and the Lord for the body....

Flee from sexual immorality. All other sins a man commits are outside his body, but he who sins sexually sins against his own body. Do you not know that your body is a temple of the Holy Spirit, who is in you, whom you have received from God? You are not your own; you were bought at a price. Therefore honor God with your body (1 Cor. 6:13,18-19).

But among you there must not be even a hint of sexual immorality, or of any kind of impurity, or of greed, because these are improper for God's holy people. Nor should there be obscenity, foolish talk or coarse joking, which are out of place, but rather thanksgiving. For this you can be sure: No immoral, impure or greedy person—such a man is an idolater—has any inheritance in the kingdom of Christ and of God (Eph. 5:3-5).

Put to death, therefore, whatever belongs to your earthly nature: sexual immorality, impurity, lust, evil desires and greed, which is idolatry. Because of these, the wrath of God is coming (Col. 3:5-6).

It is God's will that you should be sanctified: that you should avoid sexual immorality; that each of you should learn to control his own body in a way that is holy and honorable, not in passionate lust like the heathen, who do not know God; and that in this matter no one should wrong his brother or take advantage of him. The Lord will punish men for all such sins, as we have already told you and warned you. For God did not call us to be impure, but to live a holy life. Therefore, he who rejects this instruction does not reject man but God, who gives you his Holy Spirit (1 Thess. 4:3-8).

The best antidote to sin is scripture memory (Ps. 119:9-11). For that reason we suggest parents have their children learn one verse of scripture a week. Write them on three-by-five cards and review them frequently. High on that list to be memorized should be 1 Corinthians 6:15-20. Then, incorporate some of the verses listed in this section.

ADDITIONAL HELPS FOR PARENTS IN RAISING SEXUALLY PURE TEENS

Personal Letter from Dr. Tim LaHaye to Your Teen ($4.00)

Dr. LaHaye has prepared a warm and friendly three- to four-page personalized letter for your teen. This letter reinforces your teachings and may bring in some things you have omitted. Since it comes addressed personally to your teen, it is highly probable he or she will read it at least once and perhaps several times. It covers some of the things in this book and gives further details based on talks he has given young people. The cost is only four dollars. Please supply the information requested below (feel free to photocopy the form) to help Dr. LaHaye make the letter more personal.

To order the personalized letter for your teen, please fill out the following profile and send it, along with $4.00, to Family Life Ministries, P.O. Box 2700, Washington, DC 20024:

Name: _____

Nickname (if applicable): _____

Address: _____

City:_____ State:____ Zip: _____

Age:_____ Grade:_____

Church name:_____

Youth pastor's name:_____

Pastor's name: _____

Name of high school: _____

Does he/she like school? Explain.

Is he/she a good student?

What are his/her plans for after high school?

Is he/she currently dating?

If so, is his/her girlfriend/boyfriend a Christian?

"Welcome to the World of Dating" cassette tape ($6.00, specify for girl or boy)

This interesting cassette was professionally produced and is based on Dr. LaHaye's talks to teens on this subject. Drawing on his years of experience as a Christian counselor, minister, author, and educator, he has prepared this fascinating talk that includes some of the material in this book and some of what he learned in his discussion groups with teens. He covers "What girls need to know about boys," "What boys need to know about girls," "The importance of virtue before marriage," "How to say no," and much more.

Love, Sex, and Dating by George Eager ($9.95)

Dr. LaHaye considers this the finest book of its kind for teens. Mr. Eager, a high school teacher who talks teenagers' "language," has written a book teens are likely to read. Complete with interesting diagrams and drawings, this book would serve as an excellent follow-up to your talks about sex and the challenge to virtue.

Raising Them Chaste by Dr. Richard C. Durfield and Renee Durfield ($8.95)

For a more thorough description of how to present the challenge to virtue and the virtue ring or key, read this book.

LaHaye Temperament Analysis ($19.95)

For readers of this book we enclose a $10 discount certificate for Dr. LaHaye's Temperament Test which he has administered to over twenty-seven thousand people. It is an excellent aid not only for diagnosing your primary and secondary temperament but for discovering vocational aptitudes (offering fifty suggestions for your temperament combination). The analysis also lists your spiritual gifts in priority and offers twenty-five areas where you could serve in your local church. It confronts you with your ten basic weaknesses and offers steps to overcome them. Not only is this good for parents, but it is also good for teens as they begin making decisions about the kind of vocation they are best suited for. This test is appropriate for anyone fourteen years of age and older.

Currently, the analysis, which is personalized throughout its fifteen pages, sells for $29.95. The discount certificate on page 259 is good for a $10 discount on as many tests as you order at one time.

"Wait for Me!" video produced for Concerned Women for America ($19.95)

When newcomer Johnny meets someone totally out of this world, the party he's at turns into a mine field of questions—and choices. This honest and highly entertaining film looks at the decisions every teen needs to make about sex. It deals with the issues from a teenager's perspective and challenges your teen to make a commitment to wait for marriage to have a sexual relationship.

"Wait for Me" is designed for parents, pastors, or youth leaders to watch with their teens. It provides a natural starting point for frank, in-depth discussion on sexuality and what the Bible has to say about it. Activities, discussion points, Scripture references, and other material in the Parent/Leader Guide will help you—and your teen or youth group—get even more out of this video.

Finding the Will of God in a Crazy Mixed-up World by Tim LaHaye
($6.95)

One of the most important subjects for young people today is how to find the will of God for their lives. This interesting book is easy to read and will help your teen make some of the very important decisions that will confront them in the years to come. It's a book they will read and refer to when making big decisions.

The Act of Marriage by Tim and Beverly LaHaye ($9.95)

A good way to prepare your young person for marriage is to give them a copy of The Act of Marriage. This best-selling book on the beauty of sexual love in marriage is a classic. It is given by more ministers and parents to young people just before marriage than any other book in print.

The above materials may be ordered from:

FAMILY LIFE MINISTRIES
P.O. Box 2700
Washington, DC 20024
(202) 488-0700

Please add $2.00 for postage and handling.

YES! Dr. LaHaye, I would like to gain new insights into my behavior through your Temperament Analysis. Please send me a copy of your test booklet.

☐ Payment enclosed of $19.95* plus $10 discount coupon.
☐ Please charge my ☐ VISA ☐ Mastercard   Card No. _____   Exp. Date _____

* All payments must be in US dollars.

Customers outside the United States and Canada add $2 US extra postage and handling.

Signature _____

Name _____   Address _____   Apt. _____

City _____   State _____   Zip _____

Send to: LaHaye Temperament Analysis, Family Life Ministries, P.O. Box 2700, Washington, DC 20024

$10   **TEN DOLLAR SAVINGS CERTIFICATE** $10

good toward the purchase of the

LaHAYE TEMPERAMENT ANALYSIS

$10 $10